"What is post-socialism? Can we conce community and love? Rabbi Michael L overhaul the inequities and mean-spir should read this book—and incorporate social-change movements. Going beyoi we are resisting, this book not only puts ._____ a positive vision, drawing much from the wisdom of feminists and peace activists, but provides a coherent strategy for how to get there. It liberates readers to go beyond the 'be realistic' command of our ruling elites and embrace the beautiful and love-filled world that Michael Lerner proposes."

Medea Benjamin, cofounder of Code Pink

"In *Revolutionary Love*, Rabbi Michael Lerner provides a great theoretical and political service. No one that I am aware of does a better job of using love as a theoretical tool to address these issues and suggest what a politics based on a love of the other might look like. This book is not merely innovative—it is groundbreaking in its scope, depth of scholarship, insight, and originality."

Henry Giroux, Paulo Freire Distinguished Scholar in Critical Pedagogy, McMaster University

"Rabbi Lerner is no innocent romantic about love. His call for a new bottom line is of immense importance not only for my colleagues and students in the Christian and Jewish worlds but for all in the United States, Canada, and Europe who are seeking a path out of the narrow materialist, ultra-individualist, and competitive-acquisitive approach to politics that has severely limited the appeal of both Left and Right in the Western world. This book must be required reading for every opinion maker, every spiritual leader, every political leader, every college student hoping to understand American politics, and any citizen hoping to avoid the drift in Western societies toward reactionary nationalism, fascism, and the destruction of the life-support system of Earth."

Walter Brueggemann, William Marcellus McPheeters Professor Emeritus of Old Testament, Columbia Theological Seminary

"Love is the thread that connects and heals us all. Rabbi Michael Lerner's *Revolutionary Love* shows us a meaningful path toward healing our hearts, minds, souls, society, and planet. Highly recommended."

Dean Ornish, MD, Founder and President, Preventive Medicine Research Institute, and Clinical Professor of Medicine at University of California, San Francisco

"*Revolutionary Love* is a much-needed antidote to today's hardball politics of cynicism and self-interest über alles. Drawing from Rabbi Michael Lerner's spiritual wisdom and lifetime of social activism, it provides a treasury of practical tools to counter the drift to domination and violence and to build a more caring and sustainable society for us all."

Riane Eisler, President of the Center for Partnership Studies and author of *The Real Wealth of Nations: Creating a Caring Economics*

"Michael Lerner is a tough-minded, bold, and intellectually brilliant writer and speaker. Read this book, and he will show you that survival as a nation and a planet depends on not being so embarrassed by the concept of love that you dismiss it as too soft. It isn't. He spells out a detailed plan for a new way of living in which love is taken seriously and soberly. I feel that my brain cells, speaking metaphorically, have been rearranged by this energetic book that inspires with its clarity and visionary power."

Thomas Moore, author of *Care of the Soul: A Guide for Cultivating Depth and Sacredness in Everyday Life*

"This visionary and hopeful book's argument for the fusion of love, compassion, and politics counters narrowly economistic progressivism, narcissistic spirituality, and the reigning forces of oppression. Its model of respect and care should be widely read, widely discussed, and—because it would work beautifully in the classroom—widely taught."

Roger S. Gottlieb, author of *Morality and the Environmental Crisis*

"Bringing together the critical with the theological in purposeful and humanitarian ways, this book benefits from Lerner's evident passion. It is sufficiently grounded in a number of the philosophical debates and does a very good job of proposing love as something that can have real and tangible effects."

Brad Evans, coauthor of *Histories of Violence: Post-War Critical Thought*

THE S. MARK TAPER FOUNDATION

IMPRINT IN JEWISH STUDIES

BY THIS ENDOWMENT
THE S. MARK TAPER FOUNDATION SUPPORTS
THE APPRECIATION AND UNDERSTANDING
OF THE RICHNESS AND DIVERSITY OF
JEWISH LIFE AND CULTURE

The publisher and the University of California Press Foundation gratefully acknowledge the generous support of the S. Mark Taper Foundation Imprint in Jewish Studies.

Revolutionary Love

Revolutionary Love

*A Political Manifesto to Heal
and Transform the World*

RABBI MICHAEL LERNER

UNIVERSITY OF CALIFORNIA PRESS

University of California Press, one of the most
distinguished university presses in the United
States, enriches lives around the world by advancing
scholarship in the humanities, social sciences,
and natural sciences. Its activities are supported
by the UC Press Foundation and by philanthropic
contributions from individuals and institutions.
For more information, visit www.ucpress.edu.

University of California Press
Oakland, California

Library of Congress Cataloging-in-Publication Data
First paperback printing 2022
Names: Lerner, Michael, 1943– author.
Title: Revolutionary love : a political manifesto to
    heal and transform the world / Rabbi Michael
    Lerner.
Description: Oakland, California : University of
    California Press, [2019] Includes bibliographical
    references and index. |
Identifiers: LCCN 2019017920 (print) |
    LCCN 2019021719 (ebook) | ISBN 9780520973138
    (ebook and ePDF) | ISBN 9780520389755 (pbk : alk.
paper)
Subjects: LCSH: Politics, Practical—United States. |
    Right and left (Political science)—United States. |
    Interpersonal relations—Political aspects—United
States. | Conduct of life—Political aspects.
Classification: LCC JK1726 (ebook) | LCC JK1726 .L47
    2019 (print) | DDC 320.6—dc23
LC record available at https://lccn.loc.gov/2019017920

Manufactured in the United States of America

26   25   24   23   22
10 9 8 7 6 5 4 3 2 1

For Cat Zavis, my partner, wife, and empathic guide through a challenging period

And for those who seek a world of love and generosity

CONTENTS

Acknowledgments   *ix*

Introduction   *1*

PART I. TRANSCENDING THE CRIPPLING DYNAMICS
OF OPPRESSION   *31*

1. A World of Pain, a Hunger for Love   *33*

2. Fear and Domination, or Love and Generosity?   *65*

3. Toxic Self-Blaming and Powerlessness   *79*

4. To Change a Society, You Must Respect Its People   *100*

PART II. STRATEGIES FOR BUILDING THE CARING SOCIETY   *139*

5. Overcoming the Dictatorship of the Capitalist Marketplace   *141*

6. Major Institutional Changes for Building a Love and Justice
   Movement   *198*

7. The Caring Society in the Twenty-Second Century   *228*

Afterword   *241*

Notes   *249*

Bibliography   *255*

Index   *261*

I am grateful to Niels Hooper for his helpful editorial advice, to Susan Whitlock and Kathleen MacDougall for editing this entire book, and to the staff of the University of California Press for their assistance in publishing this book. I'm also grateful to the staff of *Tikkun* magazine, including Chris Philpot, Chantal Tom, Andrew Hiyama, Hannah Arin, Madison Wheeler, and Robin Kopf, and to Tikkun Institute Fellow Ben Case for their contributions to the editing of this book.

Everything in this book has been mightily influenced by my personal mentors, Abraham Joshua Heschel and Zalman Schachter-Shalomi, and by the teachings of Richard Lichtman, Herbert Marcuse, Wilhelm Reich, Thich Nhat Hanh, Keeanga-Yamahtta Taylor, Omid Safi, Martin Luther King, Jr., Pope Francis, Carol Gilligan, Arthur Waskow, Michael Sandel, Michelle Alexander, Richard Sennett, Erich Fromm, Marianne Williamson, Harvey Cox, and James Cone. In addition, I have relied on the writings of many contemporary feminists, including Judith Plaskow, Rachel Adler, Susannah Heschel, Marge Piercy, Catherine Keller, and Tirzah Firestone. And I am grateful to the many hundreds of authors of articles in *Tikkun* magazine and to the dozens of interns and the evolving staff of *Tikkun* (and before that the staff of the Institute for Labor and Mental Health), all of whom contributed to the development and refinement of these ideas and the research on which they are based.

In particular, Peter Gabel, a founder of Critical Legal Studies and one of the most creative thinkers I've ever met, has been my partner in working out, through *Tikkun,* many of the ideas in this book. He is my close ally in building a movement for revolutionary love.

Cat Zavis was a lawyer and trainer in empathic communication before she joined *Tikkun* as the Executive Director of the Network of Spiritual Progressives. She helped me name, refine, and extend many of the key concepts presented here. She has shown me how empathy can be a central part of societal transformation; her ideas contributed greatly to the content of this book and to my falling in love with her. We are now happily married as well as ongoing partners in the work of healing and transforming our world. I dedicate this book to her with deep rejoicing at her presence in my life and for the beautiful way she embodies revolutionary love.

Introduction

> We need much more than a political revolution; we also need a moral, cultural, and spiritual revolution—an awakening to the dignity and value of each and every one of us no matter who we are, where we came from, or what we've done. . . . It is this revolutionary spirit—a revolutionary love for all people and for life itself—that will ultimately determine our collective fate.
>
> Michelle Alexander

We earthlings need to build a fundamental change of consciousness in ourselves and in every part of our national and global society, in order to achieve the economic and political changes necessary to prevent the destruction of the life support system of Earth; to end global and domestic poverty and wealth inequality; to defeat racism, sexism, homophobia, and other forms of xenophobia; to protect human rights; to achieve social, economic, and environmental justice; and to achieve lasting global peace. This new consciousness is possible, and can emerge through embracing revolutionary love, the struggle for the caring society, and a new bottom line in all our economic, political, legal, educational, and cultural institutions. This manifesto is written to show you how this can happen and how you can help make it possible.

Liberal and progressive movements need to move beyond a focus on economic entitlements and political rights to embrace a new discourse of love, kindness, generosity, and awe. This is not some New Agey "smile and be nice" formula or a "let's get into self-transformation before we change society" kind of thinking. I am calling for both our American and global societies to embrace a new bottom line so that every economic, political, societal, and cultural institution is considered efficient, rational, and/or productive—not according to the old bottom line of how much these institutions maximize money, power, or ego but rather how much they maximize love and generosity, kindness and forgiveness, ethical and environmentally sustainable behavior, social and economic justice. This new bottom line seeks to enhance our capacity to transcend a narrow utilitarian or instrumental way of viewing human beings and nature, so that we respond to other people as embodiments of the sacred instead of thinking of them primarily in terms of how much they can serve our interests, and also so that we respond to nature not solely as a resource for human needs but rather through awe, wonder, and radical amazement at the beauty and grandeur of this universe.

I call this new consciousness revolutionary love, and its goal is to create the Caring Society—Caring for Each Other and Caring for the Earth. The vehicle to create this new consciousness we will call the Love and Justice movement (and eventually, the Love and Justice Party).

The revolutionary possibility of love is the kind of love that breaks through those distortions of consciousness that make it difficult to implement a rational environmental policy or to end the many forms of oppression that permeate our world. To really embrace revolutionary love requires us to develop a strategy way beyond anything currently being given serious attention in the media, the political parties, and even many of the social change movements. And it requires us to move beyond what seems realistic in terms of the contemporary frame of discourse. Yet there is no alternative if we are to solve the environmental crisis and prevent our society in the coming decades from moving further and further into reactionary nationalism and repression of our humanity. We need a global mobilization of billions of people to solve the problem, and this manifesto outlines the first steps for making possible such a mobilization.

To understand the urgency, let's consider our current environmental crisis.

In 1992, thousands of scientists issued a collective statement warning of the impending dangers to the life support systems of planet Earth. Twenty-five years later, in December 2017, 15,364 scientists from 184 countries signed a new statement, which reads in part:

> Since 1992, with the exception of stabilizing the stratospheric ozone layer, humanity has failed to make sufficient progress in generally solving these foreseen environmental challenges, and alarmingly, most of them are getting far worse. Especially troubling is the current trajectory of potentially catastrophic climate change due to rising GHGs [greenhouse gases] from burning fossil fuels and agricultural production—particularly from farming ruminants for meat consumption. Moreover, we have unleashed a mass extinction event, the sixth in roughly 540 million years, wherein many current life forms could be annihilated or at least committed to extinction by the end of this century.
>
> Humanity is now being given a second notice. We are jeopardizing our future by not reining in our intense but geographically and demographically uneven material consumption and by not perceiving continued rapid population growth as a primary driver behind many ecological and even societal threats. By failing to adequately limit population growth, reassess the role of an economy rooted in growth, reduce greenhouse gases, incentivize renewable energy, protect habitat, restore ecosystems, curb pollution, halt defaunation, and constrain invasive alien species, humanity is not taking the urgent steps needed to safeguard our imperiled biosphere.[1]

And in October 2018, the United Nations Intergovernmental Panel on Climate Change released a new study showing that climate change is happening at a faster rate than previously anticipated. If it continues at the current rate, there will be disastrous consequences for much of the world's population.[2] Despite denials from U.S. President Donald Trump, his administration's Global Change Research Program issued a statement in November 2018 affirming that climate change was accelerating. "Climate change threatens the health and well-being of the American people by causing increasing extreme weather, changes to air quality, the spread of new diseases by insects and pests, and changes to the availability of food and water," said the report. "Human health and safety, our quality of life, and the rate of economic growth in communities across the U.S. are increasingly vulnerable to the impacts of climate change." Trump responded by saying he simply didn't believe this report. But rational people do!

To implement the changes scientists say are needed would require an overall transformation of domestic and global economic arrangements. It would require the elimination of many products as well as the factories producing them, a fair distribution of wealth, the overhaul of our transportation and energy systems, a dramatic reduction in the production of unnecessary consumer goods, the rejection of the notion that "growth" of production is in itself a societal good, the curtailment of military expenditures and armament production, and the dedication of trillions of dollars to repairing the damage already done to our planet. In short, the human race would have to find ways to cooperate in dealing with the number one problem facing us all: survival of the life support system of Earth.

In this context, growing numbers of people feel powerless and in despair about the future—feelings reflected in higher rates of suicide and lower rates of childbirth. What they intuit is that a global struggle among competing national and international economic imperialist groupings flourishes without any effective counterforce. Corporate power needs to be replaced by people power, but that cannot happen until money is removed from politics. And so far in the United States, social justice and environmental movements have been too limited in their focus and have failed to explicitly endorse the goals scientists tell us are necessary.

Even more narrowly envisioned goals for short-term steps are likely to be frustrated. *Tikkun* magazine and the Network of Spiritual Progressives have joined with many other groups to support a Green New Deal proposed to Congress by the courageous Alexandria Ocasio-Cortez in the House, Ed Markey in the Senate, and sixty-five other Congressional sponsors. The January 10, 2019, letter to Congress from 626 organizations describes the following vision for a Green New Deal:

Halt all fossil fuel leasing, phase out all fossil fuel extraction, and end fossil fuel and other dirty energy subsidies. The science is clear that fossil fuels must be kept in the ground. Pursuing new fossil fuel projects at this moment in history is folly. Most immediately, the federal government must stop selling off or leasing publicly owned lands, water, and mineral rights for development to fossil fuel producers. The government must also stop approving fossil fuel power plants and infrastructure projects. We must reverse recent legislation that ended the 40-year ban on the export of crude oil, end the export of all other fossil fuels, and overhaul relevant statutes that govern fossil fuel extraction in order to pursue a managed decline of fossil fuel production. Further, the federal government must immediately end the massive, irrational subsidies and other financial support that fossil fuel and other dirty energy companies (such as nuclear, waste incineration, and biomass energy) continue to receive both domestically and overseas.

Transition power generation to 100% renewable energy. As the United States shifts away from fossil fuels, we must simultaneously ramp up energy efficiency and transition to clean, renewable energy to power the nation's economy where, in addition to excluding fossil fuels, any definition of renewable energy must also exclude all combustion-based power generation, nuclear, biomass energy, large scale hydro and waste-to-energy technologies. To achieve this, the United States must shift to 100 percent renewable power generation by 2035 or earlier. This shift will necessitate upgrading our electricity grid to be smart, efficient, and decentralized, with the ability to incorporate battery storage and distributed energy systems that are democratically governed. In addition, Congress must bring the outdated regulation of electricity into the twenty-first century, encouraging public and community ownership over power infrastructure and electricity choice, as well as permitting distributed energy sources, including rooftop and community solar programs to supply the grid.

Expand public transportation and phase out fossil fuel vehicles. As the transition away from fossil fuels occurs, our transportation system must also undergo 100 percent decarbonization. To accomplish a fossil-fuel-free reality, Congress must require and fund greater investment in renewable-energy-powered public transportation that serves the people who need it most. The United States must also phase out the sale of automobiles and trucks with internal fossil fuel combustion engines as quickly as possible and phase out all existing fossil fuel mobile sources by 2040 or earlier. Federal credits for electric vehicles must be expanded.

Harness the full power of the Clean Air Act. The Clean Air Act provides powerful tools that have proven successful in protecting the air we breathe and reducing greenhouse pollution. It can also serve as an important backstop to ensure climate targets are met. Congress should harness the full power of the statute by setting strict deadlines and providing adequate funding for EPA to carry out all its duties under all applicable sections of the Act, including implementing greenhouse pollution reduction requirements for cars, trucks, aircraft, ships, smokestacks and other sources, as well as a science-based national pollution cap. The Act has successfully reduced many air pollutants and can do the same for greenhouse pollution.

Ensure a Just Transition led by impacted communities and workers. In effectuating this energy transformation, it is critical to prioritize support for communities who have historically been harmed first and most by the dirty energy economy and workers in the energy sector and related industries. We support a comprehensive economic plan to drive job growth and invest in a new green economy that is designed, built and governed by communities and workers. Building new energy, waste, transportation, and housing infrastructure designed to serve climate resilience and human needs; retrofitting millions of buildings to conserve energy and other resources; and actively restoring natural ecosystems to protect communities from climate change are but a few ways to build a sustainable, low carbon economy where no one is left behind during this change.

Uphold Indigenous rights. The United Nations Declaration on the Rights of Indigenous Peoples (UNDRIP) must be upheld and implemented, along with treaties, instruments and decisions of international law that recognize that Indigenous Peoples have the right to give "free, prior and informed consent" to legislation and development of their lands, territories and/or natural resources, cultural properties and heritage, and other interests, and to receive remedies of losses and damages of property taken without consent.

Further, we will vigorously oppose any legislation that: (1) rolls back existing environmental, health, and other protections, (2) protects fossil fuel and other dirty energy polluters from liability, or (3) promotes corporate schemes that place profits over community burdens and benefits, including market-based mechanisms and technology options such as carbon and emissions trading and offsets, carbon capture and storage, nuclear power, waste-to-energy, and biomass energy. Fossil fuel companies should pay their fair share for damages caused by climate change, rather than shifting those costs to taxpayers.

Medea Benjamin and the Code Pink movement that she helped lead for many years is encouraging climate activists to add the following stipulations to the Green New Deal: a major transition away from the environmental destruction of war and war preparations, including the closure of most U.S. military bases abroad and within the United States and the thorough cleanup of the land and water in those locations.

All these programs make a great deal of sense and most are likely to be blocked on the national level—yet they fall short of the more dramatic changes I outline in the second part of this book. Even forceful local initiatives are often blocked by the disproportionate power of the fossil fuel industries. The *New York Times* reported on one such defeat in the 2018 midterm election:

Faced with what they saw as an existential threat to their businesses, BP, Valero, Phillips 66, the Koch brothers and other members of the fossil fuel fraternity dumped more than $30 million into Washington State to crush a ballot initiative that would have imposed the first taxes in the nation on carbon emissions. Backers of the proposal hoped it would serve as a template for similar action elsewhere and perhaps for the country as a whole. But the theoretical elegance of a carbon tax, which most economists and scientists believe is the surest way to control emissions on a broad scale, was no match even in reliably Democratic Washington for relentless fearmongering about job losses, higher electricity bills and more expensive gasoline.[3]

WHY WE NEED A NEW KIND OF REVOLUTION

Why have decades of Left activism failed to produce the kind of world we seek, and know we need?[4] Liberal and progressive strategists and social theorists often mention the following reasons.

Failure to Understand Basic Needs

In *Listen, Liberal*, Thomas Frank contends that because Democrats are loyal to what he and others call "the professional class"—who often are in the top 20 percent of wealth holders—they are unable to seriously address income inequality or understand the struggles the bottom 80 percent have in meeting their basic needs.[5] As a result, the rest of society perceives *them* as "the elites"—although most Democrats do not perceive themselves as elite and are astounded that others see them that way. Yes, this is part of the problem.

Inept Funding Strategies

The Right has more money to spend on politics and institutions and the Left can't compete financially. Many progressives argue that money controls American politics. And, for decades, the Right has successfully financed candidates, educational institutions, religious organizations, media companies, and research and policy institutes. The Left often complains that they just can't match that kind of strategic investment. I want to challenge that notion. Because the difference here is not who has money: there are billionaires on the Left and the Right. Rather, it has more to do with how the money is spent.

Right-wing funders see the importance of spreading their worldview, so they tend to give more money to educational, media, and policy institutions that unashamedly promote that worldview. Left-wing funders are too often narrowly pragmatic, so they insist that the community organizing projects and national organizations they fund be issue-, rather than worldview-, oriented, and that they achieve measurable results within relatively short periods of time. Thus, the Right has funded a wide variety of explicitly Christian colleges that unashamedly teach students a right-wing version of Christianity far removed from the wisdom of Jesus, instilling in them capitalist values as if they were religious values; while leftist alternative colleges, such as the now defunct New College of California in San Francisco, and Antioch College in Yellow Springs, Ohio, as well as alternative think tanks, have failed or been forced to severely curtail their programs for lack of funding. True, many liberal colleges have added classes that teach the history of African Americans and offer majors in women's studies and other identity-based curricula. These, however, are not enough to teach a worldview that contradicts the key tenets of capitalist society to which most students have been subjected for most of their lives—hyper-consumerism, looking out for number one, and making it economically. And while some liberal colleges may have mission statements and invite graduation speakers who articulate a vision of the good society, most would be shocked at the idea that they should promote a coherent idealistic worldview, much less one that challenged the core values of the competitive marketplace, and indeed the oversight accrediting institutions would forbid it. Without ever being exposed to an alternative ethical and political worldview that challenges the logic of the competitive and "me-first" logic of global capitalism, and having no idea of how they could make a living serving others, students increasingly have moved away from humanities and much of the social sciences toward fields like economics, business, computers, and technology-related studies or science because the culture in which they've grown up tends to see education as valuable primarily to the extent that it helps students get the skills or connections that will help them be successful in the marketplace. Liberal funders have rarely sought to create colleges that would embed in their curricula and through the people they hire a systematic challenge to the capitalist system and its notion of the old bottom line and its portrayal of what is or is not "realistic."

Campaigning on the Wrong Messages

Meanwhile, if you ask many liberals or progressives why many middle income people vote against their rational material self-interest by supporting right-wing candidates, they likely will respond that it's because those people are racist, sexist, homophobic, Islamophobic, xenophobic, or anti-Semitic. My response: clearly racism and sexism play major roles in how some people vote. But it's also true that a majority of voters gave their votes to Barack Hussein Obama in 2008 and 2012, and to Hillary Clinton in 2016. Obama and Hillary Clinton faced racist and sexist attacks throughout their public lives, yet a population decisively committed to white supremacy and/or unrepentant patriarchy would never have given a woman or an African American man the majority of votes in a presidential election. On the other hand, it is well to remember that, due to their elitism and fear of the majority, and fear that a democratic society would overturn slavery and other "privileges" of the wealthy, those who drafted the U.S. Constitution were compelled to create an Electoral College to determine the final choice for the presidency, which could overrule the popular vote.

The question remains, why has the Right dominated American politics on the state and national levels for much of the past forty years?

Failure to Address Fairness for All

There are, naturally, more nuanced responses than simply assuming that people are being evil or irrational. In her masterful book *Strangers in Their Own Land*, Arlie Russell Hochschild describes one reason some white working-class men have disdain for liberals. They see themselves being constantly moved to the back of the line for economic advancement and political and societal caring while liberals, largely through affirmative action programs, slip their own favored groups ahead of them. These white men believe they are being discriminated against because they have been waiting patiently for economic opportunities and benefits they feel they have already earned. What they experience is that the system set up by liberals is unfair to them.[6] While this complaint does focus on material well-being, it is often shared by working people who have not lost jobs and are not in immediate economic distress. They are moved by issues of justice and fairness even when they are not suffering materially. This perception of injustice, exaggerated by the Right, became a central theme in the growth of the Right and in the subsequent development of racist, "White Lives Matter" movements.

Bill Clinton and Barack Obama, who together totaled sixteen years in the White House, made disappointingly few attempts to use their bully pulpits to address racism, sexism, and classism in American society, much less take seriously *Tikkun* magazine's proposal to make federal support for public schools dependent on these evils being challenged at each grade level of our education system. Their presidencies failed to help more Americans in the lower 70 percent of income earners or wealth holders recognize that their situation was a product of the shared, radical inequality and class structure in this society, not, as the Right would have it, a product of the minimal affirmative action attempts that have been made to rectify previous unfairness toward women and people of color. Liberal forces could have made important advances had they consistently challenged economic inequality, vigorously educated Americans about the legitimacy of affirmative action for those who had faced systemic discrimination and oppression for centuries, and appointed progressive judges in the first two years of the Clinton and Obama administrations, when their party held majorities in the Senate and House of Representatives. Compare that with the destructive boldness of

Donald Trump, who used his first two years in office to dismantle much of the good done by generations of reformers, environmentalists, and social justice advocates.

Today, the Democrats offer a simple solution to our environmental and other dilemmas: put us back into power by giving us control of Congress and the White House and we'll fix it all. Sadly, this will not be sufficient. When the Democrats were in power, they did not fix it. Though they put in place some efforts to expand environmental protections and develop solar energy, they never touched in any serious way on what environmental scientists told us was needed: a challenge to uneven material consumption, rapid population growth, the role of an economy rooted in growth, defaunation, or the incentivization of farming ruminants for meat consumption; nor did they limit the power of corporations to move their operations from cities, states, or even countries that seek to impose stricter environmental measures.

Democrats and Business as Usual

The Democrats are really two parties: one the champions of the pro-corporate policies of the Clinton and Obama years, the other a more progressive force that reached its best articulation in the campaign of Bernie Sanders in 2016.

Commenting on the electoral defeat in 2018 of Democratic party Senators who took centrist positions, such as Claire McCaskill of Missouri, African American Studies scholar at Princeton Keeanga-Yamahtta Taylor opined on Jacobin's website that "we now have tangible proof that you can't beat neo-Confederate, white nationalism with mealy-mouthed middle-of-the-road appeals to civility and good governance. Conservative and centrist Democrats found that voters won't waste their time with cheap knockoffs. The only chance we have to bury the Trump nightmare is a radical political agenda that provides an actual and real alternative to the status quo."[7]

The "Blue wave" in 2018 brought in more progressive Democrats at the local level and in the House of Representatives. But they are still a minority of elected Democrats and lack control of the party as a whole. With this split unresolved, even a Democratic Party-dominated Congress in the 2020s will find it difficult to overcome much of the massive environmental and human-rights damage done by the domination by corporate-oriented politics over the past forty years. Partial measures—for example, re-affirming the Paris environmental agreements from which President Trump has threatened to withdraw—are already understood by environmentalists to be far too limited to address the global crisis we face.

Further, even a Democratic president and a Democratic majority in both houses of Congress would face the strong likelihood that legislative or presidential attempts by executive order to put environmental and human rights restraints on the free market would be overturned by a right-leaning Supreme Court. For the next twenty years the Court will likely remain in the hands of a conservative bloc committed to protecting the current distribution of wealth and power in the United States. The past decisions of these justices and their ideological orientation will continue to prevent them from imposing serious restraints on the power of corporations, or reversing the disenfranchisement of poor and minority groups, the dismantling of material, safety, and health protections won over the course of the past sixty years, and the loss of important rights for women and minorities.

Given this context, our best bet to taking the decisive steps scientists say are absolutely necessary to save the environment would be to write constitutional amendments that not only overturn specific past Supreme Court decisions but essentially institute changes that the Court could not then block. But to pass any such needed constitutional amendment would require that progressive forces gain a two-thirds majority in both houses of Congress, elect a progressive president, and win a progressive majority in two-thirds of the states. This seems exceedingly unlikely unless they take a radical turn toward a new kind of politics described in this revolutionary love manifesto.

To take over the Democratic Party and unabashedly challenge the capitalist system, its materialist worldview, its belief that growth of an economy is a critical aspect of economic efficiency and health, and its championing of individualism, selfishness, and chauvinistic nationalism, progressive forces would have to learn to address the unmet spiritual and psychological needs that the capitalist system is unable to acknowledge, much less satisfy, but about which the Left has been tone deaf. Respectfully and empathically addressing these needs would allow us to win a majority of Americans to effectively challenge global capitalism and its destructive impact.

Could it happen? Some people look at American politics and see the growth of the Right, its powerful financial resources, its ability to play to racism, sexism, homophobia, and fear—and they despair of fundamental change. They point to the increase in mass shootings, assaults on African Americans and Jews, Muslims and immigrants, and conclude that their fellow Americans really are bad people or intractably reactionary. Others, more hopeful, point out that millions more people vote for liberal or progressive candidates nationwide than for reactionaries and that local activism has grown and achieved significant victories, developing local institutions that could become the foundation for a post-capitalist order. Moreover, they observe a significant section of younger people between the ages of eighteen and thirty-five seeking new ways to do politics, in part with the goal of saving the planet. Both pictures are partially true, partially exaggerated. In the 2020s we will see both tendencies continue to be important aspects of our world. But we can't afford to wait while elections tilt one way one year, another way two years later, in endless rotations.

This manifesto is a call for all people to come back to their own highest and most love-oriented hopes and instincts. To have the kind of world we really want—a world that would nurture the most ethically coherent, joyous, compassionate, and hopeful parts of our souls while simultaneously repairing the global environment and healing the racist, sexist, xenophobic, homophobic, and reactionary nationalist distortions that are flourishing—we will need to purge ourselves of all the fear, pain, and distortions that have led us to give up hope.

I recognize that pessimism about our fellow humans runs deep, in part a product of Trump's administration and the reemergence of fascistic movements in Europe and elsewhere. For reasons that I will explain, such pessimism has been part of class and patriarchal societies for the past ten thousand years, and has been promoted by the powerful to keep us from uniting and changing the world. But the very pain that these societies cause has often produced revolutionary transformations in the past, and can do so again.

POST-SOCIALISM

This manifesto could reasonably be read as a nonviolent strategy to replace global capitalism with a very different and post-socialist kind of world. Or we could call it a "socialism of the heart" or a "spiritual socialism."

I was one of the founders, in 1971, of an organization called the New American Movement and published a call for the Left to "Put Socialism on the Agenda." The New American Movement eventually merged with Michael Harrington's Democratic Socialist Organizing Committee to form the Democratic Socialists of America. Yet the post-socialist or socialism of the heart orientation I'm proposing is several steps more radical.

Why "post-socialist"? I've found those who yearn for a second try at socialism or communism do not really understand the aspects of those systems that are problematic. They correctly point out that none of those movements actually created the democratic control over the economy that was supposedly the defining feature of a communist or socialist society, and they blame the failures on Stalin or Mao or some other perverse or self-interested leaders. But they rarely ask themselves what was lacking in those movements that made it possible for such totalitarian leaders to gain popular support and control. Nor do they wonder why social democratic reforms in European countries generated so little enthusiasm that people later voted in conservative governments that dismantled some (not all) humanistic and egalitarian reforms that had brought European social democrats to power originally.

Certainly, it would have made a significant difference if those movements had actually been democratic at every level. The Democratic Socialists of America place a healthy emphasis, as do I, on making sure that much of the economy should be democratized, but not by concentration of all power in some national bureaucratic and elitist government. Wherever possible, decentralized and local decision making must be prioritized. Yet to save the environment there will have to be some decisions made on the national and international levels and, unlike the Paris Agreement on environmental issues, they must be enforceable. Transportation, energy, and the extraction of resources need to be supervised by those who worry about the well-being of the planet and of future generations. The post-socialism that many of us seek would favor worker-owned cooperatives or publicly owned enterprises managed by workers and consumer representatives, as well as local worker-owned enterprises (though many consumer-goods industries might be best run as cooperatives) and market mechanisms to determine the demand for many consumer goods.

This is a long way from the failed socialisms of the past. But the core problem of these past movements went deeper. Historically, socialist and communist movements (and their remnants in some contemporary movements like the British Labour Party) focused almost entirely on the external realities of life, the economic and political arrangements, ignoring the inner realities, the need to place love, empathy, and genuine caring for each other, for all of humanity, and for the planet at the top of their agenda. They did not recognize the importance of what I call "meaning needs"—being connected to higher values for one's life than simply satisfying material wants and needs. They did not ask themselves how to shape an economy and political system that embodied and promoted that kind of caring. In short, they, like many aspects of the New Deal in the United States in the 1930s, focused on objective caring but not on subjective caring. Subjective caring involves helping people actually feel respected and treating them as important and deserving of care.

I propose a democratization of the economy that goes far beyond the tepid attempts at economic democracy that left most Europeans uninspired. But I also insist that such a transformation will only be viable when done in the context of a society that constantly nurtures our ethical and spiritual capacities to care for each other and the planet, and that facilitates our ability to give meaning to our lives that transcends material satisfactions. These concerns must be placed at the center not only of a program for the future, but of how we treat each other now, and this reorientation is not yet part of most of contemporary liberal, progressive, or radical social change movements. That is why I don't call what we need "socialism" but rather a spiritual socialism, a socialism of the heart, or a post-socialist world.

WHAT WILL IT TAKE TO GET THIS KIND OF A POLITICAL MOVEMENT?

To create a political force that truly addresses the American people with compassion, psychological sophistication, empathy, and spiritual sensitivity, we will have to repair some of the central misconceptions that flourish among many (not everyone) in the liberal and progressive social change movements. Much of the first part of this book addresses these issues.

The most important such misconception is the materialist reductionist view of the American public articulated by James Carville, advisor to President Bill Clinton, in 1992: "It's the economy, stupid." All that people really care about, according to this belief, is their economic well-being. This has been a major subtext of liberal and progressive politics ever since a crude materialist-reductionist and dumbed-down version of Marxism permeated the labor movements in the late nineteenth and much of the twentieth centuries (even while they rejected the more revolutionary and humanistic strands that a few Marxists sought to preserve but which never got any traction in the major communist and socialist political parties).

I reject this materialist reductionism. No matter how poor some people are, or how little job security they have, they are not thereby reducible to caring only about money. Members of the American working class have the same range of fundamental human needs as those in the middle and upper middle classes. The notion of a hierarchy of needs is belied by human experience in which even people starving to death in concentration camps sometimes put their solidarity and caring for others over their chance to get enough for themselves.

The tired yammering of TV talking heads often explains that the Democrats lost the 2016 presidential election because they "don't speak to the white working class." This is usually understood to mean that the Democrats failed to deliver what the white working class "really" wants: more material benefits. This materialist reductionist account is mistaken and disrespectful. Yes, the Democrats failed to deliver, but as Hochschild shows us, what they failed to deliver was not only relief from financial insecurity, but equally important, a modicum of caring and respect—dimensions of the human psychological and spiritual needs with which too many liberals and progressives often seem to be out of touch in their public life (though in their personal lives these dimensions are often very important to them). I argue that the denial of respect and the denial of a life connected to higher meaning, community, and love create pain that the Left ignores and the Right addresses, albeit in a very distorted way.

Here is a methodological guide to understanding human behavior in politics and elsewhere: whenever you see millions of people acting in apparently irrational ways to achieve goal X (for example, economic security), consider the possibility that they might actually be giving higher priority, without articulating it, to goal Y (such as, respect and genuine caring), or goal Z (a sense that one's life is connected to some higher meaning and purpose). While many who have moved to the Right in recent years can be seen as irrational if one assumes that their highest value is material security, they may be seen as far less irrational if their highest values are acknowledged as lying elsewhere.

Princeton sociologist Robert Wuthnow demonstrates the folly of economic reductionism.[8] Rural Americans (whom Wuthnow defines as farmers and those living in towns with populations of 25,000 or fewer—some 44 to 50 million people) have consistently voted for Republicans for the past several decades, during which many of their towns have faced declining populations as younger people move away to find better jobs. Wuthnow urges us to think of these people as living in "moral communities"—not in the sense of good, right, or virtuous, but in the sense that people living there "feel an obligation to one another and to uphold the local ways of being that govern their expectations about ordinary life." What leads them to be angry at liberals is their own "almost inexpressible concern that their way of life is eroding, shifting imperceptibly" and that they are "being discredited and attacked from the outside." In other words, rural Americans are afraid for the well-being and sustainability of their communities that have given them a sense of meaning and purpose and a location in which they get respect.

Wuthnow's argument underscores my contention that most people need community and a sense of higher meaning to their lives than they can achieve through the socially sanctioned pursuits of money or fame. Valuing this sense of meaning and community, which people rationally seek, is usually not addressed by liberals and progressive movements—even though it is precisely these kinds of needs that brought many people into progressive movements.

Sadly, for example, I didn't find much understanding of the psychological and spiritual needs of Americans in what was otherwise a beautiful moment of upsurging, revolutionary energy during the Occupy movement in 2011. I spent many nights at Occupy encampments, where young and idealistic men and women sought to live their own highest ideals while challenging the financial powers that were responsible for so much economic suffering. Their lasting contribution was to highlight the disparity of wealth and power between the top 1 percent and the 99 percent of the rest of us. Yet they disappeared after a few months, in large part because they refused to put forward a vision of the world they wanted, or any transitional demands. Fearing the co-optive power of electoral politics, they failed to do in the Democratic Party what right-winger Tea Partyists subsequently did in the Republican Party—organize themselves into an electoral force that took control. And though they presented themselves as speaking for the 99 percent, their process—meetings that required consensus and hence lasted late into the night—made it impossible for those with families and jobs to be included.

Nor have I heard the needs I am talking about seriously discussed by speakers at wonderful events like the mass mobilization for the environment sponsored by 350.org or the beautiful and impressive Women's March that began the day after Trump was inaugurated in 2017. I've attended endless conferences, living room conversations, public and private colloquia; listened to many TED Talks; read a wide variety of liberal and progressive magazines and websites; watched wealthy foundations and individuals give huge amounts of money to liberal and progressive organizations. Yet I've found very few willing to address the psychological and spiritual crisis in America or to encourage the visioning of a new society that could energize the hope necessary to inspire people to spend their time and energies on something more than winning the next election for the most palatable candidates, or passing some modest voter initiatives, or organizing narrowly focused single-issue campaigns.

Democrats in the United States will likely achieve electoral victories in the early part of the 2020s, based in part on growing reactions against the sexism, racism, xenophobia, and hate that has characterized much of the Trump agenda. Yet even if an extremely progressive person becomes president in 2020 or 2024, the Democrats could once again follow the script that inclines them to look for the middle ground between the apologists for American's ruling elites and those who have been badly hurt by them. If the Democrats raise hopes for more meaningful change only to disappoint again, we might see a backlash similar to the one we experienced in 2016; and the outcome might be an even more oppressive right-wing movement in the 2030s than the Trumpists delivered!

To prevent these dynamics from leading to a truly fascist America (elections suspended, critics of the regime jailed without trial or murdered, media critical of the regime forcibly closed, demonstrations of protest prohibited or facing violence and mass shootings), we will need a movement in the 2020s that can address powerfully and empathically those suffering from the psychological and spiritual crisis that the Right has recently manipulated so successfully. *Revolutionary Love* offers not just a salve for the pain, but a way to clearly see what is happening in our world and move beyond the Left's list of complaints, first to help people understand the connection between the pain in their personal lives and the ethical dysfunction built into the dynamics and worldview of the competitive marketplace, and then to articulate a vision of the world we actually want.

WHAT CAN A THERAPIST DO WHEN MAJOR PARTS OF ONE'S SOCIETY SEEM TO BE GOING CRAZY?

I became a psychotherapist in 1976 in part because I had already noticed American society becoming increasingly unbalanced. What should therapists do today when they encounter a growing psychological depression generated not solely by unresolved childhood traumas or chemical imbalances but by the internalization of fear and despair as the human race continues to destroy the life support system of the planet and, by extension, its own future? What should therapists do when our own society elects and puts into power as president not only someone who many therapists believe is a malignant narcissist (and some see him as on the border of being a socio-path) but also a team of people whose careers have been built on undermining the rights of racial minorities, supporting sexist practices, or dismantling environmental protections and public education systems? Or when tens of millions of people vote for candidates who tell them that refugee caravans of mostly women and children from Central American countries fleeing violence, rape, and murders in their own country will be an existential threat to the safety of the most powerful country in the world and that their attempts to get here is "a national emergency" requiring military troops and violation of the Constitution's mandate of separation of powers? What are those of us in the healing and teaching professions to do when the pathologies in our society and in the larger world are so toxic that they deepen despair and make treatment of the smaller pathologies almost (not totally) beside the point?

Most therapists are trained to avoid discussing the larger pathologies of society. I often think of the endless hours that many Jews spent in therapists' offices in pre-Holocaust Europe during the 1920s and early 1930s while managing to avoid, both in therapy and in the rest of their lives, the growing hate movements that would eventually murder them and everyone they ever knew. What a shame that psychotherapists didn't use some of their expertise to help people see more clearly the destructiveness growing around them— and use some of their time to help people develop skills that might have helped win over (or back) those Europeans who were not yet firmly locked into a fascistic movement of hate before the Nazi movement took power! To those who say that's not the job of a therapist, I would respond that if people are blind to the dangers threatening their existence, the emotional blocks to seeing those realities must become a central issue for the helping professions, particularly those that explicitly deal with emotional blocks.

Clearly these challenges are not new. They were faced by Sigmund Freud and others in the wake of World War I, by the Frankfurt School of Critical Theory during the rise of Hitler and Stalin, and then again after World War II by those who studied the authoritarian personality. Erich Fromm, Herbert Marcuse, Robert Jay Lifton, Hannah Arendt, and many others grappled with similar issues during the height of the Cold War, the Vietnam War, and subsequent global struggles. And yet, these thinkers do not provide sufficient instruction for how to approach the coming decades as the economic, psychological, and spiritual failings of global capitalism intensify.

The call to create the caring society promoting what I and others call revolutionary love that this manifesto presents emerged for me from what I learned as a psychotherapist working at the Institute for Labor and Mental Health. In my role as the principal investigator of a National Institute of Mental Health-funded grant to study the dynamics of stress at work and in family life, I encouraged our research team to learn about the psychodynamics of American society for middle income working people. In particular, I asked them to probe why many American workers had moved from supporting liberal policies that offered them economic benefits to more conservative ones that sought to reduce or eliminate those benefits. What was leading otherwise healthy people to be attracted to reactionary political and religious movements?

I discovered while doing this research what social theorists, theologians, and many psychotherapists already knew: that most human beings have a part of them that wants a very different kind of world but have been convinced that getting to such a world is impossible. Our desire for meaningful change remains powerless as long we are "realistic," accepting what the media, major political leaders, and even our own family and friends tell us is possible. And it can then be twisted into something very different by leaders who purport to share our values and goals.

Every major change in our world has happened because a small group of people started to talk and act, in the name of higher values, in ways that challenged the so-called realists of their day. In this historical moment, that challenge requires rejecting the notion popular in many liberal and progressive circles that most people are either evil, racist, sexist, homophobic, xenophobic, anti-Semitic, Islamophobic, ultra nationalist, white supremacist, patriarchal, religious extremist, or just plain stupid. Instead, we must recognize that the hurtful attitudes and behaviors we see are the results not of individual, deformed personalities but of systemic practices and consciousness fostered for thousands of years in class societies. Elites who sought to consolidate their own power over others and secure free or very low-cost labor used these oppressions to divide those whom they ruled, impoverished, and exploited. And in the past few hundred years, the creation of a world of work so frequently rewarded selfishness and materialism while setting people against each other in ruthless competition that caring for others began to seem like a unique achievement rather than the norm of human reality.

Revolutionary love seeks to reunite all sections of the population into a democratic force capable of healing and repairing our world (the Hebrew concept of *tikkun olam*) and saving it from environmental disaster. But to accomplish that, we must make major strides in overcoming the fear, the pain, and the traumas that often cripple our abilities to see clearly what is happening in our world or what we could do to change things. Without meaning to, we make the pain worse when we blame people for getting some rewards from the existing, oppressive system, which they did not create and which they have never been encouraged to think about how to change or encouraged to seek people in their vicinity who might want to be involved in that conversation. Before we can win people back to a world of justice and environmental sanity, we will first need to change some aspects of the elitist and condescending cultural and societal assumptions that flourish within the liberal and progressive social change movements and among the tens of millions of people who identify with them.

Revolutionary love is not, therefore, about winning the next election—it is about a fundamental transformation of thinking and acting. Most young people born in the last forty years have no historical experience of the possibility of such large-scale change. Many take for granted, for example, the existence of a powerful global movement for women's rights; they don't realize that just fifty years ago the tiny group of Second Wave feminists concentrated in a few cities and college campuses in the United States, France, and England were seen as completely unrealistic when they sought to overcome patriarchy. No, that battle has not yet been won (nor were their efforts without shortcomings, especially in their inability to include working-class white women and women of color), but the current status and power of women in almost every culture in the world has changed almost unimaginably in five short decades.

Revolutionary love is *not* a variant of New Age claims such as "If each of us changes how we think, the world will be healed" or "If only we were more loving, everything else would work out." Unless we simultaneously transform our economic and political arrangements to overcome class-stratified society, patriarchy, and racism, our compassion, empathy, and generosity will not stop the destruction of the Earth. The path forward is a new kind of activism described in the first four chapters of this book.

I have deep appreciation for the creativity, energy, and ethical seriousness of millions of people who march and campaign to resist the worst crimes of the Trumpists and in favor of human rights and for an environmentally sane world. I believe that their activism helped create the climate in which many women and people of color were elected to the House of Representatives in the 2018 midterm election. At the same time, I've witnessed (and participated in) movements that have acted in self-defeating or self-marginalizing ways. So I'm going to challenge some of the ways people in social change movements have unintentionally weakened their own effectiveness even while I celebrate their ethical seriousness and courage.

Revolutionary love provides a picture of a world that could work for everyone. It could save the life support system of the planet; support the human race to overcome its current spiritual and psychological depression and be filled with joy, gentleness, emotional awareness, and caring for each other; and help humanity reclaim awe and wonder at the grandeur and mystery of all life. Revolutionary love requires giving up the so-called common sense of capitalist society, thus allowing each of us to become a champion of a new way of thinking and a new way of relating to each other, to our brothers and sisters of the human race, to animals, and to the planet Earth.

Revolutionary love faces a challenge: how to help people overcome the psycho-physical illness that novelist and healer Deena Metzger describes in a January 3, 2019, article titled "Extinction Illness: Grave Affliction and Possibility" (available on Tikkun's website) and which I've described in *Tikkun* as a global psycho-spiritual depression. Metzger writes that the environmental crisis is now so pervasive that everyone has a part of them that knows that "we are all going extinct. The animals know this and now all humans know this as well. Sensing the imminent death of all species, the cellular understanding of our common fate is making us ill. Our nervous and physical systems cannot bear this terrible knowledge . . . all human people and all beings, animals, trees, birds, insects, fish, know this. And all of us are being driven to some form of madness, pain, or dysfunction . . . We humans know, with or without awareness, that we are responsible. And so, we, entirely crazed, become a species that commits ecocide even as we die of it." Revolutionary love offers us a path out of this horror, but it is a path that requires fundamental transformation and a rejection of all the voices that tell us to be realistic, which de facto means to continue on the path toward destruction of the planet upon whose life-nurturing energies our lives depend. As the Torah teaches: "Choose life." That is what this manifesto is really about.

HOW TO READ THIS BOOK

I suspect that if you've read this far you may already be someone who recognizes that an effective social change movement needs to manifest caring for everyone—including those not yet seeking justice for all. I know well that most people engaged in liberal or progressive change movements, and the many who have never been engaged but in their minds and hearts support them, are beautiful human beings. You've given what you could, taken risks for your ideas, perhaps been arrested, lost jobs or job promotions, even lost friends and family members, and yet you've often been underappreciated. You deserve recognition, honor, and support. You try to be the highest embodiment of your ideals while still dealing with all the challenges of everyday life. Think of this book as inviting you to take one more courageous step toward overcoming classism and embracing the possibility of building what I call the caring society. Far from being a utopian fantasy, the caring society is actually the necessary next step for the survival of Earth and the victory of social justice.

In the first part of this book I discuss the human needs that go beyond economic security and individual rights, and how liberals and progressives need to change internally to effectively address those needs. Yet I do so without abandoning the concern for material well-being, which people also need. The second part of this manifesto presents a strategy for how to build a different kind of world, including programs, demands, guidance on practices, and some utopian speculations about where that could ultimately lead. Programs and policies based on revolutionary love will bring dramatic improvements in addressing not only people's psychological and spiritual needs but also their material needs. If we want people to engage in the process of building a new world, we need to begin now to articulate our visions of what such a world will look like.

I ask you to suspend your disbelief and your inclination to believe that anyone writing about love and other spiritual values must be either intellectually challenged or a religious fanatic. I am neither. I've been involved in social change movements since 1964. Now, as an Elder, I want to share some of what I learned that might be helpful to anyone who wishes to counter the reactionary movements that have arisen in the United States and around the world.

Allow yourself to imagine a social change movement for the 2020s and 2030s that addresses not only the economic suffering of some, but the psycho-spiritual deprivation for all that comes from living in a world in which people are in constant competition. Global capitalism encourages us to believe that life is about the accumulation of power, money, fame, and/or sexual conquest, and we blame ourselves for not succeeding economically or having the kind of friendships, loving families, or supportive communities for which we hunger. A movement for revolutionary love would teach people empathy, both for themselves and others in their lives and for people with whom they seemingly or authentically disagree.

Our movement would seek to transform the Democratic Party from within while simultaneously building the infrastructure for a Love and Justice Party in case the Democrats become as stuck in their insensitivity to this movement as they were in dealing with Bernie Sanders in 2016. Our movement would not only promote a world of love and justice, but embody those notions in nourishing ways toward both its members and those who will at first ridicule and demean it. Such a movement would soon, over the course of the next several decades, win the mass support needed to defeat the reactionaries and proto-fascists; save life on the planet; undermine the racism, sexism, classism, homophobia, anti-Semitism, ageism, xenophobia, and Islamophobia that have been used to divide us; and relieve the depression and powerlessness that paralyze so many people today.

The Love and Justice movement (or whatever it might come to be called) would have a strong backbone and a prophetic voice that challenges those who speak lies and those who cause, or turn their backs on, the suffering of others. We would not play the game of politics that compromises with the powerful rather than letting them face consequences for their actions. We would see the humanity of those with whom we disagree, but we would not soften the tones of the prophets of ancient Israel who insisted on confronting the evil around them. The prophets we honor spoke out loudly at the cynicism of those who worshipped religiously but then refused to care for the hungry, the homeless, the powerless, and the refugees.

Without such a movement, we can expect more decades of alternation between high-minded but spineless liberal forces compromising on their ideals in order to be realistic, and ultra-right-wing and white nationalist and Christian fundamentalists groups whose views are increasingly articulated by congressional Republicans. No matter which of these two is in ascendancy at any given moment, the destruction of the life support system of the planet will intensify, and classism and racism and sexism will find new paths to flourish.

We can't scare people into the rational behavior needed to protect the life support system of Earth. We need to replace the globalization of selfishness with the globalization of generosity and caring—caring for one another and caring for the Earth. We need to overcome the ways that liberal and progressive movements and the Democratic Party have alienated people who might otherwise have been on their side. And we need to paint a picture of a very different kind of world that is not only possible but necessary for global survival. If this manifesto succeeds in generating this conversation, gives you some tools to help you better understand the psychodynamics of daily life and their impact on American politics, entices you to join me in joyfully embracing what the media and leaders and opinion shapers tell us is "unrealistic," and perhaps provides a foundation for a new kind of progressive movement, it will have succeeded. So I offer these ideas in a spirit of humility, knowing that I will have left off many important points, and hoping that you will absorb what is valuable in this book and transcend my limitations.

PART I

Transcending the Crippling Dynamics of Oppression

CHAPTER ONE

A World of Pain, a Hunger for Love

We live in a world whose people are in deep pain.

Some of this pain is a product of economic inequality. Approximately 842 million people suffer from hunger worldwide, and nine million people die of hunger each year. According to recent studies, over 10 percent of people in the world live on less than two dollars a day. In the United States, inequality has grown dramatically over the past four decades, ever since both political parties participated in gradually weakening the New Deal's social safety net that had been put in place during the 1930s and 1940s. In 2016, the richest 1 percent of families controlled a record-high 38.6 percent of the country's wealth, according to a Federal Reserve report published in November 2017. That's nearly twice as much as the bottom 90 percent of families, who now hold just 22.8 percent of the wealth, down from about 33 percent in 1989 when the federal government started tracking this statistic.[1] And all this does make a difference. Dr. Sandro Galea, dean of the Boston University School of Public Health, writing in the February 2019 issue of *Fortune* magazine, reports that "the wealthiest 1 percent of Americans can now expect to live 10 to 15 years longer than the least well-off 1 percent. . . . Inequality not only denies the majority of Americans access to the material fruits of wealth; by denying them these resources it also denies them health."

Yet the pain I focus on in this book is often less obvious, though not unrelated to our global economic system. This pain is a result of a worldwide deprivation of love, generosity, respect, and community. People hunger deeply for a higher purpose in life than the search for material well-being, power, fame, and sexual conquest, and they feel real suffering when they are unable to find meaning either for themselves or within a community that puts these transcendent values above those that they encounter daily in the competitive marketplace and mass media. If we call the economic crisis of the 1930s the Great Depression and the economic crisis of 2007–2011 the Great Recession, then I suggest that this psychological and spiritual pain, which cripples billions of people worldwide, should be called the Great Deprivation.

The Great Deprivation may have begun as far back as the emergence of patriarchy and class society (in some cases, as long as 8,000 to 10,000 years ago) in the newly forming city-states in Mesopotamia, China, Greece, India, and elsewhere. Mythology and tribal collective memories preserve the notion that at an earlier point in human history people lived in groups that shared their resources in relatively equal ways. It took violence to coerce people into accepting inequalities to satisfy the lust and selfishness of the few. The subsequent development of patriarchal and class societies enshrined the notion that violence and inequality were natural, and that wars and oppression were built into the inescapable structure of human society and human nature. People began to lose their memories of a more cooperative and sharing way of life.

From the start of the Great Deprivation, however, people also found ways to hold on to their best ideals. Many communities remembered or evolved religious rituals that provided some relief from the increasingly exploitative realities of life and work. They built forms of resistance through beliefs in a world to come after their death (such as a heaven or hell) in which injustice would be overthrown. And even when, over time, religions were undermined by their subservience to the ruling elites who funded them, most people in both ancient and medieval times worked in outdoor rural settings that provided opportunities for direct and unmediated spiritual and transcendent experiences in nature.

But the use of violence to maintain unequal power in the newly imposed class and patriarchal societies required human beings to suppress more and more their inborn ability to see and directly experience the nobility and goodness of others, particularly those who were being dominated. The clerics, philosophers, teachers, poets, entertainers, and authors supported by the ruling classes, who dominate most societies past and present, produced both elite and mass cultures that justified the selfishness and emotional disconnection that would allow people to impose pain on others. Among these cultural systems, racism became one of the most effective, and it remains a central reality in contemporary politics.

The practice of enslaving human beings began in the ancient world, including forced marriages imposed on women or the conquest of one tribe by another in struggles to control land as agriculture emerged as an easier solution to getting a steady supply of food than had been available in hunter-gatherer societies. Enslaving others had become the new normal form of organization of society at least by the time of Sumer in Mesopotamia some 6,000 years ago, spreading to European, African, and Asian societies (through a caste system in India and in the class structures of ancient China). Forms of slavery in Athens and then in Rome shaped the destinies of millions of people in the empires imposed on those whom the conquering elites called "barbarians" around what we'd now call the Middle East and much of Europe, and later evolved into feudal relations of subservience in which serfs became property of the landowners. As European, Muslim, and African societies sought to expand in power and land, the slave trade itself became a major economic foundation for the flourishing of European countries and their colonies in the Americas and Africa. As always, the exploiters sought to

A World of Pain, a Hunger for Love

demean those whom they dominated, developing ways to avoid seeing the humanity of those they were enslaving (or, in the case of the indigenous peoples of North, Central, and South America, murdering them with impunity in large numbers). They did so in part to suppress their own more natural instinct to see the enslaved as human beings and hence treat them with respect and to teach their children to avoid having compassion for those being oppressed, recognitions that might have undermined the system that was otherwise providing them with some benefits.

Keeanga-Yamahtta Taylor, who teaches in the African American Studies department at Princeton University, explains that "Racism in the U.S. has never been about abusing Black and Brown people just for the sake of doing so. It has always been a means by which the most powerful white men in the country have justified their rule, made their money, and kept the rest of us at bay. To that end, racism, capitalism, and class rule have always been tangled together in such a way that it is impossible to imagine one without the other."[2]

Each new system of mistreatment has increased the Great Deprivation for all people, since all get taught to justify their participation by valuing various systems of material compensation and to ignore their loss of connection to any higher ethical purpose and meaning. Martin Luther King, Jr., underlined the need for a fundamental transformation when he wrote in his "Testament of Hope," in the weeks before his assassination, "America must change because twenty-three million black citizens will no longer live supinely in a wretched past. They have left the valley of despair; they have found strength in struggle. Joined by white allies, they will shake the prison walls until they fall. America must change."

Sadly, in the fifty-plus years since King's assassination, the huge energy of the civil rights movement has been focused on extending the benefits of civil rights legislation without giving equal energy to dismantling the racist consciousness so deeply ingrained in Western societies. Like so many liberal and progressive movements, the civil rights movement has focused on external change, like the integration of schools, without for instance, insisting that every school in America educate young people about racism to break down emotional distance and help children understand why so many societies used racism to prevent people from uniting against whatever system of oppression existed at the time. Affirmative action did bring African Americans and Latinos into work places and universities, and Barack Obama's presidency gave some the illusion that equality had finally been achieved. But it was an illusion: the failure to focus on dismantling racist assumptions, even about the legitimacy of affirmative action, left an opening for the Right. Racist forces soon mobilized, first in the white racist Tea Party and eventually in the national leadership of the Republican Party which, in its quest for a sustainable path to national political power after decades of relative powerlessness in the shadow of the New Deal, had adopted what aides to Presidents Richard Nixon and Ronald Reagan termed a Southern Strategy (catering to the legacy of slavery and segregation while pretending in northern states that they still sought to honor notions of equality for minority groups). With the emergence of the Tea Party in 2009 (and later, the growing power of Trumpists), this pretense was being abandoned while the Obama administration—and the mainstream of the Democratic Party, which followed Obama's lead—worried that the resurgent racism would be strengthened if it was openly confronted, and hence did little either through legislation in its first two years in power, or through executive orders and effective use of its bully pulpit, to help white working people understand why racism actually worked against their interests.

The emergence of the #BlackLivesMatter movement in response to ongoing assaults on African Americans—particularly murders of blacks by police, who regularly are not held accountable—has been a hopeful sign that a new generation would no longer be satisfied with (usually unfulfilled) promises of economic mobility alone. As Keeanga-Yamahtta Taylor declares, "The day to day struggles in which many people are engaged today must be connected to a much larger vision of what a different world could look like."[3]

For me, this call echoes Malcolm X's universalist vision, which grew out of his conversion to Islam. It took a different form yet rang with the same universalist aspirations when it was articulated to me by Huey Newton and Bobby Seale when I met with them to try to bring the Peace and Freedom and the Black Panther parties into alliance in 1968. What made Malcolm X, and after his assassination, the Black Panthers, so dangerous to America's ruling elites was precisely their combination of passionate advocacy for their own African American community linked to a universal vision that could speak to the needs of both middle income and working class whites, inviting a solidarity that could effectively challenge not only racism but classism. Huey Newton explicitly used these terms in our discussion and I later experienced the solidarity enabled by such a universalist consciousness when the Panthers sent word to their followers at the Terminal Island Federal Penitentiary to ally with me and provide protection against white nationalist extremists who sought to attack me while I was incarcerated as one of the Seattle Seven (for contempt of court, a charge later overturned by the U.S. Ninth Circuit Court).[4]

That same universalist consciousness led me to bring members of *Tikkun* magazine's interfaith and secular-humanist-welcoming Network of Spiritual Progressives to show up in solidarity at African American churches around the United States on Sundays after the murder of African Americans; and it led many pastors who appreciated that symbolic act to show up in return when eleven Jews were massacred in a Pittsburgh synagogue by a white nationalist supremacist in October 2018. This kind of solidarity for victims of racist violence has been repeated in many churches, synagogues, and mosques whenever such atrocities occur.

We cannot get to the world we need without sustained attention to the roots of racism, sexism, and class domination. Each of these systems is fortified not only by economic and political inequalities but by a system of emotional and spiritual deprivation. A great mistake of liberal and progressive forces is their tendency to direct their righteous indignation about systems of oppression not only toward those who have the greatest wealth and power, but also at anyone who they believe is materially benefiting from systemic injustice, no matter how slight those material benefits really are (in the United States, the target then becomes all whites and all men). To achieve the transformation of American and global politics our world needs, while continuing the struggle against every form of inequality and oppression, equal attention must be focused on how much racism, sexism, homophobia, ageism, and classism continue to produce a huge loss in the quality of almost everyone's lives, including the lives of most whites and most men, on how much we are losing as the global environmental crisis deepens, and on how much we would benefit from a society based on repairing the Great Deprivation with revolutionary love. Much of this and the next three chapters illuminate this claim.

WHAT IS REVOLUTIONARY LOVE?

Revolutionary love is the love of life and all beings, embracing this world with all its complexities, heartaches, and joys. It is an approach that is respectful and caring toward everyone on the planet, even those whose behavior we hope will change, and toward the Earth in all its magnificent diversity as well. It is recognizing oneself and all others as part of the fundamental unity of all being—and caring for the welfare of every part of that unity. It is transcending one's own narrow self-interest to experience others as manifestations of the sacred, and recognizing that a world where all are treated with respect and nurturance, both material and emotional, is in fact in one's own self-interest as well. It is finding meaning in one's life through relieving the pain and suffering of others, and joining with them in joyous and mutually nourishing relationships.

We see this kind of love again and again in heroic actions throughout the world. People running into the collapsing World Trade Center to help others escape. People jumping into flooding waters to save people, and even animals, from drowning. People chaining themselves to trees to protect forests from the devastation of logging. Native Americans and their allies facing freezing water hoses, rubber bullets, and arrest as they joined together at Standing Rock to demand that oil companies and big banks halt the laying of environmentally destructive pipelines and the fracking that is destroying significant sections of North America. It is joining with these indigenous peoples in demanding that banks and investment companies stop funding the extraction and use of fossil fuels and instead only fund development of alternative sources of energy like the wind and the sun to run our transportation systems, our communication systems, and our agricultural systems.

Revolutionary love affirms what we experience in personal family and romantic love, deeply values that kind of love, and yet moves beyond these personal experiences to an affirmation of the unity of all humanity and a genuine caring for all sentient life. Revolutionary love is closer to love as understood in the Torah's commands to "love the Other/the stranger as yourself" (Leviticus 19: 33–34) and to "love your neighbor as yourself."

It may seem overwhelming to make oneself so vulnerable to the needs of so many others. Yet caring for others often renews us. And we can act in ways that affirm their sanctity and preciousness, and we can build an economic and political system that embodies and sustains that kind of universal caring. Doing so will involve creating larger periods of open time in our lives, in part through a decrease in the hours spent at work, so that we may transcend our customary goal-directed activities—the driven consciousness fostered by a world of material scarcity—and instead aim to create a world in which people spend more time inhabiting states of playfulness, creativity, and joyful celebration. Rather than manifesting only in a long-term relationship with a spouse, partner, or friend, revolutionary love also manifests in an ever-growing consciousness that finds joy in learning about each other and our world through science, literature, art, music, religion, and dance. It expands through genuine caring for the Earth combined with awe at the mysteries of consciousness and being itself, whether addressed through art and music, philosophy, religion, psychedelics, or other sources that lead to an awakening to the necessity of sharing, cooperation, generosity, humility, and joyful celebration of life.

Revolutionary love repudiates domination, instead cultivating a fervent commitment to healing ourselves and others, to ending psychological as well as physical suffering, and to fostering the values of nonviolence so eloquently articulated by Mahatma Gandhi and Martin Luther King, Jr. It recognizes hurtful behaviors—such as violence; hoarding and consumption beyond any physical hunger or survival need; or the endless search for more power, more possessions, more sexual conquests, and more obedience from others—as evidence of an absence of real connection with others. All these are manifestations of an intense cry from within that has been stifled and misdirected into destructive paths, leading to war and exploitation of others and of the planet.

As it embraces the sacred core of all being, revolutionary love manifests within us as an intense desire to heal those hurts rather than simply demean or punish those who act out their pain on others. To heal effectively, we must recognize that every one of us has been wounded in some way and needs forgiveness, atonement, and personal transformation.

All of us? Yes, this also means reaching out to the 1 percent along with the 99 percent, even those who have actively and consciously participated in economic arrangements that hurt the rest of us; or engaged in acts of cruelty; or financed media that spread misinformation and lies while refusing to publicize the ideas of those who challenged their wealth; or knowingly supported candidates and social movements that demean others; or financed pipelines and fracking while opposing environmental programs that would benefit the health of humanity and the well-being of the Earth; or engaged in what Naomi Klein calls "disaster capitalism" (exploiting the pain and the trauma of collective shocks—like superstorms or economic crisis—in order to build an even more unequal and undemocratic society); or even, like President Donald Trump, tweeted both overt and covert messages that encourage violence, racism, sexism, homophobia, anti-Semitism, and hatred of "the Other." These oppressors too are part of the human race, however distorted their current consciousness; and so even as we must work to delegitimize their ideas, dismantle their power, redistribute their wealth, and in some cases punish their misdeeds with prison sentences, we can still feel compassion for whatever childhood pain and adult life seductions led them to lives utterly detached from beautiful and nurturing ethical and spiritual wisdom, loving relationships, and the joyous human-connectedness that continue to provide spiritual sustenance and fulfillment to so many whose lives are shaped by a commitment to higher goals than money, power, or conquests. Being aware of that suffering dimension of the lives of many of the most brutal and uncaring of the rich and powerful may make us more effective and not one ounce less committed to stopping them from hurting anyone more than they, as well as those who do their bidding and the global capitalist and patriarchal systems they serve, already have done.

Revolutionary love is aimed at building what I call the Caring Society—Caring for Each Other and Caring for the Earth. When we embody that kind of revolutionary love, we are capable of connecting with, fully recognizing, and empathizing with others in all their complexity, and building lasting relationships with them; deepening our understanding of the complicated, multilayered, and interconnected nature of this planet Earth; caring for others without fear that there won't be enough caring to go around; generously sharing our talents and our material resources with others; sharing responsibility for the raising of empathic, joyous, and curious children, and for the care of elders in ways that affirm their worth; taking pleasure in our own bodies and minds and in the bodies and minds of others, and creating respectful, consensual relationships, both platonic and erotic; respecting individual differences and alternative life paths; and connecting our personal lives to a higher meaning or transcendent reality that serves the well-being of humanity, all life forms, and Earth. Some mystics would call revolutionary love "God-ing," that is, a manifestation of the sacred, creative, and transformative energy of the universe (though one need not be religious or a believer in God to seek a world shaped by revolutionary love).

This is the love for which most people intuitively yearn, the answer to the Great Deprivation. Yet most of us simultaneously believe it to be impossible, and suppress our yearning for reasons I explore below. The conscious reclamation of this kind of love, and the ensuing struggle to realize it in every aspect of our global society, is the key to a global transformation that would not only defeat the militarists, religious and nationalist extremists, white supremacists, champions of patriarchy, and global elites who benefit most from our corrupt economic and political arrangements; it would also reawaken *tikkun*—the idealism, hope, and commitment to heal and repair the world that are the keys to saving the human race from further destroying ourselves and the life support system of Earth. Only a full-scale embrace of revolutionary love will save our world. This love must manifest in actions to transform the economic, political, social, cultural, religious/spiritual, and environmental realities of our global society and must constantly link each of our particular actions to our larger vision of the world we want, even as we work on changing ourselves.

I remember how I hated being told by rock stars at antiwar rallies in the 1960s, "I love all of you." I believed then that it was impossible to love people you didn't know, if by "love" we mean the narrower version of romantic love. But you *can* feel revolutionary love for all of Earth's people, and its animals and plants and geology and atmosphere, and you can act on that love.

Revolutionary love is recognizing, feeling, and acting upon the truth that we are all interconnected. This love manifested powerfully in the horrified responses to President Trump's order to ICE (U.S. Immigration and Customs Enforcement agency) to separate children and nursing babies from their refugee-seeking parents and place those children in cages. Suddenly the normal political divisions disappeared as Baptists, Evangelicals, and many Republicans joined with progressive Catholics, Jews, Unitarians, mainstream Protestants, Muslims, Buddhists, atheists, and many Democrats and social change activists to attempt to force Trump to back down. The memory of their own precious experience of attachment to a parent, the love that they shared and in many cases subsequently lost, led them to gather as a mighty, united force to demand that separation of families at the Mexican border not happen to the children of refugees. When people get back in touch with the revolutionary love that has always been a part of their essence, they are willing to put aside their own narrower needs and creature comforts and even risk their lives for something greater than themselves. When we do so, we become spiritual progressives and love revolutionaries.

To take revolutionary love seriously, we will all have to overcome our internalization of the many constraining ideas our current political and economic system has planted in us, especially those that keep us from believing that the world we want really is possible.

CHALLENGING DOMINANT FORMS OF ECONOMIC REASONING

In ancient Greece, the economic concern was on how to build a functioning household (defined within patriarchal assumptions). Later, as market societies rose to dominance, economics became more focused on how corporations as well as powerful individuals could accumulate more power and more money, in the belief that this was the path to happiness. Yet those who do well in market societies rarely find happiness just in accumulating money and material goods. Meanwhile, the psychological and spiritual costs of pursuing the goals of global capitalism are devastating. Caught like King Midas of legend in a frenetic pursuit of wealth, power, and fame, many lose the nourishment that comes from loving relationships based on real intimacy—and also their ability to connect spiritually to the universe. By the same token, spiritually alive people who question the pursuit of wealth and power often risk marginalization, finding their alternative ways of thinking dismissed as irrational or as "merely" religious. They are effectively excluded from or ridiculed by the prevalent public discourse in media, politics, and the academy.

The dominant intellectual, political, and economic worldviews of Western societies rest on two key beliefs, which are foundational to the present justification of class societies. Most people in Western societies have internalized these beliefs as "common sense."

The first foundational premise is what has been called radical empiricism: if one cannot show how one's claims can be measured, verified, or falsified, then the claims are literally meaningless and have no place in public discourse.

Physical science and exploration solidified the dominance of the empirical approach, which is the foundation of modern scientific inquiry and has given us such great advantages as indoor plumbing, heating and cooling, electricity, computers, advanced means of communication and travel, ever-improving medicine, and scientific knowledge about the devastation of rapidly increasing climate change. We humans owe a deep debt of gratitude to science and scientists.

But it is important to distinguish between science and scientism. Science is the attempt to understand the aspects of nature that operate according to publicly observable and repeatable laws. Scientism, on the other hand, is a belief that everything that exists or can be known can *only* be known through empirical methods or measured (at least in principle). Scientism is the inappropriate extension of legitimate science into a radical empiricism that seeks to reduce all human realities to those that science can describe

A World of Pain, a Hunger for Love

and measure. This is a reductionist materialism that narrows and distorts our understanding of the human world.

For instance, let's look at the realm of ethics. From a scientistic perspective, ethical judgments are not scientifically verifiable, cannot be measured, and hence should not be the basis for our public life. Since true knowledge, in the scientistic account, is based only on what we can empirically observe or measure, ethical reasoning lacks gravitas and intellectual foundation. Everything else is dismissed as religious fantasies or as meaningless metaphysics that has no claim on our respect and no place in shaping our public lives.

Yet, ironically enough, the worldview of radical empiricism that has frequently been used to minimize, marginalize, or even at times discredit ethical reasoning, all spiritual or religious thought, and all talk of meaning in life, is by its own criterion religious in nature. Consider its founding belief: that which can be known, and that which is real is that which can be subjected to empirical measurement, verification, or falsification. Yet this statement itself cannot be subjected to empirical verification or falsification nor can it be measured. No set of experiments or observations demonstrates its truth. Nor can there be any such demonstrations. By its own criteria, then, scientism is either false or meaningless.

Some defenders of scientism say that their adoption of radical empiricism is only a methodological principle, not a claim about reality. Fine. But that is what ethicists and religious people do also—except that they adopt a different methodological principle. Both are without empirical foundation, and both have outcomes that are at times valuable, and at times destructive.

I celebrate science, and want no part of those on the Right who dismiss scientific knowledge about climate change or the way humans and capitalist societies have contributed to it, but I don't worship at the church of scientism. When it comes to matters of fundamental human aspirations or desires, sociological or psychological research can tell us what people do in fact think but are useless in assessing what we should believe or do. Human reality is based on consciousness, which is only somewhat accessible to external observation and which does not fit into the regularity and order that science seeks in nature. It has not been and cannot be reduced to a set of deterministic laws. Its essence is freedom and transcendence.

The universe evolved in such a way that human beings developed a consciousness that manifested freedom and choice. While science may certainly study the details of our nervous system and brain and rightly contends that at least on this planet or perhaps in this galaxy consciousness is dependent upon certain kinds of physical and chemical prerequisites (e.g., a body like ours), science will never be able to reduce that consciousness to the bodily states that make it possible. Human freedom belies scientism.

To the extent that human freedom is carefully constrained by societal norms communicated through educational and mass media indoctrination, and these constraints are incentivized with material rewards, people will act in ways that society or powerful members of that society want them to act. Consequently, economists and social scientists can predict with a degree of accuracy how people will behave. In fact, the predictions themselves can play a role in shaping future behavior, to the extent that people wish to act as they believe they are expected to act (and will be rewarded for so acting).

But the moment people begin to break out of those constraints, social science and economic predictions prove useless, and their supposed laws of human group behavior will fail time and time again. When social movements emerge and make fundamental changes in economic and/or political arrangements, some economists and social scientists scramble to come up with explanations after the fact. The same scholars warn people that changes are impossible before they happen and then try to show that they were "inevitable" once they have happened.

Some of the best social scientists of the past several decades have given up on trying to find laws of human behavior and instead turned to emphasizing qualitative research, in which researchers talk to people in depth and over time. Getting to know people, being exposed to their consciousness, and hearing how they understand their world and their desires are prerequisites for helping us all understand the complex yearnings and inner dynamics of human beings and our ever-present possibilities for transcending and transforming ourselves and our world.

I experienced this transcendence and transformation during the antiwar movement of the 1960s. I helped create a teach-in against the Vietnam War and was so moved by what I learned that I joined with hundreds of others to try to stop the troop trains taking young men off to bootcamps to become soldiers. Then in 1967 I joined thousands of others to shut down the Army induction center in Oakland, and sent my draft card back to my draft board with a note saying I would not serve in that immoral war. None of this was easy for me. When I first heard the United States labeled an imperialist country, I resisted it. I didn't want to believe it, and I didn't want to ruin my potential career as a professor of political philosophy. My twenty-one-year-old self graduating from Columbia in 1964 would never have imagined I would turn into a social change activist—nor would any of the people who knew me then. Yet the more I learned, the more I was forced to acknowledge the truth of the Left's perspective on the war in Vietnam.

Similarly, most political scientists and sociologists did not and could not predict the eruption of revolutionary energy in Paris in May 1968, the Second Wave of feminism in the mid and late 1960s, the spread of lesbian-gay-bisexual awareness, the growing acceptance of transsexual people, or many other subsequent movements. The empirical method simply does not work well to the extent that we are dealing with the possibilities of human emancipation. Yet it is often used to convince people that such liberation is impossible, and to discount the whole realm of ethics, spirituality, and religion. Nevertheless, the revolutionary possibility of love may yet empower human beings to save human and animal life from almost certain destruction if we keep accommodating to the world as it is, and dismissing radical new ways of organizing our world, out of the depressive certainty that nothing much can be changed and "no one will take us seriously" if we propose such changes!

Take all this into account as I now present the second key belief of Western capitalist societies—the foundational notion that I call the old bottom line. It is the central mantra of the capitalist order: any economic system, corporation, government policy, legal system, educational system, or even personal life is considered "rational," "productive," "efficient," or "successful" only to the extent that it maximizes money or power.

There is no proof that the maximization of money or power is an appropriate measure of rationality, productivity, or efficiency. These criteria are merely the values that the powerful claim to be essential to running a society. Yet most economists religiously uphold these values of capitalist society, assuming they are shared by everyone. They then teach their theories in universities and in the mass media, and their underlying assumptions are repeated in tens of thousands of editorials, opinion pieces, and speeches by publicly recognized "authorities" on society, politics, psychology, and human relations until the message is unconsciously repeated even by those in social change movements who ostensibly want a different kind of society.

Those who adhere to the old bottom line have two things going for them. First, money is the easiest thing to count and, hence, to measure and verify. Second, when a single religious worldview dominates, its fundamental assumptions seem obvious and appear to be universal—so how could anyone dare to challenge them?

Yet in interviews conducted at the Institute for Labor and Mental Health, these assumptions were discovered not to be so universal after all. Although the thousands of people interviewed mostly repeated what they had heard over and over again in their lives, namely that what everyone wants "really" is more money and power, they also told our researchers that money and

A World of Pain, a Hunger for Love

power are not *their* bottom line, not really what *they* most want or value—but only what *everyone else* really wants and values. When asked if this were true of most of their friends, the majority answered with some variant of the following: "Well, it's true of some of my friends, but no, it's not true of most of my friends, because I couldn't be friends with people who really valued money more than they valued love, generosity, and caring for others." They still insisted that *everyone else* was really selfish, self-centered, and looking out for number one, because in the media, at work, and in school they had learned that these traits were basic to human nature.

A world where our global economic and political arrangements reward selfishness and materialism tends to undermine our confidence that we can bring about a new way to live—a loving, generous, and environmentally sustainable way. It confuses us. No matter how much our inner ethical consciousness tells us differently, after years of experience in the world of work where we (and everyone else) are seen as valuable only to the extent that we increase the money and power of those who run the institutions in which we work, or at least contribute to their ego gratification, many of us come to believe that the only rational way to live in this society is to maximize our own interests and look out for number one. If we don't, we often find ourselves losing the chance for more income or a job with greater satisfaction. Since everyone around us is telling us that this is the only way we can deliver the material goods needed to feed, clothe, house, and educate ourselves and/ or our families, and when so many movies and TV shows simply assume as obvious that everyone is following the path of maximizing self-interest, we re-learn daily what it means to be "realistic" in a competitive market society.

Of course, the people who surround us, who look at us primarily in terms of what we can do for them, rather than seeing us as beings with intrinsic value and worth, have come to believe that this is how everyone sees *them*. They have accepted that the only rational way to be in such a world is to live by its rules, unconsciously going against their own deepest yearnings. When people feel safe to open up to family, friends, therapists, counselors, or researchers, they often report feeling frustrated and disappointed. They admit feeling that something critical to a good life is missing.

People try desperately to compensate for these painful absences in their lives—which are really absences of connection and higher meaning. They try by creating personal solutions—in a tight family unit; in psychotherapy; in churches, synagogues, mosques, zendos, communes, or nationalist/political communities; even in identity groups, sports teams, or political parties. But they often find that the values of the larger society seep in and undermine their best attempts to create what Peter Gabel calls a "parallel universe" with alternative values. Sadly, the pursuit of money, fame, power, and sexual conquest often bubble up in the very places where people had hoped to escape them, leading some in despair to turn to alcohol, drugs, opioids, or addiction to social media.

But there is hope. Just as the predictions of radical empiricism in the societal order can be outwitted by transformations in consciousness, the economic assumptions that deprive us of love, solidarity, respect, and a sense of higher meaning can also be challenged. A nonviolent, systematic replacement of the economic, political, cultural, and psychological distortions foundational to most Western societies would enable us to replace the old bottom line by a new bottom line.

I propose a new bottom line that judges the productivity, efficiency, and rationality of our society and its institutions—including corporations, government policies, our legal system, our political system, our educational system, and even our own personal choices—by the degree to which these institutions and preferences enhance our capacities to be loving, respectful, compassionate, empathic, generous, and caring toward each other; supportive of economic, environmental, and social justice; able to treat other human beings as manifestations of the sacred rather than merely as vehicles to achieve

A World of Pain, a Hunger for Love

our own ends; and capable of responding to the Earth and the universe with awe and wonder rather than treating it as nothing more than an instrumental resource for human needs.

"But wait," some will say. "How can you measure love or generosity or compassion or awe and wonder? And if it can't be measured or verified, how can it possibly be useful in the public sphere?" Here we are back to the empiricist religion of capitalist society—scientism—and its insistence that everything real must be subject to measurement or intersubjective verification. The U.S. Supreme Court faced a related problem when lawyers argued that there is no objective measure of pornography. The justices of the Supreme Court responded, "We know it when we see it." Then let us respond in a similar way about other aspects of our public life: we know it when we see beauty in a powerful work of theater, art, or music; we know we feel compassion and outrage at injustice when we see people being hurt by racist tropes, workers being disrespected, or women or children being emotionally or sexually abused—even though none of these responses is easily measured or verified. Better that we ask ourselves whether a given societal practice, government policy, corporate behavior, or cultural activity can be justified in terms of the new bottom line or only by the old bottom line!

How soon we successfully create the caring society based on the new bottom line, and whether it can happen before the current system destroys much of the life support of the planet, depends on you, reader, and the people you can reach and mobilize. To that end, my heart, solidarity, and revolutionary love are with you, as we move away from the narrow vision of human needs that our capitalist order has tried to coerce and seduce us into supporting and enacting. We are bonded together by something beyond what our current consciousness can even begin to conceptualize but which we nevertheless intuit through poetry and song, dance and ritual, mythology and novels, meditation and mindfulness; something we find in community gatherings and celebrations, in long walks in the natural world or in seeing the night sky filled with stars, and in private moments in which suddenly we are overwhelmed with joy and yearning for a different reality than the world as it normally is presented to us.

WHY WE CAN'T CREATE THE WORLD WE WANT SOLELY BY INNER CHANGE

Revolutionary love is a path to the caring society. I'd call revolutionary love an ethical psycho-spiritual strategy, but I'm wary of associating this strategy with versions of pop psychology or pop spirituality that focus solely on each individual achieving inner equanimity and mindfulness while dismissing social change concerns as distractions.

These self-focused practices can be important components in providing inner strength and in my view should be incorporated into the practical strategies of most social change movements. My objection is with any strategy that claims, "Change yourself and the world will be changed." This claim neglects the powerful impact of capitalist indoctrination in the workplace, the media, and our experience of other people who have accommodated themselves to oppressive realities, along with their tendency to tempt us not only into individualism (that is, caring only for ourselves) and consumerism, but also into believing that social change must wait until we've overcome all our personal limitations.

There are some people who, by virtue of their incomes or inheritances or lucky breaks, spend most of their day practicing meditation, mindfulness, yoga, or psychotherapy, isolating themselves from the daily realities of the economic system the rest of us live in. Many working people see those with the privilege to live a life freed from socioeconomic pressures as a perfect example of selfishness, since the privileged are content to enjoy their own lives while giving little time to changing the economic and political structures that continue to constrain the lives of the majority. They do not have to see others come home from work every day exhausted and emotionally depleted.

For many of the top 20 percent of income earners, those who earned over $100,000 in 2018, internalization of the ethos of the capitalist market looks less like hardscrabble reality than it does for the rest of us. Many of them have opportunities for collaboration and creativity, ways to use their intellect that are acknowledged and financially rewarded. They may see themselves as resisting societal and cultural pressures to look out for number one, and as not giving in to the competitive ethos. What they miss noticing is that they are already on top. Society seems great, recognizing their talents and giving them reason to feel good about themselves, because they have bought the flattering lie that they deserved it and earned it. Meanwhile the vast majority of the lower 80 percent of income earners too often suffer from job insecurity, and often also mind-narrowing and spirit-crushing work.

Thus the "change yourself and the world will be changed" mentality too easily masks the effect of unequally distributed resources, opportunities, and spiritual and psychological rewards. Worse, it implicitly assigns blame to the individual if everything doesn't go well.

Instead of buying into individual solutions for change, we need to recognize the external realities that constrain us. In fact, the worldview promoted by conservatives and neoliberals alike is the biggest stumbling block to change. As Martin Lukacs writes, in the July 17, 2017, issue of *The Guardian:*

> The political project of neoliberalism, brought to ascendance by [England's former prime minister] Thatcher and [U.S. president] Reagan, has pursued two principal objectives. The first has been to dismantle any barriers to the exercise of unaccountable private power. The second has been to erect barriers to the exercise of any democratic public will.
>
> Its trademark policies of privatization, deregulation, tax cuts and free trade deals: these have liberated corporations to accumulate enormous profits and treat the atmosphere like a sewage dump, and hamstrung our ability, through the instrument of the state, to plan for our collective welfare.
>
> Anything resembling a collective check on corporate power has become a target of the elite: lobbying and corporate donations, hollowing out democ-

racies, have obstructed green policies and kept fossil fuel subsidies flowing; and the rights of associations like unions, the most effective means for workers to wield power together, have been undercut whenever possible.

In short, no matter how much we as individuals change our attitudes or our patterns of consumption, corporations (protected by both conservative and liberal politicians) determine what is being produced, persuasively advertised, and consumed.

This is not an argument against inner spiritual work! But throughout history, spiritual prophets have understood that their messages calling for world transformation had to be pursued on both internal and external levels (read Abraham Joshua Heschel's *The Prophets* to see how this path was pioneered). Separating the two would make either level of transformation deeply limited and flawed. As Ron Purser and David Loy explain in their article "Beyond McMindfulness," when the Buddhist practice of mindfulness is stripped from its ethical and religious roots and sold to corporations as a way to increase productivity, it is decontextualized "from its original liberative and transformative purpose, as well as its foundation in social ethics . . . Rather than applying mindfulness as a means to awaken individuals and organizations from the unwholesome roots of greed, ill will and delusion, it is usually being refashioned into a banal, therapeutic, self-help technique that can actually reinforce those roots."[5]

The transformation we need cannot happen internally without also happening in the way we live our lives externally in the worlds of work and politics. Likewise, the need for external transformation must not preclude inner psychological and spiritual development. The two must go hand in hand. The inner work on ourselves must be valued and encouraged by love revolutionaries, but we must be vigilant not to let that become the sole focus, replacing mass political action. See the second part of this book for more details.

Revolutionary love encourages people to develop a compassionate attitude as well as an intense desire to end mutual suffering by changing the economic, political, and cultural realities that make it so hard for people to most fully embody the loving energies they wish to actualize in the world. So yes, revolutionary love is an ethical psycho-spiritual strategy—*and* a social/political path.

PERSONAL RESPONSIBILITY

There are some elements of a caring society that cannot be produced by the important psychological, economic, political, and cultural transformations described in the rest of this manifesto. These are places where individual decisions are key to manifesting revolutionary love. Both governmental and care-oriented social arrangements cannot take the place of our personal responsibility for the ethical and spiritual choices we make.

For example, zero population growth as well as the reduction of the current global population are necessary goals for our survival, but they must be achieved in ways that are not coercive. We can build a societal ethos that sees sexual connection as a sacred moment to be treated with great care for oneself and one's partner. But individuals will have to take personal responsibility for reducing the number of children we bring into the world—at least until the number of people in future generations does not exceed the environmental capacity of the Earth to provide food, clothing, shelter, and energy for everyone. Government has no role in this kind of decision. While government should provide easily available family planning information and aid, it must avoid the horrendous suffering that China's one-child policy caused, or any other such intervention into our personal sexuality and reproductive decisions.

We can encourage each other and ourselves to be empathic, compassionate, generous, forgiving, grateful for the amazing ways that we benefit from the work and thinking and writing and creativity of people all around our planet and their generosity of spirit. But we will inevitably make mistakes. And we must each take responsibility for our own personal and communal missteps, learning how to make amends for consequences of unintended hurtful behavior and how to generously forgive others. We will adopt practices for reflection, gentle self-criticism, repentance, and atonement. I suggest that each of us set aside a time each day to forgive those who have offended or hurt us, and then spend a few minutes thanking the universe (or God if you believe in a god) for all the goodness and beauty in it, for the amazing ways life has evolved on this planet, and for the freedom and consciousness we have to celebrate all the goodness that surrounds us. Some of these skills would be taught in schools in the world we hope to shape, as well as reinforced by mass media and embodied in the ethos of the workplace. But ultimately each one of us must take these practices seriously and make them integral to our own lives.

Christian theologian Dietrich Bonhoeffer warned against "cheap grace"; similarly, Diana Butler Bass warns against the way much "that passes for gratitude today appears to be a sort of secular prosperity gospel" that suggests saying "thank you" enough times will make the universe reward us with health and wealth.[6] I would say the same danger applies to all our spiritual practices and psychological and political actions. It is important to avoid the cheap version of love and caring that is given only as a way to "earn" material or relationship rewards.

I sometimes hear speakers telling a crowd that the revolution they want must be "fun." While I'm all for fun, and have been blessed to have a lot of it in my life along with a lot of suffering, I'm also aware of the immense capacities of ruling elites to undermine some of the fun of social change movements with violence, imprisonment, and public ridicule; of the strategy of placing undercover agents into an organization to cause disharmony, spread negative stories about the most effective activists, or advocate for violence. And if we don't stand up and develop ways to prevent acts of violence in our name, we have to be prepared to take responsibility when our movements are unfairly accused of being violence prone. Similarly, if we don't stop people from putting each other down or causing pain to members of our own movement, we have to take responsibility for our movements losing members and ultimately failing to make the societal changes needed. To get a full sense of how this happens, I have interviewed several people who resent the way they were treated in social change movements.[7]

We must approach the building of a compassionate and loving society with humility, recognizing our capacity to make serious mistakes. This is why generosity and empathy are imperative when dealing with one another, those with whom we have political differences, those within our movement, and even with ourselves.

Revolutionary love compels us to oppose legislation on issues of personal responsibility, but we do not agree that they have no place in the public arena. A movement can foster an ethos as well as legislation—one need look no further than the movements that built an ethos of respect for women, LGBTQ people, and minority groups to see how impactful these changes of consciousness can be. Yet I've also heard some people using the term "revolutionary love" in a way that is completely divorced from a strategy to heal and transform our world by changing its economic, political, and cultural arrangements through an overt commitment to replacing capitalist and patriarchal practices and institutions—and this is a slippery slope back into the self-indulgent forms of "changing oneself" that those who critique "McMindfulness" are correctly warning us against!

A side point: being serious about revolutionary love may help you receive a message from the universe or an unfamiliar part of your unconscious—perhaps in a dream, while watching a movie or television show, in a conversation with a friend or family member, or while reading this book—opening you to the possibility of seeing what your personal path to a life of deeper meaning or purpose might be. Often it will be an insight on how you might best use your skills, your talents, your money, your connections, and your loving nature to participate in *tikkun* (the healing, repair, and transformation) of our world. That path may require responsibility and even some sacrifice, but it may well in the long run give you your greatest satisfaction: to become aligned with the most important task facing humanity today, which is creating a world of love, generosity, social justice, and environmental sanity that will save life on Earth!

THE CHALLENGE OF BEING SEEN
AS WEAK OR GIRLY

The revolutionary love I talk about is at the heart of the teachings of the ancient prophets of Israel, as well as the teachings of almost every surviving religion from the past few thousand years. It is equally at the heart of the practices of many secular humanists and atheists who are engaged in struggles for peace and for social, economic, and environmental justice. Yet, the selfishness-as-rationality ethos of the competitive marketplace has been so powerfully internalized by most people that many fear even speaking about building a world based on love and generosity will make them appear weak, foolish, or unintelligent.

Moreover, the fear of appearing weak has a definite gendered component. In the midst of the Republican National Convention in 2004, Arnold Schwarzenegger, the former bodybuilder and Hollywood actor who became governor of California, chided Democrats for being "girly men." The phrase fit well into the rhetoric of the Republican Party's campaign to present itself as the tough and courageous men who stood up to the threat of terrorism manifested in the September 11, 2001, attacks. Democrats, and the progressive forces with whom they were identified, had long been criticized as weak on national defense, and as people the country couldn't trust to provide protection when Americans were under attack. They were thus like girls, the supposed weaker sex, and ought to learn how to "man up." Until they did that,

Schwarzenegger implied, they would need protection from "real" men, like the Republicans claimed to be. It was that same kind of discourse, coming from Fox News commentators, that led President Trump to shut down sections of the federal government in late 2018 and early 2019 rather than appear "weak" by accepting a budget that did not fund his proposed wall on the border with Mexico to prevent asylum seekers from entering the United States.

Why didn't the progressive world critique this sexist trope that women and girls are the weaker sex? What I discovered in my earlier research as a psychotherapist was that many men on the Left had lived through childhoods in which their own ethical values inclined them away from engaging in fights in the schoolyards and playgrounds where the so-called tough boys often shaped the discourse. These more sensitive, nonviolent boys were called fags or other demeaning names. When these same boys grew older and began to recognize the evils of American imperialism and racism, many of them refused to fight in Vietnam and subsequent misguided wars. Again they were taunted—this time by the Right, who called them cowardly and unpatriotic. Because many of these liberal men carry with them the fear that they will once again be seen as weak, they tend to grab on to something that feels to them to be protection: facts, figures, and a rational discourse that often ignores the values and the emotional needs of those whom they had hoped to organize. People want to feel their leaders' authenticity but instead too often only encounter in the liberal movement and its activists an array of policy positions devoid of the ethical and emotional content that had led these men to develop their progressive policies in the first place. Afraid to reveal who they really are, including their deepest hopes and fears, too many liberal or progressive men present themselves to the public as stick figures rather than as authentic, loving, caring, kind, and generous human beings with whom one could connect.

The media are filled with images that honor tough men: police who fight crime or members of the military who fight foreign enemies. There are very few media images of people being treated as heroes for using their talents to resist the undoing of civil liberties or human rights, much less trying to build a caring society. Liberal and progressive think tanks, political movements, journalists, elected officials, policymakers and public opinion shapers all often feel they have to show that they are really tough and not too "girlish."

When we at *Tikkun* approached male activists, they had a visceral reaction to the idea that the people of our world hunger for meaning, purpose, love, and generosity, sometimes meeting us with such sentiments as "Sure, I agree with you that those values underlie my commitment to liberal or progressive politics. But I don't want to be seen as identifying with love, caring, and generosity, because I don't want to be seen as 'weak'. That would make it hard for me to be taken seriously by the powerful whose policies I wish to change."

Even women in some of the big progressive policy-oriented organizations and charitable foundations had the same reaction—they feared that being identified with a movement that called for a world of love would reduce their credibility with policymakers. By the last decades of the twentieth century and the first decades of the twenty-first, many women had entered corporations and government by presenting themselves as "just as tough as men"—often because they believed it was necessary to their success in those fields. The last thing these women wanted was to be associated with caring.

Yet what our world really needs are movements that can be courageous and powerful in advocating for a world of love and generosity. And that will require affirming that those qualities that have been stereotypically associated with women and girls are actually the best basis for building a decent, just, ethically coherent, and sustainable world.

Though one major strain of contemporary feminism, often labeled "bourgeois feminism," has encouraged women to assimilate into institutions of economic and political power, adopting the same competitive and ethically challenged tactics as the men in those institutions, another strain has argued that a commitment to loving and caring relationships is at least equally important. While rejecting any essentialist attempts to say that being loving is what women "naturally are," care-oriented feminists have pointed to the experience of raising and nurturing children as imparting a kind of knowledge that could become the basis for a more just and peaceful world. Even though, under patriarchy, the assignment of childrearing to women as unpaid labor has been oppressive, the experience of being caregivers in families has given many women knowledge and skills to resist the selfishness-oriented values of the capitalist order. In sharing what they've learned, these women (and sometimes men as well as non–gender-conforming folks) are able to contend against those who see love through the distorted lenses of pop novels, TV, and movies, with their inherently narrow assumptions.

Carol Gilligan's writings paved the way for an understanding of the centrality of caring in women's development.[8] She challenged the more mechanistic theory developed by Harvard developmental theorist Lawrence Kohlberg by insisting that women's moral development is shaped by their focus on caring for others. When I first read Gilligan's research I found myself wishing that we men could have allowed ourselves to learn from women this developmental capacity, and I now feel that doing so is a survival necessity for the planet. If women can be pushed by the champions of the capitalist order to "lean in" to learn how to be like a tough man in the world of work, then those of us who want to save the life support system of the planet need to encourage men to lean into the capacity of many women to think in terms of caring and responsibility. Gilligan puts it this way: "Within a patriarchal framework, care is a feminine ethic. Within a democratic framework, care is a human ethic. A feminist ethic of care is a different voice within a patriarchal culture because it joins reason with emotion, mind with body, self with relationships, men with women, resisting the divisions that maintain a patriarchal order."

Nel Noddings, in her work in philosophy of education, sought to build into the educational system a feminist ethics that privileged caring for others. Noddings taught that it is the acts of caring and the memory of being cared for that create the possibility for altruism in daily life.[9] Both Gilligan and Noddings were thus responding to the widespread and deep intuition that being a loving and care-giving person is an amazing gift that should be esteemed.

In a society based on revolutionary love, caring would be an emotion and activity fostered in the daily life of both men and women. Childrearing would be shared across all genders and sexual preferences, and extended families and communities would be involved in what would be perceived as the amazing privilege of contributing to the raising of the next generation. I had that privilege as a single dad raising my son by myself for several years, and even though it was difficult to do while being financially marginal (and also I made many mistakes), I still consider that experience to have been among the most fulfilling in my life.

To get there, we need to help men, and the women who think that their own success depends on being seen to be "like men," feel safe enough to fiercely embrace these caring qualities. Ironically, it was often this very yearning for a loving and caring world that inclined them to embrace progressive politics in the first place. We need to help them overcome fear and encourage them to publicly embrace the very beautiful part of themselves that led them to want to heal and repair the world. Now is the time to encourage both women and men to be tough in standing up for kindness, gentleness, empathy, compassion, and generosity! In so doing, they will make it easier for many others who really want that kind of a world to feel empowered to say so and to fight nonviolently for such a world! Lean in to that struggle rather than the struggle to make yourself or your business or corporation more wealthy or powerful and you'll find your life much more fulfilling!

In the meantime, we owe a debt to transgender and nonbinary people who are leading the way in showing us that gender is both a lived experience and a social construct, and as such, can be reimagined.

I advocate for the Caring Society—Caring for Each Other and Caring for the Earth as the central tenet of a new kind of politics. In this sense, revolutionary love is the "taking seriously" of feminism that is the next stage in the healing and repair of the human race.

I do not believe that the triumph of revolutionary love is inevitable, but only that it is possible. The accumulated weight of societal conditioning and all the other disempowering and self-destructive factors described in this and the next three chapters have great power. But also powerful is the yearning for a life of higher meaning and purpose, of love and respect, of community and caring. The Rev. Dr. Martin Luther King, Jr., said that the arc of the universe bends toward justice. I don't believe that that is necessarily true with regard to planet Earth but only with regard to all conscious beings. If that bend toward justice does not play out on this planet, it will eventually play out somewhere among the hundreds of planets in the universe where conscious life has either already developed or may yet develop in the coming several billion years. The good news is that we have the opportunity to make it happen here. The challenge that I present here is this: to bring about the transformations required to save the life support system of Earth, we need more than a "justice" movement—we need a "love and justice movement" that draws not only on the rich traditions of past struggles for justice and the important critiques that help us understand their limitations, but also on that part of the psychological and spiritual wisdom of the human race that could contribute to liberation and environmental sanity. To make that happen, please read the strategies proposed in the rest of this book.

CHAPTER TWO

Fear and Domination, or Love and Generosity?

If you want to change the political world, you need to grasp the underlying dynamics that shape how people understand their own realities. We began that discussion in the previous chapter. In this chapter we look at two world-views that have been in a tug of war throughout history: a worldview of fear and domination and a worldview of love and generosity. No matter how harshly or subtly ruling elites may try to impose the worldview of fear and domination, they have never fully extinguished human beings' yearning for a world of love and generosity; human aspirations continually erupt and push for full liberation. Our task is to support each other in that push.

FEAR AND DOMINATION

The worldview of fear teaches us that at birth we are thrown alone into a world where people are essentially interested in maximizing their own advantage without regard for the well-being of others. This worldview under-girds the capitalist world of work, in which we all live. And it can seem all-pervasive, reinforced at every level of our lives. At a personal level, well-meaning parents and teachers often tell us that to protect ourselves from others, we need to learn to get power over them before they dominate us. As many parents say, "It's a dog-eat-dog world, so you'd better be prepared for it. Everyone is out for themselves, so be careful and don't let others take advantage of you." At a national level, this worldview leads to a similar strategy for what we used to call "foreign policy" but now call "homeland security." To protect your own country, either your country's leaders must control the means of domination, or your country must become part of some alliance taking the steps necessary to dominate others before they dominate you.

Some anthropologists believe that there were hunter-gatherer tribes and indigenous cultures in which this domination worldview did not flourish. Once "civilization" and its accompanying structures of power and oppression developed in ancient societies, however, the worldview of fear and domination quickly took over and became entrenched, even in mythology and theology. Gods were portrayed in frequent struggle with each other for domination, and human beings sought to enlist these gods in their own struggles for health, wealth, power, and security.

The Italian social theorist Antonio Gramsci has helped us understand that these "necessary domination" ideas and the societal practices they reinforce have an important role in supporting the ruling elites.[1] If those elites can secure cultural hegemony—can make the rest of us believe that life is just a struggle for advantage, for example—they then do not have to depend solely on violence to keep their power and wealth. Through their hegemony, we are taught to see existing oppressive systems as "natural."

Over the course of thousands of years, ruling elites in the emerging tribes and city-states of Asia, Africa, and Europe recognized the tremendous joy people got from tribal spiritual experiences of awe and wonder at the grandeur of the universe as well as daily rituals of celebration, and so they slowly began to embrace those experiences and institutionalize them into what became fixed religious practices, reshaping them in the image of the existing realities of the emerging patriarchal and class societies, and not infrequently removing from them their spiritual essence, the sense of unity with all beings, the imperative to share, the ecstatic dancing and sexuality, the valuing of women's insight and connection to the sacred, and other experiences that they could not control. As those societies clashed with others, religious worldviews of fear and domination slowly began to replace awe and wonder at the center of religious life, and war began to be seen as having a spiritual value, while outsiders were increasingly seen as essentially evil and predisposed to violence. When those religions were replaced thousands of years later, first with monotheistic religions, and then in the past five hundred years with more "enlightened" visions of the world that discarded gods of any sort, philosophers, social scientists, college professors, and even some novelists became the priests of a new secular religion supporting the next stage in the evolution of class and patriarchal societies, and these too often envisioned human reality as one in which people sought power and domination over each other.

Thomas Hobbes, the founding father of Western political philosophy in the seventeenth century, described a "state of nature" that was a struggle of all against all. Seeing how the emerging competitive marketplace was shaping people who cared only for themselves, he attributed this to a preexisting human condition. The only way to relieve the struggle, he posited, was through a monarchical sovereign power that could keep people safe from the "natural" desire to dominate others. Thus Hobbes justified the ruthless struggle of the emerging capitalist order, and the power of the elites, by branding them inevitable. Many concluded that only a fool would seek to change something as fundamental as competition or domination.

Hobbes's vision of the world allows economic and political elites to warn people not to challenge current societal arrangements, because to do so would go against "nature." Moreover, it lets them instill a fear among the dominated that any kind of rebellion could empower new elites as the de facto sovereign and they would be even more oppressive, or bring about an even more restrictive world. Very handy for those who wish to maintain their position of dominance! When Jean-Jacques Rousseau in the eighteenth century posited a state of nature in which people were born free and cooperative and described the legitimate "sovereign" in society as being the totality of the people who were "everywhere in chains" because of the existing social order, his ideas became the subject of massive attacks by the intellectuals of the next several centuries who served the elites.

When modern social science developed in the nineteenth and twentieth centuries in universities run by representatives of the elites, ideas justifying elite power were given a pseudo-scientific basis. Scientific works that preached various forms of the domination worldview received acclaim both within academic settings and in the mass media. Some embraced a Social Darwinism, which took the notion of "survival of the fittest" as a justification for the exercise of power, both in the class societies of the newly industrializing countries of the West and in these countries' colonial possessions. The idea of racial superiority—that is, racism—was seen as a natural outgrowth of evolution. Others postulated that something inherent in the human psyche pushed us all to seek power over others, even going so far as to propose the existence of a "selfish gene" (Richard Dawkins) or a propensity toward a death instinct (see Sigmund Freud at one point in his thinking).[2] Still others suggested that hierarchical relationships were necessary for maintaining the complexity of a social organization that made civilization possible.

Significantly, though these thinkers' descriptions of domination-oriented behavior are often quite accurate, the alleged necessity and inevitability of such behaviors are always a postulate that lies beyond empirical foundations. Erich Fromm's masterful work *The Anatomy of Human Destructiveness* is one of many studies demonstrating the intellectually (and ethically) untenable ways that domination belief systems have been given pseudo-scientific justification.[3]

LOVE AND GENEROSITY

Fortunately, another worldview emerged thousands of years ago with a different message—one that gained prominence among the Abrahamic religions as well as other spiritual paths. This worldview sees human beings as fundamentally capable of responding to each other in generous and supportive ways, capable of building lasting, loving relationships and solidarity in communities. In the Hebrew Bible, we are enjoined to "love your neighbor as yourself" and "love the stranger/the Other." According to this worldview, homeland security could be achieved through generosity: caring could be the norm of interaction, generating a feeling of safety with others. In the second part of this manifesto, I present a global Generosity Plan as an example of what a strategy of generosity should include.

The worldview of love and generosity is built on the recognition that we don't come into this world alone—each of us comes into it through a mother (and she through her mother). Your ability to survive the first few years of life was possible because your mother (or some "mothering other") loved, nurtured, and cared for you. Without that care, you would have died. Psychologist René Spitz studied infants and discovered that those who were given roughly the same amount of objective care—in the form of food and medical necessities—nonetheless showed differences in behavior according to how much affection or loving care they received from a mother, father, or other caretaker. Those who received less subjective care were disabled physically and emotionally and even died at a dramatically higher rate than infants who were held, hugged, or shown other signs of affection. Spitz's studies, conducted in the 1940s and published in 1952, eventually led to what psychologists today call attachment theory, the notion that loving attachments formed in infancy and early childhood (with a mother, father, or other mothering caretaker) are central to our ability to form healthy and lasting adult relationships.

In the forty plus years since I earned my Ph.D. in psychology, I've told this story many times to large groups of students and practitioners in the caring professions. Occasionally, people say to me, "Rabbi Lerner, you don't know how neurotic my parents really were." I reassure them that I am not denying the existence of neuroses that parents often pass on to their children,

Fear & Domination, or Love & Generosity?

nor that their parents or parenting-others may have been very screwed up. But I do claim that physical survival becomes impaired or impossible without what British psychoanalyst Donald Winnicott described as "good enough mothering"—or parenting in which you got enough loving touch and care from someone—something more than objective care.[4]

If we were to reframe these insights using more capitalistic language, we might say that your mother did not have a reasonable expectation of a good return on her investment of loving energy toward you. She was at least to some extent "giving to give," not "giving to get." Her loving care was not a calculated utilitarian move based on the assumption that she'd get back from you what she needed at some later point. Of course, parents sometimes will say or imply that their children "owe them" for raising or supporting them, but this is often a result of feeling inadequately loved themselves rather than a reflection of feelings that they had when their children were infants or toddlers.

We can see this same kind of loving care being given by other primates as well. The desire to give and care for others is intrinsic in both humans and some primates (indeed, some contend that similar behavior can be found in all mammals).

On the foundation of this experience of loving care, people over the centuries built families, clans, tribes, and eventually towns or cities; they engaged in peaceful trade and commerce with other people who spoke different languages and had different customs. Those experiences gave rise in turn to worldviews, first religious and then secular, that affirmed the centrality of ethical behavior, trust, compassion, and the possibility of a world of love, generosity, and peace among all nations.

WHAT MOVES US TOWARD FEAR OR LOVE, DOMINATION OR GENEROSITY

The truth is, most people carry both the domination and the generosity worldviews in their conscious or unconscious minds. We have heard versions

Transcending the Dynamics of Oppression

of both, and either has the capacity to shape our response in any interaction. The Hebrew Bible, edited by many human beings, contains both voices, as do the New Testament, the Koran, and the texts of many other religious traditions; the classics of Western literature and philosophy; and the works of liberation theorists (including Karl Marx, Sigmund Freud, Simone de Beauvoir). Both perspectives are there in all of these religious and secular traditions, sometimes both uneasily together in the teachings of the same prophet, philosopher, visionary, literary genius, poet, songwriter, filmmaker, therapist, or secular revolutionary.

The way people approach others is shaped by which worldview dominates their thinking at any given time. Most of us can shift from one perspective to the other depending on our interpretation of verbal, facial, and action cues. Consider the circumstances in which we meet a new person, go on a date, or encounter people out in the world. Depending on our mood or our past experiences, we might start a conversation guardedly, wondering if this person is someone looking out for only their own interests, someone who might want to use or take advantage of us. We might then be delighted to find that the person defies our assumptions and opens up to us in ways that make us feel safe enough to do the same. Or, we might start with a very open attitude and then notice responses that sound alarms, causing us to move away from our trusting inclinations and closer to the fear/domination worldview and the behavior it dictates. Many of us are unaware of these shifts when they are happening, though on reflection afterward we can become aware that the shifts took place.

Of course, some people are so attached to one or the other of these worldviews that they always approach others from the standpoint of either openheartedness or deep suspicion and distrust. But most human beings can best be understood as on a continuum between the worldview of love and generosity and the worldview of fear and domination. Where we are on that continuum at any given moment depends in part on how much and how long the nurturing energy of our parents prevailed before their more fearful, self-interested, and goal-directed needs began to emerge.

But these conflicting worldviews don't come just from parents. In predicting where a person will fall on the continuum between domination and love, we also have to ask these kinds of questions:

How much was your schooling, and the way you were treated by other children and teachers, nurturing or destructive? Did you feel recognized for what was good about you, or did you have to struggle for recognition, respect, and caring? When you reached out to someone in friendship, did you feel seen and accepted or unseen and rejected?

What are your adult relationships like? Have you met people who see how wonderful a human being you are, or have they mostly seen you in narrow utilitarian terms? Have your friends been loyal, or have you been disappointed when people who seemed close to you acted as if they did not really care about you?

What are the ideas to which you have been exposed in school (elementary through high school, college, postgraduate, or professional or vocational training) and through mass media and politicians? How have they reinforced your inclination toward hope, love, and generosity, or toward fear, control, power, or domination over others?

How have you experienced societal energies when they tilt toward fear or hope? When they lean more toward fear, have you been inclined to see all ideas about trusting others and creating a world based on caring as utopian and irrational? When they lean toward hope, have the stories and ideas you've heard affirming the possibility of trusting others, caring for them, and building a world based on love begun to sound more plausible?

All of these experiences have a major impact on where one's consciousness will fall on the worldview continuum. Using this series of questions, you may develop an understanding of how long-forgotten experiences of humiliation from relationships in childhood, perhaps re-stimulated by experiences of being ignored, demeaned, manipulated, used, or oppressed in your adult life in the competitive economic marketplace and more generally in a patriarchal and racist society, may push you and others toward fear, suspicion, and despair.

Keep these two worldviews in mind every time you watch a TV show, whether a scripted show like *Law and Order, Girls,* or *Transparent,* a reality show like the one that made Donald Trump a household name, or a series on PBS. Keep them in mind when you watch a movie or hear a speech on YouTube, read a book, listen to a teaching in a religious space or a lecture by a respected cultural or intellectual figure, listen to a podcast, read an article being widely circulated on Facebook, or get a message on Instagram or Twitter. Always ask yourself, is this experience, communication, or message more likely to move me and most people who hear or see it toward fear and the conviction that "everyone is selfish or hurtful or not to be trusted," or toward trust in the possibility of a loving and caring world?

Are you bombarded with stories of violence and pain, but given only faint opportunity to learn about the goodness and cooperation that is happening around you? Do you get endless updates on social media from people who seem so narcissistic and emotionally dead that you wonder if they are able to really see or appreciate the world around them? Despite all this, do you *still* find yourself checking and rechecking social media in hopes that it might bring some relief from the anxieties of the world? If so, don't be surprised if the voice of fear is getting nourished inside your consciousness even as you search for the voice of hope and love and generosity.

In the midst of writing this section, my wife runs into my room crying in response to new descriptions of U.S. patrol agents on the Mexican border teargassing children who are part of an exodus from Central American countries and who with their families are now seeking asylum in the United States after facing violence, rape, and murders in their own home countries. Momentarily I too am startled by the inhumanity of the governing people in the Trump administration who gave these orders, just as I was when learning of the children killed by the bombs dropped by drone attacks on suspected terrorist locations in the Middle East authorized during the Obama administration. I momentarily feel despair, sadness, and even a few minutes of depression, and have to work this through to come back to hope.

All over the world, psychotherapists are beginning to notice a pervasive depression in many patients. People feel hopeless about the possibility of saving our planet and are more inclined to abandon any involvement in societal processes other than extracting as much pleasure for themselves as possible before our planet becomes unlivable. The conditioning is so pervasive that often it takes a huge amount of conscious attention and support from others to diminish the already powerful impact of fear and distrust on each of us. But depending on how they are presented, challenging truths do not have to be emotionally debilitating. Those same truths can empower hope and love if they lead to joining others who are working to repair what has gone wrong.

To be sure, some aspects of our world are in fact dangerous (e.g., the accelerating destruction of the environment, the reemergence of quasi-fascist political movements, and the racist violence that is always a potential threat to people of color as well as Jews and Muslims and many other demeaned groups). No matter how loving and generous we are, it is sometimes rational to protect ourselves and our loved ones from these real dangers. Knowing when such protection is rational and when it is a product of our own internal distortions or excessive fears takes careful discernment. Certainly Europe during the rise of Nazism or Chile during the dictatorship that overthrew the legitimately elected government of democratic socialist

Salvador Allende were moments when fear was rational and stopping the domination of an oppressive, aggressive leader was necessary. But seeing every situation through that framework is mistaken and debilitating. In order to build a more just and environmentally sustainable world, we must help ourselves and others move toward a deeper capacity for trust and the skill to experience disappointments without letting them make us feel personally humiliated for believing in the possibility of a different kind of world.

SOCIAL ENERGY

Another factor that can push us toward more fear or more hope, more love or more domination and control, is where social energy is moving at any given moment. I define "social energy" as the sum total of feelings and thoughts radiated from each person to every other person they meet, which gets circulated around the entire society in which we live.[5] It is somewhat analogous to the way air surrounds us. We are all deeply impacted by the social energy field I am describing, though usually we are not aware of how and when.

When social energy moves exceedingly far toward fear, be alert to increases in violence from police, government, and people affiliated with hate groups, militarist groups, or militia; and to moves by courts or government to reduce civil liberties and civil rights. It may be easiest to recognize these moves when made by a Trump administration or other overtly reactionary forces. But they can be just as destructive of hope when enacted more subtly by an ostensibly caring liberal or progressive regime. So, for example, when President Obama failed to bring to trial those engaged in torture during the war in Iraq, dramatically increased the number of undocumented immigrants his administration deported (more than all the previous presidents combined), escalated the use of drones that murdered not only suspected terrorists but also many innocent civilians, and prosecuted rather than rewarded whistle-blowers who were revealing the lies and human rights violations in U.S. army and intelligence agencies, he actually undermined hope and set the stage for people's fear and despair to reemerge powerfully.

If fear and despair are not actively challenged, some of the most decent people begin to fear for their own safety and turn inward. Some survivors of Nazism in Europe have commented that the greatest danger of fascism comes not from the fascists themselves but from the "good people" who don't want to get involved and hence stay silent or passive. This passivity is often a product of the despair-generated social energy that gains ground in the face of a society moving toward deeply oppressive policies. Thankfully, a movement of resistance has emerged during the Trump presidency that has countered some of that despair and passivity, and undoubtedly will continue to function no matter who takes power in the 2020s.

Do societal events determine the direction of social energy? No, not completely!

Consider, for example, the national mood after the September 11, 2001, attacks. We were told that the destruction of the World Trade Center and the deaths of several thousand people was the work of an Islamic terrorist group operating around the world, seeking to destroy Western civilization. Most Americans, and hundreds of millions of people around the world, were saddened and mourned for lost loved ones and their families. When the towers came crashing down, social energy moved dramatically toward fear, strengthening our tendency to see other people and the larger world through that lens.

But the framing of that event, which ultimately led the United States into war, first in Afghanistan and then Iraq, was not an inevitable consequence of the event itself. Imagine if instead of using this horrific attack to justify wars, a different president and vice president than George W. Bush and Dick Cheney had urged Americans not to believe that we lived in a world of cruelty and evil. They could have focused on a different part of what happened on 9/11: the thousands of police, firefighters, and others risking their lives for those trapped in the flaming towers, and the tens of millions of people around the world who grieved with Americans and sent public messages of solidarity. Imagine a president saying, "My fellow Americans, the first responders who risked their lives, and the hundreds of them who actually lost their lives trying to save others should remind us that we live in a world where most people really care about others. The way to honor them is to affirm the goodness of people, not only here but around the world. The terrorists wish us to believe that the world is unsafe. We will take dramatic actions to make our borders and our airplanes safer. But we will not let them win by adopting a false narrative that tells us that most people are basically evil. They are not. The goodness of the people here in the U.S., and the goodness of people all around the world, millions of whom from almost every country have sent messages of comfort and solidarity, must remain at the center of the way we honor all of those who lost their lives or are recovering from painful physical or psychological wounds. The terrorists choose violence, but we choose love, generosity, and caring for all the people of the world—and, combined with strong security measures, this is the way to defeat terrorism and honor those whom we have lost." That kind of message, affirming a solidarity among human beings that crosses political and national divisions, could have pushed America and humanity toward a hopefulness that would have prevented the war in Iraq. Had it not been for the war in Iraq, there would be no ISIS or widespread growth of terrorism. Those most fully immersed in the worldview of fear would still have asserted that 9/11 vindicated their sense of the pervasiveness of evil and desire for power. But if the people who were closer to the worldview of hope had been able to mobilize themselves, and had on their side a political party fully committed to emphasizing the message of hope, social energy could have moved in a very different direction than it did.

My main point here is that the facts of a situation, even a horrific situation, rarely determine how it is going to be understood. The way such situations enter consciousness is mediated through existing frameworks of understanding, and the prominence of fear or love in those frameworks in turn shapes the direction in which social energy will move.

Social energy is a central aspect shaping our collective lives even though we cannot objectively measure it with some empirical gadget like a thermometer. All of us have a role in shaping that energy, though those with greater access to the means of communication and production have a much greater impact than the rest of us, unless we are organized and vigilant about putting forward a different message. We spiritual progressives have a plan for such an organization, and this manifesto is an invitation for you to consider it and, if it makes sense to you, join with us to make it happen.

What can an organized, progressive social change movement do to strengthen the movement of social energy—both within each of us and within society as a whole—toward the construction of economic, political, and cultural realities that will reinforce our deep though often unconscious desire for a world of love, generosity, sustainability, and justice?

A first step is to challenge the claim that Western capitalist societies are meritocracies and to put an end to the self-blaming and powerlessness that arise when we internalize the meritocratic vision as a justification for inequality and other disappointing aspects of our lives. We turn to these topics in the next chapter.

CHAPTER THREE

Toxic Self-Blaming and Powerlessness

From the 1950s onward, self-fulfillment became a major cultural theme in Western societies. Though World War II's victories against fascism and subsequent battles against various forms of European colonialism created the possibility for a surge in hopefulness, the establishment-oriented intellectual elite in universities, publishing houses, television, radio, and most major newspapers used details of cruelty imposed by fascism and Stalinism to highlight human evil and to discredit the possibility of fundamental social change. Indeed, America's ruling elites, fearing the militancy that a vigorous labor movement had forged in the 1930s and 1940s, mostly welcomed a rebirth of extreme anti-communism that took the form, pioneered by U.S. Senator Joseph McCarthy, of charging liberal thought with being soft on communism and many liberal activists as being actual communists themselves. As McCarthyism spread through the country, many liberals, fearful of being labeled "communist" and losing their jobs, sought to situate themselves within the celebration of Western values and nationalist rhetoric that had become a motivator for building and then using the atomic bomb against Japan and potentially against the Soviet Union. While a handful of principled liberals refused to sign loyalty oaths that were being foisted on many Americans as a condition of continued employment or promotion, many others succumbed to the pressure as social energy moved dramatically toward fear.

Major corporations, aided in part by fast-growing technologies such as television that made advertising ever more effective, now tried to convince the public that they would achieve "the good life" without reliance on the labor struggles and social change movements popular in the 1930s, but instead through focusing on consuming commodities and accumulating money, sex, or fame. People were encouraged to find the meaning of life in individual fulfillment, not in societal repair; this vision was sold to the public by Hollywood, book publishing, radio and TV, and the record industry, but also in evangelical churches, and in slightly more sophisticated forms by universities, pop psychology, and pop spirituality. Only the courageous struggles of African Americans in the late 1950s and 1960s seemed to reawaken a section of young people to a new sense of ethical community and the need for collective struggles for social justice.

This mentality—of aiming to become a healthy (and consuming) individual instead of, or at the very least before, pursuing any larger social change—emerged as the new common sense: its most popular foundational formulation was that because we create our own reality, if we want to change anything we first must change ourselves. The larger economic, political, and cultural structures that shape our daily lives were made invisible (and even today remain invisible, for most people). The inevitable and discouraging conclusion that thoroughly disempowered social activism was the mantra "We have no one to blame but ourselves if our self-created reality isn't fulfilling!"

This way of understanding the world was a perfect fit for our capitalist system, with its "free market" claims that a person with talents and energy could become anyone they wanted to be. Supposedly, the possibilities were endless. The newly forming global class-stratified society needed a way of justifying its radical and systemic inequalities, so it was promoted as a true meritocracy: wherever you ended up in the social and economic hierarchies was now deemed a function of your own individual worthiness (or worthlessness). And like any hegemonic idea, this one was flexible enough to accommodate some challenge. In response to the civil rights and feminist movements of the 1960 and 1970s, for instance, some corporations, some media, and many colleges and universities started to open up academic degrees to women and people of color, and the hiring of a few in prominent positions undergirded the (mostly misleading) impression that anyone could become rich, powerful, or influential if they had the intelligence and energy to try.

PROBLEMS WITH CAPITALIST "FREEDOM"

The capitalist organization of society and work created significant problems and incited rebellion early in its history. Spread in part by the American and French revolutions, it nonetheless could not meet the latter's promises of "liberty, equality, and fraternity" (note that these promises were at first only offered to white men and in practice, only to a small percentage of those men).

By the middle of the nineteenth century, working people were discovering that liberty referred only to the freedom to sell their labor for whatever factory owners were willing to pay. Now that the land on which people had previously raised their food became private property, and the Commons where they had brought their animals to graze and drink water were being "enclosed," that is, reserved to those who had documents claiming ownership as the inheritors of feudal rights, many agrarian dwellers had no choice but to give up their financially marginal but still sufficient lives (given their rural ethos of helping out their neighbors) and try to find a job in the emerging big cities while competing with other equally desperate, displaced workers.

As for equality, working people learned that they weren't going to be given equal amounts of money or capital with which to compete—instead, the wealthy from the previous feudal order mostly kept their wealth in the new capitalist order and lent money to the poor at high rates of interest. Equality meant "equal under the law," which, as one writer described it, meant that the poor and the wealthy were equally forbidden from sleeping under a bridge at night.

And fraternity? Well, that too seemed largely a fantasy, since the new order kept on breaking down human relationships of solidarity. Each person was encouraged to compete with everyone else for the few places available to attain some social mobility, usually only to rise into jobs that would ultimately serve the needs of the powerful and the rich. Social solidarity was replaced by the competition for jobs so that workers could provide at least a marginal life for their families.

As people began to understand the downsides of capitalism, more and more became angry at the ways they had been deceived by the cheerleaders for this new economy. Some were attracted to communist and socialist ideas about how to transcend capitalist society. These movements were put down in a variety of ways, mostly through violent repression, but also by a global system of colonialism and imperialism that eventually allowed the capitalist countries of the West to bring home wealth from the so-called undeveloped world, some part of which, it was promised, would trickle down to the working classes of the Western world (if in no other way, then by joining the armies that enforced these colonial or imperial armies or by getting work in the factories that produced the armaments needed to suppress the revolts of those whose countries were being colonized).

But by the middle of the twentieth century, after the armies and economic engines of colonizing countries had been weakened by World War II and their populations had momentarily grown weary of the xenophobic nationalism necessary to justify continuing to try to impose colonialism in Africa and

Asia, capitalism's cheerleaders needed a new strategy to undermine anti-capitalist anger. The self-blaming engendered by the notion that we all live in a meritocratic society played an important role in disempowering working class people in Western countries who might otherwise have continued the pre–World War II struggles for significant redistribution of wealth and power.

The meritocratic fantasy was bolstered by the reality that the system did offer real, though very limited, mobility. Most of the positions in the higher ranks of society remained in the hands of people who had won the birth lottery—those whose families were in the upper 20 percent of income earners, with enough money and power to secure their children's class status through elite schooling and/or broad social networks. But a few of the most ambitious born into the lower 80 percent could scale the class ladder to assist and even join the elite through a combination of skill, luck, education, hard work, and intense loyalty to the powerful. Those who were able to make it, moving into jobs that either felt more satisfying and meaningful, or at least paid more money and hence provided them with the opportunity to become better consumers, often did so by taking the place of others, so that the upward mobility of some was balanced by the downward mobility of others. Those who were able to rise had a stake in believing that their own success proved that capitalism was a meritocracy; this belief insulated them from survivor's guilt at leaving behind so many others for whom there was no room at the top, for example, people they had known in their childhood, or former friends, or members of their own extended family.

At the same time, the notion of meritocracy was celebrated by groups of liberal intellectuals and academics who fiercely defended the capitalist order; in large part they felt certain that any system that recognized them as brilliant was amazingly discerning and merited their loyalty. Meanwhile, I watched with sadness as many exceptional thinkers with more progressive views, who had not yet earned academic tenure or places of influence in the major intellectual magazines, newspapers, radio, and television, were ignored or even booted out of major American universities and in most cases denied access to the media's attention.

To further secure their loyalty, working people were encouraged to think of themselves not as the working class but as the middle class. And it is true that the advanced industrial societies did expand their own wealth (often at the expense of countries of the global South and East), and incomes did rise somewhat even for the working class, enabling them to enjoy luxuries such as new automobiles, color televisions, machines to wash clothes or dishes, computers, stereos, and eventually even handheld phones with intriguing video games. These small, but for many significant, gains gave people the (false) impression that the capitalist class structure was permeable. As long as the system was expanding, with growth understood to be the highest value, and few recognizing that environmental damage was increasingly to blame for polluting the air and waterways, most people in the Western world could be convinced that capitalism was working well.

But things are changing. Even the limited mobility that characterized the period from the end of World War II to the 1970s is now disappearing. A report published by the Washington, D.C., Center for Equitable Growth in the fall of 2016 on research done by Michael D. Carr and Emily E. Wiemers, two economists at the University of Massachusetts in Boston, found that lifetime earnings mobility has declined since the early 1980s as inequality has increased.[1] Though mobility has declined for people across all income and education levels, one striking feature Carr and Wiemers note is the decline in upward mobility among middle class workers, even those with college degrees. "Across the distribution of educational attainment," Carr and Wiemers report, "the likelihood of moving to the top of the earnings distribution for workers who start their career in the middle of the earnings distribution has declined by approximately 20 percent since the early 1980s."

Nonetheless, even during this more recent period, tens of thousands of Americans, Brits, and others in advanced capitalist societies have in fact moved up the class ladder. In addition to the tried-and-true paths created by family connections and education, some have been lifted by new inventions that allowed for new markets and new job opportunities, as in the case of Silicon Valley and the dramatic rise of the electronic data-processing technology executives. These lucky tens of thousands are showcased frequently to the tens of millions for whom no such possibility exists. The message to the rest of us is that if we had been as smart and worked as hard as those who succeeded in the high tech industry, we too would have made it. The implication is that capitalist society could easily have made all of us into CEOs of billion-dollar corporations or at least made each of its several hundred million citizens into multi-millionaires if only we had worked harder and been smarter. No way! The class structure and inequalities of wealth and power make this impossible.

Many Americans who heard presidential candidate Donald Trump talk about "making America great again" associated greatness with that brief mid-twentieth-century period when many working people experienced an expansion of their economic well-being. But significantly, as the Center for Equitable Growth notes, the mid-twentieth century was also characterized by public policies and societal norms that fostered broad prosperity, including a rising minimum wage, firm labor rules for paying time-and-a-half overtime wages, strong private-sector unions, and cultural and political taboos against high pay and bonuses for executives in the face of layoffs.

By contrast, the decades since 1979 have been characterized by an erosion of the minimum wage and overtime standards, a decline in unionization, and cultural and political acceptance of excessive executive pay and accumulation of huge wealth for the top one-tenth of 1 percent of the population. The growing political power of elites made these changes possible.

Elites have been able to shape the media, convince working class people that technological changes would eventually benefit them, and also control the discourse in both major political parties by funding candidates who supported the interests of the biggest corporations, banks, and investment companies on Wall Street. Calling themselves New Democrats and labeling their worldview as neoliberalism, a significant section of the Democratic Party (most notably Presidents Bill Clinton and Barack Obama) promoted outsourcing and free trade. In particular, President Obama enabled the United States to sell its agricultural and other products to developing countries, in the process underselling local farmers in these countries, forcing them to seek employment in already overcrowded cities, and eventually, for many, to become the undocumented workers desperately trying to cross U.S. borders in the hope of finding employment here or safety from the violence of U.S.-backed regimes in their native country. With neoliberal policies making it easier to ship jobs overseas, a growing percentage of U.S. and European workers faced the choice of reduced wages, dramatic reductions in previously negotiated retirement benefits, or bleak unemployment. Austerity rather than upward mobility has been the fate for large portions of the working people of the advanced capitalist societies.

Meanwhile, the U.S. Supreme Court has ruled that corporate money in elections is a form of speech protected under the First Amendment, thereby giving the wealthy greater opportunities to shape the outcome of elections. The Supreme Court also dismantled the heart of the Voting Rights Act and allowed many states to make it harder for poor people and people of color to vote. Moreover, Republican legislatures and a handful of billionaires have created innovative ways to push people off lists of registered voters whom they suspect would support Democrats—a plan documented in the 2016 version of Greg Palast's *The Best Democracy Money Can Buy: A Tale of Billionaires & Ballot Bandits*. And most recently, to seal the power of corporations, the Supreme Court has ruled to allow employers as a condition of employment to keep employees from joining together in class action suits, thereby eliminating one of the few ways that workers could challenge unfair employment practices.

Most of the commentators who have weighed in on why former Democratic Party voters recently defected to the Republican Party or did not bother to vote at all focus primarily on the economic impact of this inequality—the closing of American factories and the loss of jobs. They argue that working-class people were simply responding to material deprivation, which (irrationally) they hoped the Republicans would rectify. Trump's election in 2016, in this view, was easily explained as a reaction against Democrats who had failed to use the opportunity of the Great Recession to bail out those millions of people who lost their homes, their jobs, and/or their savings while instead bailing out the very banks and investment firms that caused the 2008 collapse of the economy.

It's certainly true that the Bill Clinton administration dismantled many of the carefully constructed post–Depression-era regulations on banks and investment companies. This, in turn, allowed many corporations to borrow or lend monies without any serious checks and balances for financial responsibility, making the 2007–2011 Great Recession virtually inevitable. This proved once again that the capitalist economy is not self-regulating, as its cheerleaders in both major political parties have contended.

And it is also true that with millions of people losing their homes and jobs in the Great Recession, the Obama administration, his hand-picked economic team composed of many who had shaped or shared the corporate-oriented assumptions that guided the Reagan, Clinton, and Bush presidencies, focused its bailout on the needs of the very institutions that had caused the crisis rather than on the people who were suffering most intensely. The betrayal of working people was astounding! So why was anyone surprised when many people who had previously voted for Democrats abandoned them, some by voting for Republicans, others by simply refusing to vote at all?

Yet what this assessment fails to take into account is that there have been previous periods in American history when people who faced equal, if not more intense, economic deprivation responded by building a militant labor movement focused on working class needs, supported Franklin Delano Roosevelt's New Deal and pushed it in progressive directions that at first FDR was reluctant to take on, joined the socialist and communist movements, or engaged in mass demonstrations and militant strikes. So, what has happened in these past few decades that made unlikely the emergence of a radical labor movement, a progressive political party supported by a majority of working people, or even the nomination of Bernie Sanders as the Democratic Party's presidential candidate in 2016?

These were the questions we at the Institute for Labor and Mental Health raised with thousands of working people beginning in the years of the Ronald Reagan and George H. W. Bush presidencies when many former supporters of the New Deal began abandoning the labor movement, the Democratic Party, and many liberal and progressive movements. In particular, we ran occupational stress groups for eight to twelve weeks each. Our participants were drawn from a wide array of unions, from the Communication Workers of America and Service Employees International Union (SEIU) janitors, hotel, and restaurant workers to the Teamsters, the United Auto Workers, and government employee unions, as well as nonunion workers in Silicon Valley's high tech industry, unorganized nurses and medical technicians, secretaries, bank tellers, and many more. The groups were usually equally populated by men and women, Caucasian people and people of color, gay and straight people, and were mostly people whose parents were born in the United States, though there was also a scattering of first-generation Americans and some new immigrants. We screened out people who needed psychological counseling. And to meet National Institute of Mental Health requirements, we did quantitative testing and pre-, post-, and post-post-followups in order to record data that was measurable and legible to the scientific community.[2]

Our most interesting conclusions, however, arose from conversations in the groups. We learned that over the past fifty years the ethos of global capitalism has taken hold of the conscious and unconscious lives of many Americans. Negotiating the worlds of work and home, these workers have absorbed two destructive ideas: that people don't care about anyone but themselves, and that economic insecurity is one's own fault—as, by the way, is everything else that is wrong in these workers' lives. Instead of feeling bad about a society that continually preaches these destructive ways of thinking, they felt bad about themselves. Their feelings disempowered them by making them feel that they were not entitled to a larger share of the societal wealth that they and workers before them had helped create.

This is not surprising given what these workers are up against. Tens of millions of people every day soak up the larger message of this society that shapes the dynamics of most workplaces, namely, "To be rational is to maximize self-interest, regardless of how that impacts others. If you are clever enough, you can hide the ways that you are seeking to advance your self-interest, precisely because hiding your self-interest is in your self-interest!" Acting on this message often does prove materially rewarding for working people, who are pitted against each other in hierarchies of power in both for-profit and nonprofit workplaces and pitted against working people in other countries around the world. But when a whole society rewards this kind of thinking and behavior day in and day out and even elects a president who embodies this way of thinking, we end up with a society in which many people have a tough time trusting anyone else. "Looking out for number one" becomes the guiding principle and appears for many to be the only rational way to live. And the value of other human beings is reduced to what they can offer that might help us advance ourselves and our chances for promotions, higher incomes, and public honors.

Needless to say, this consciousness leads people to feel lonely and isolated, because they (often partially correctly) feel that everyone else is just out for themselves, and hence can't really be counted on or trusted. Many feel this alienation even in their most intimate relationships, specifically that since a spouse or friends have learned to be rational maximizers of self-interest, one can never be sure that others will be there when they are most needed.

Even romantic relationships can be shaped by this kind of instrumental consciousness. Single people often encounter a marketplace of potential partners in which they are encouraged, as in a supermarket, to sample one product, and then the next, and then the next—and for many this can go on through much of their twenties and even their thirties. Dating apps and websites, Facebook and other social media, all make it easier to confront the challenge of finding a partner as a solitary (and often unsuccessful) entrepreneur in the free market of relationships. For some, the thrill of conquest or being seen as attractive to many potential partners starts to lose its appeal over time, and at a certain point many decide to settle down with one person. But given their own conditioning, their choice of a partner is often based on a conscious or unconscious evaluation that person X will satisfy more of their needs than anyone else who is likely to be open to a committed relationship with them. Thus even marriage comes to feel relatively insecure and hollow—not just the 42 to 45 percent of marriages that end in divorce, but almost all marriages—because one never knows if one's partner will at some point find someone else they believe can satisfy more of their needs and hence decide to leave the marriage. The societal result is a deep fear that one might end up with no one at all to be there for you when you are sick or weak or aging. And in a society that has allowed pensions to be weakened, social security to deteriorate, and long-term medical care to be available mostly to the wealthiest, friends may abandon you, disappearing into their own anxieties.

RAISING CHILDREN IN A SOCIETY BASED ON SELFISHNESS AND MATERIALISM

Imagine people in this society—that is, ours—trying to raise children. Having felt lonely for real friendships that transcend the "Oh, I'm fine" superficiality often put forward with co-workers and casual friends, and not so sure whether partners or spouses can be counted on in the long run, many adults turn to their children to find the emotional connection that they are not getting elsewhere. For some, that works. For most parents, however, the stress and frustrations of work and economic insecurity combine to make it hard to be fully present to their children. Stress from the world of work is hard to shake off in the few waking hours most parents have when they get home. Children feel that distancing. Not knowing anything about how their parents have been emotionally wounded both in their own childhoods and then again daily in the competitive marketplace, many children simply feel unseen. They intuit that instead of being responsive to the children's needs, their parents want to feel validated in some way by their own children.

In myriad ways, parents who wish to communicate love to their children may also simultaneously display their own neediness and their fears that they are not enough. This ambivalence may interfere with a parent's ability to see what their child actually wants, namely a fully present and mothering or fathering caretaker who sees them as the miraculous being they really are. In response, children at an early age will cry. The parent, having no idea what the child really wants, rushes to soothe and hush the crying child because they believe that their child is in pain. In this process, repeated frequently during the child's early years, both the parent and the child learn not to express their emotions. Rather than meet their child with an authentic connection, parents may offer inadequate substitutes such as food, games, or television, or in some cases, even punish the child for crying. Children, in response to sensing that they are not delivering what their parents need, internalize this gap and assume something is wrong with themselves because they can neither help their parents nor elicit from them the attention, recognition, and love they themselves so badly need.

Very few children are able to figure out what responses their parents need to feel validated in the ways their world of work does not provide. Nor are most parents aware that they are bringing home into their relationship with their young children the pain that they have tried to avoid feeling, the multiple messages they have absorbed that they are not enough and have only themselves to blame. Often, they respond with puzzlement or anger toward their children, who need something from their parents that the parents don't know how to provide. The parents may try to avoid noticing the absence of genuine mutual connection with their children, because to the extent that they notice this, they process their failures with their children through the same self-blaming framework that they've already internalized from their work world. Children in these situations have no way of learning that their parents' unsatisfactory responses at home are not their own fault but rather the outcome of feelings of inadequacy generated by class society and its meritocratic fantasy.

There is yet another way parents may try to show their love—they prepare their children for a competitive, selfishness-oriented society by encouraging them to develop the skills and toughness that will make it possible for them to "succeed." For instance, ask yourself if your parents ever communicated some version of the following messages: "You will not be happy unless you are successful in the world of work or unless you marry someone who can provide you with financial security"; "Make us proud of your accomplishments"; "Don't trust most people—they only want something from you." These are all ways parents pass on their own sense of fear and insecurity. And if children resist, preferring play and fun over performance and goal-directed activity, their parents will sometimes communicate anger or disappointment—or just give up on their children.

This same dynamic often plays out in rich families just as much as in financially struggling families, because wealth and fame are never enough to overcome feelings of inadequacy inherited from unsupportive childhoods. Here is the cycle: children find it impossible to deliver what their parents consciously or unconsciously want from them; this causes pain and often makes children blame themselves for their failure to secure the loving care they need from their parents. Then children interpret this lack of loving to mean that they themselves are not worthy of love, a feeling that generates a deep and painful humiliation, which they then may bring into relationships with their own children.

In other words, the absence of understanding by both parents and children and the absence of classes in schools that could teach children about why parents often don't give them the love they deserve almost guarantees that these children will grow up with negative feelings about themselves. They then enter the economic marketplace primed to blame themselves, making it all the easier for them to absorb and believe class societies' meritocratic fantasies and the ethos of selfishness that will lead them into even deeper self-blame.

CHALLENGING THE MESSAGES OF SELF-BLAME

To protect themselves from reexperiencing childhood's humiliations later in life, many people adopt a skeptical stance toward others, particularly those who reawaken in them the desire to be fully seen and loved. They feel safer with those who have a similar suspicion of others and similar emotional walls that keep them from being vulnerable to new disappointments and humiliation.

Most people still have a deep yearning for a world of kindness and generosity and higher meaning. Nevertheless, some will strongly deny the possibility of such a world and deny that they want it, at least on a conscious level, forcefully repressing their desires. They can become angry or even violent when they encounter people who say that this kind of a world is possible, because to take the possibility seriously would force them to feel vulnerable again to a basic need that has never been fulfilled. At all costs they wish to avoid the potential humiliation that would come from opening themselves and then once again being disappointed and feeling that they yet again have failed in the one relationship in which they've spent so much time—their childhood family. They feel much more comfortable in a conservative milieu in which these yearnings are dismissed as childish fantasies or channeled into a vision of a god and heaven where these needs will be fulfilled.

Others who have some inkling of these yearnings inside themselves join liberal or progressive movements to find a different world. Yet to the extent that they too have been wounded by not getting the love and respect they needed as children, they can become disruptive to those movements. I've witnessed many progressive organizations and movements crippled by participants who are so deeply needy for recognition that they interrupt meetings with impossible demands, raise irrelevant ideological disputes, or put down others or the organization that they joined, in the process making others question their desire to be in that movement. Many people have told me they stopped being activists because they had hoped to find in the Left people who embodied high ideals but instead only found people who were deeply wounded; they explained that they want to spend their limited time outside of work with healthier people.

My response has always been that if you want to change this society and save the life support system of Earth from the destructive impact of what I call the globalization of selfishness (a.k.a., global capitalism and its ethos of endless growth), you have to work with wounded people, because there is nothing else on this planet. All of us have had some degree of childhood wounding that is in need of repair, in ways we may not yet fully acknowledge to ourselves or others. These wounds are part of what Richard Sennett and Jonathan Cobb called the hidden injuries of class.[3] It can take patients years in therapy to recognize and overcome those wounds, a process that is often undermined by the societal message that it is rarely safe to be emotionally vulnerable. The more hidden and entrenched the dynamic of self-blame is in any given individual, the more he or she is attracted to the worldview of domination as common sense. Still, even people who were deeply hurt as children may end up choosing the path of love and generosity, if they find a way to heal.

In our occupational stress groups at the Institute for Labor and Mental Health, we created safe environments in which people could admit to feelings of deep shame and pain at a lack of love, caring, support, and success in their lives. Fearing that they would be seen as losers if they revealed the full extent of their self-blame, the middle income working people we interviewed rarely told their stories in full at first. However, they were able to see self-blaming in others in the group settings and sought to help these others see how inappropriate it was; that, in turn, helped them over time open up themselves. They reported that either they or people they knew turned to various distractions to stay out of touch with these feelings, immersing themselves in frenetic activities, sports, exercise, religious or spiritual practices, or in various addictions such as television, drugs, alcohol, sex, or more recently, social media.

Most people will deny their self-blaming story, and researchers conducting opinion surveys or quantitative studies will rarely pick up any hints of self-blame. On the contrary, developing egotistical or even narcissistic defenses against acknowledging to oneself any inadequacy is often taken to be a sign of strength in capitalist firms, or by professionals or politicians. It takes a process like the one we created at our institute to provide the emotional safety necessary for people to look at themselves honestly and reveal to themselves and others the details of their own particular self-blaming story. Through these occupational stress groups, we have demonstrated that stress could be reduced by social support if that support is deep and real, measured not by the number of people in one's network of friends and family or by the frequency of interactions with those people, but only by the quality of these interactions. Always, our goal is to steer toward the question "Is it reasonable to say you created this reality?" and some variation of the answer "No. Although we make our own choices, we do so in the midst of social arrangements that we did not choose and which constrained our ability to imagine alternatives."

As we moved the groups' discussion to the isolating nature of competition in the world of work and even in schools, participants poured forth stories of loneliness and being misunderstood, now seeing themselves not as failures but as suffering from a system they had never before fully grasped.

And then we talked about the ways that media and culture lead one to believe that everyone else is competing effectively, and that only losers are not finding successful relationships and gratifying family lives. Suddenly, when our groups turned to that discussion, a massive anger and sadness appeared as participants began to understand how they had been made to feel bad about themselves. As this began to sink in, many people started to dissolve their self-blaming. They began to reflect in a new way on the massive and often impossible task of navigating the challenges they faced in their lives, which include the following:

Finding a partner to love who is not primarily out for themselves in a society that teaches everyone to maximize self-interest? Not so easy!

Having children who offer respect and really want to learn from you? Also not so easy, especially when children are taught that their highest goal must be to achieve maximum autonomy at the earliest possible moments in their lives.

Finding a job where your intelligence is fully recognized and respected, and your creativity is given room to manifest, and where you can genuinely feel that you are serving a higher purpose, giving back to the world, and connecting to some higher meaning for your life? Extremely rare!

And yet, these were precisely the things that most of the people in our groups really wanted for themselves: love, respect, and work that provides a sense of meaning and purpose.

Few of our researchers expected to hear about hunger for higher meaning. This wasn't a goal that we professional observers had been taught would motivate so-called ordinary Americans. Indeed, we had been taught that only we, the upper middle class professionals—as the intellectuals, the presumed "new class" that was inheriting the world—had needs for meaning and purpose, whereas they—the working class, those we were observing—had mostly material needs. And we realized that this failure of perception was part of the problem: the Left couldn't understand why so many workers were failing to organize and instead were moving to the Right when the Left surely would better serve their material needs. Now, suddenly, we were finding an answer. The slogan "It's the economy, stupid!" was actually not true and continues to not be true. Beyond material needs, all people have a hunger for love, respect, and a higher meaning. If they aren't hearing this hunger addressed by the Left, then they are motivated to seek it on the Right.

Overcoming this society-induced self-blaming empowers people to join with others in efforts to fundamentally change the selfishness-generating society in which we live. As became clear to us at the institute as we saw dramatic changes during these group discussions, the yearning for a world of love and justice has never been and can never be fully absent, even if the fear of trying to build such a world leads many to say that it is impossible or undesirable. Once the self-blaming decreased, many participants were open to rethinking other aspects of their internalization of the patriarchal, racist, and homophobic values they had previously embraced. Some white men, for example, began to acknowledge the racist ideas they had for so long held on to, and began to express a strong rejection of them. Others, listening to the self-blaming stories of women in the groups, expressed a new openness to feminist ideas that had previously angered them. Of course, there were some who could not yet take those leaps in consciousness.

It will take a much larger and consistent effort over several years for a campaign against the capitalist forms of self-blaming to have any society-wide impact. Moreover, while we recognize the major impact that societally-generated self-blaming has in making people feel powerless, we do not want to eliminate the rigorous self-examination called for in most religious traditions and many psychologically based therapies, which encourage people to learn how to take personal responsibility for choices damaging to themselves and others, at least in those situations where they do have the power to change. Yet we also helped people in our occupational stress discussion groups to see that many of their self-destructive (or other-destructive) choices were made in a societal context where selfishness was (and is still) being rewarded pervasively, with ethical choices often mocked as "idealistic" and "unrealistic," and options to behave differently often unclear in situations where people made choices that they later regretted. What we witnessed was the way undermining self-blaming could be amazingly empowering. When they recognized that a significant part of the disappointments in their lives at work, in friendships, and with family were often a product of the unconscious internalization of the psycho-spiritual distortions of the globalization of selfishness (the ethos of the capitalist marketplace), they felt empowered and less stressed, and less inclined to anger toward the societal "demeaned others" who had previously been blamed for what was not working in their lives.

The women's movement is an example of amazing transformations, created within just a few decades. Millions of women have been enabled to stop blaming themselves and to understand that the sexism that suffused their experience in the worlds of work and family life was the fault of a patriarchal social order. Today, even some of the most traditionally trained therapists are able to make successful interventions based on this understanding; thirty years ago they would have resisted such a tactic as inappropriately "political." The strategy of revolutionary love owes a tremendous debt to the work of feminists, who have showed that they could challenge gender roles previously considered immutable, as just "human nature," and in the process have changed the practices of psychotherapists and others in the helping professions. Our movement is really an outgrowth of theirs, aiming for similar results in what we might call classism and its underlying belief systems, of which self-blaming is a major component. Self-blaming disempowers people from challenging the system that both puts them down and causes their pain. Undermining self-blaming through empathic communication and discussion groups like those we ran at the institute is a crucial first step in the revolutionary possibility of love to build the caring society.

But wait. What if the movements seeking change are themselves infused with shaming, blaming, and put-downs of the very people they need to attract? How does that happen, in what ways does it manifest? And what changes are needed in liberal and progressive movements so that they undermine rather than reinforce the values of the capitalist marketplace? These questions are the focus of the next chapter.

CHAPTER FOUR

To Change a Society, You Must Respect Its People

The coming decades offer an unprecedented opportunity for a Left that understands and effectively articulates the relationship between the ethical and spiritual distortions of the capitalist marketplace and the pain that results when people internalize the values and ideology of that marketplace and try to live by them.

Why hasn't that happened yet? Sadly, the Left has been missing the mark in part because it has itself internalized some of the assumptions of the capitalist marketplace critiqued in the previous three chapters and continues to rely on elitist ways of seeing their fellow citizens. There are essentially four corrections or repairs the Left needs to accomplish in order to gain and/or regain the trust and engagement of people who don't vote or who have moved toward and are supporting the Right. Let me be clear that I am not speaking about the smaller percentage of Trump supporters, likely 15 to 20 percent of American voters, who are deeply racist, sexist, homophobic, classist, ageist, Islamophobic, and/or anti-Semitic. Nothing in this chapter or in this book is suggesting that we spend our energies trying to influence them or win them over to support the caring society. Instead, I am referring to those Americans who aren't fundamentally stuck in prejudice and hate but are so fed up with failed politics and the Left's dismissive and often elitist discourse that they are willing to vote for candidates who articulate the anger, distress, and fear they so deeply feel. Here are the four corrections the Left needs to undertake, in order to reach these discouraged voters:

Emphasize our shared humanity rather than projecting leftist activists as somehow on a higher level than the people whose support and votes we hope to win.

Honor diversity of faiths and overcome leftist disdain for or suspicion of religion, spirituality, or even using the word "love" in public pronouncements.

Overcome versions of identity politics that demean others and instead embrace a version that affirms the value of those who don't fit into the Left's idea of who is the most oppressed.

Articulate clearly what the Left stands for and not just what it is against. (See chapters 5 and 6 for this positive vision.)

My suggestions on how to achieve this final correction are presented in the second part of this manifesto; the first three corrections are discussed in the rest of this chapter.

EMPHASIZE OUR SHARED HUMANITY

We are seeing a rise in hate crimes spread throughout our country. These are scary and unsettling times. The inability and refusal of many people on the Right to see the humanity of immigrants, feminist women, refugees, people of color, LGBTQ people, Muslims, Jews, and/or others is deeply disturbing and dangerous. We must continue to stand up to attacks on people's lives and liberty, reject policies and practices that are hurtful or even violent toward the victims of past and/or present oppression or discrimination, and if necessary nonviolently put our bodies on the line to challenge or even disrupt those who are engaged in systematic practices that endanger the lives and welfare of the poor and the powerless or threaten the environment (including challenging corporations and the banks and financial institutions that fund them, as Native Americans did at the Standing Rock challenge to the Dakota Access pipeline). And no matter which political party is in power, we should be equally adamant, not allowing our desire to have Democrats, for example, win the next election to influence and soften our critique or our activism against destructive policies. In the case of Standing Rock, if only President Obama had stood up unequivocally, spoken to the nation about what we as Americans owe to Native Americans to begin to rectify the genocide committed against them, and simultaneously had informed the banks and investment companies providing financial backing for the environmentally irresponsible pipelines that the U.S. government would withdraw its financial ties to them—such a stance would have produced a very different outcome.[1]

And, I submit, we must do that with love and compassion in our hearts—not only because it is the most effective strategy but also because it is the only ethical way to live when the life support system of the planet and the well-being of our fellow citizens are in danger. The Native Americans at Standing Rock showed us that a movement could express moral outrage in a way that was respectful even toward those who are destroying livelihoods and hurting our planet. If we truly want a different world—one that uplifts rather than puts down, one that is filled with revolutionary love rather than destructive hate, one that allows for the possibility of healing and transformation rather than repeating the mistakes of our past—we must emphasize and honor our shared humanity with those who are not yet on board with progressive programs, rather than reflect back to them their own hatred or violence. If progressive ideas were no longer experienced by many as inherently linked to left-wing elitism and condescension, many of those who shut their ears to our ideas in the Midwest and Mountain states and elsewhere might enthusiastically embrace them. Not everyone, but enough to change American politics in the coming decades.

Those who wish to build the caring society must use an approach that Cat Zavis, executive director of the Network of Spiritual Progressives, calls prophetic empathy. It is prophetic insofar as it challenges the evil aspects of the systems that produce hatred, sexism, racism, classism, and environmental irresponsibility and also in calling people back to their highest selves. Prophetic empathy insists on listening to others with an open, compassionate heart and with genuine curiosity about their life experiences and feelings, and helping them articulate their deepest needs, while powerfully advocating for a loving world.

Prophetic empathy affirms the humanity of all people. It recognizes that people can be oppressors and oppressed at the same time, and that in fact most of us in Western societies are in that situation. Without softening its prophetic critique, it powerfully and lovingly teaches us how to be empathetic toward those who are not yet on our side, to recognize their humanity, and to help them discover and manifest the revolutionary love that can be the foundation for a nonviolent transformation of our world which will benefit all of humanity and the planet.

Prophetic empathy does not entail the uncritical acceptance of hateful ideas. Rather, it is asking all of us to be genuinely curious about what might lead someone who is not yet with us to choose a particular behavior, promote a particular policy, or support a particular candidate that spiritual progressives do not support. Empathy requires the ability to imagine that someone who voted for a candidate we know to be pursuing hurtful or even evil programs may only have a superficial commitment to that candidate's actual policies, and to explore with genuine curiosity what it is that underlies a person's identification with such candidates and programs—for example, how fear about one's personal well-being and security may get manipulated into fear of the Other.

It might be useful for all progressive movement activists, when speaking to people who seem hardened in their reactionary political stance, to be curious about or imaginatively picture what was done to someone in child-hood that made them close themselves off from their own suffering and later from the suffering of others; what convinced them to harden themselves so as to survive. In some cases, it may have been in the military, which they were programmed to join, and in most cases, it is likely the commitment to succeed in the competitive capitalist marketplace. What pain and what humiliations did they face? Our task is to connect with their humanity and their suppressed but still existent yearning for a different world. What did they go through to lose touch with this yearning?

The repair (*tikkun*) needed by the Left is to see the real suffering of people who may appear privileged by the color of their skin or by being a man, but who nonetheless are hurting, not only economically, but also psychologi-cally and spiritually. Unfortunately, this emphatic questioning rarely occurs. Instead of acknowledging the problem and helping people understand the connection between their own personal suffering and the distortions of our society, and particularly its classism, the Left has frequently intensified the self-blaming of the very people we need to join with us to change the world. Hopefully, this book may become the stimulus needed for a fundamental rethinking of this grave error.

And we need to remind ourselves when trying to break through to people who seem to be responding to progressives with a set of societally sponsored clichés that we need to be sensitive to the deep conditioning they've been subjected to in this society, particularly the notion that everyone is selfish, materialistic, and indifferent to the fate of others, and that if they want to be successful in any part of their lives they need to learn the skills of domination and looking out for number one even at the expense of leaving behind or injuring others, and that if they don't live this way, others will dominate them and take advantage of them. They have been taught that anyone who thinks that this ruthless mindset can or should be changed is unrealistic or even delusionally out of touch with what the dominant culture defines as reality.

Transcending the Dynamics of Oppression

Mass culture sells this approach to life as the only rational way to create an economy, the only way to live in the real world. This message is soul crushing and simply not true. Love revolutionaries, spiritual progressives, and anyone who wants progressives to be more successful must counter these pervasive messages by helping people understand that these ways of looking at the world, integral to the capitalist marketplace, are precisely a major source of family breakdown and the difficulties we have in sustaining loving relationships or even long-term friendships—and that these difficulties are not the result of personal failures but a product of the logic of the social system brought to us by class societies and patriarchy. The personal is political in this way: the pain in personal lives is often a product of living in a society in which so many have internalized the values of the competitive marketplace in ways that undermine love and caring.

Our prophetic empathy insists on the importance of helping people (and ourselves) reconnect with the basic need for a life that has higher meaning and purpose than the pursuit of money, power, fame, or sexual conquest— essentially, by proposing a vision of the caring society. A successful Left must shift its discourse, continuing to include economic entitlements and political rights but framing these social values in the terms that underlie all spiritual and religious traditions, and all ethical, moral, and philosophical teachings, and explaining how these values cannot be satisfied within the strictures and daily practices and conditioning of capitalist and patriarchal societies.

Marx and many socialists who shaped the Left of the nineteenth and early twentieth centuries believed that the critical contradiction in capitalism was that it could not satisfy people's material needs. Addressing that dimension of human needs continues to be the major focus of the labor movement and many of those in the progressive wing of the Democratic Party. It is an important dimension and I'm appreciative of their work. My own post-socialist perspective, while supporting all the struggles for economic equality, social justice, and human rights, holds that it is the yearning for a world based on love, kindness, generosity, and higher meaning for our lives, as well as the overcoming of narrow utilitarian or instrumental ways of dealing with each other and with Earth, that are the critical contradictions that capitalist societies cannot ever fully resolve. Because the word "socialist" usually conjures up a movement primarily focused on the dimensions of material well-being and human rights, and because societies that called themselves socialist democracies in Europe often ended up either susceptible to authoritarian leaders or to bureaucratic governments seemingly divorced from those other dimensions that revolutionary love addresses, I think our movement, to be successful, must at once defend the vision of socialist democracy—which has not yet been fully achieved in any of the societies that call themselves socialist—and at the same time, must differentiate ourselves by calling ourselves post-socialist or love socialists or love-based socialism or most simply, spiritual progressives or love revolutionaries. I've come to think that the best way to communicate this is to say that we are people who want the Caring Society—Caring for Each Other and Caring for the Earth. And we will fulfill this vision by building a Love and Justice movement that teaches these ideas and tries to heal and transform politics in whatever country adopts this approach.

We, the spiritual and love-oriented side of the liberal and progressive Left, want to create a society in which caring for each other and caring for the Earth are top priorities, and we want to build an educational system, a health care system, an economic system, and a political system that support those goals. We are urging the rest of the progressive and liberal social change movements to adopt this same kind of discourse. But we have to be careful to avoid the tendency to let the capitalist mindset seep into our approach. Rather than focus on winning or beating the so-called bad guys, we need to build a movement for love and justice that emphasizes our shared humanity with *all* human beings—and does not treat people (whether

Transcending the Dynamics of Oppression

within our movement or outside of it) as merely instruments for our own political success! Unless our own movement seeks to overcome our own instrumental thinking about others, and provides weekly trainings for our own activists in how to do that, there is little chance we can convince others that overcoming the capitalist and patriarchal ethos is possible. Of course, as in all other aspects of our lives, we must be gentle on ourselves and each other, encouraging each other rather than putting each other down for not doing a good enough job. Otherwise we could create a movement that is harsh with each other, that is too judgmental about who overcomes instrumental thinking best and who fails, and unwittingly we would be right back in the mode of self-blaming and other-blaming that is certain to turn people away.

We must also make it clear that we do not blame the entire American people or the people of any other country for the policies and distorted values that we challenge. Those distorted policies and values are products of economic and political systems, managed by the tiny elite that inherited these systems and whose highest priority is to maintain them. The powerful forces that uphold the capitalist system will at first ignore us, and try to keep this book from being reviewed widely or discussed on the mass media they control. If the idea of revolutionary love becomes well known, the ruling elite will likely both ridicule and demean a movement that seeks a fundamental transformation to build a society based on love, caring, respect, and justice. Or, they will manage to exalt versions of revolutionary love that are really mostly about individual consciousness change while ignoring the version presented here and emerging from the Network of Spiritual Progressives and *Tikkun* magazine. And if, despite all the ways that these ideas are kept out of public consciousness, we ever get widely known and discussed, they might use the instruments of repression employed to undermine the antiwar movement of the 1960s and early 1970s, for example, placing undercover agents in our organizations to cause dissension, or in other ways discredit, jail, or maybe even kill some of our activists.

Our chance for success depends on our ability to liberate in ourselves and in all those we encounter the deep yearning for a life filled with love and higher meaning and then to embody that loving attitude in what we do. Sometimes we will fail, will be triggered by others, or will allow new recruits to our movement to speak in harsh or even violent ways out of a misguided desire to be open to a wide variety of strategic perspectives. To the extent that we play down this yearning for revolutionary love and the caring society (perhaps in the belief that we can best win minimal reforms by avoiding being seen as too ideological, too spiritual, too prophetic, or too ahead of our time), we actually make it less likely that we can win even the less visionary reforms that the Democratic Party currently supports in principle, if not in a real struggle for them. It is precisely by speaking our deepest truth, and helping others reconnect to the yearnings that they rarely articulate to themselves (lest they once again feel humiliated by their inability—so far—to create that world) that we can build a movement capable of rapid global transformation in the coming decades—in time to repair that part of the damage to Earth's life support system that can still be reversed.

HONOR OUR DIVERSITY OF FAITHS: OVERCOMING LEFTIST DISDAIN FOR RELIGION AND SPIRITUALITY

Americans are among the most religiously connected people in the Western world. Yet the Left has inherited a strong distaste for religion. Many Western leftists have embraced the idea that religion is only for less intelligent people. This disrespectful message alienates many Americans, including a significant number of Americans who report in polls that they agree with most of the key legislative programs of the Left. But that doesn't matter as much as the feeling they get when speaking to liberals and progressives who can barely contain their disdain for people who are into religious practices and beliefs.

The liberal and progressive distaste for religion may have been strength-ened by the role of evangelical Christians in 2016 who voted overwhelmingly for Trump (different assessments put that vote at somewhere between 75 and 81 percent) and who helped Republicans increase their hold on the Senate in 2018. Moreover, a lot of the antagonism to religion on the Left is based on hurtful experiences of growing up in religious communities that were sexist, racist, homophobic, Islamophobic, anti-Semitic, anti-science, and/or anti-intellectual, and that sought to control the thinking and behavior of every-one within their religious family and community. Certainly, religious people don't have a monopoly on any of these prejudices and forms of narrow-mindedness; but encountering them through the framework of an emotion-ally powerful religious community can be particularly devastating. No won-der that many activists ran from such communities and brought with them into the secular Left a visceral distrust and anger at religious bigotry based on their own personal experiences.

But it is important to recognize that, almost always, other branches of these same religions have taken the opposite direction, encouraging their communities to struggle against racism, sexism, homophobia, and other injustices. Fortunately, we are seeing a rise in progressive religious activism since the 2016 elections. It is appropriate to criticize those parts of the reli-gious world that openly embrace oppressive values and behaviors. At the same time, we must also acknowledge the historical legacy of racism, sex-ism, homophobia, anti-Semitism, and Islamophobia in many secular move-ments of the past, including the labor movement, the nineteenth- and early twentieth-century women's movement, and the socialist and communist movements. The problem of bigotry is not intrinsic or exclusive to religions.

Religiophobes' contempt for anyone who believes in a god or other aspects of reality that cannot be supported with empirical evidence is itself based on the religion of scientism explored in chapter 1. Few religiophobes have ever confronted the lack of empirical foundation for their own beliefs.

(Please remember that one can be a passionate supporter of the scientific enterprise yet a critic of the religion of scientism.)

A Left that wants to win in the United States should unequivocally reach out to people in religious communities and embrace, whenever possible, their concerns about the values fostered by the dominant materialistic culture of Western societies. We can help many see that most of the values they deplore are not the values of the presumed special interests on the Left, as the Right would have it, but in fact are the values of the capitalist marketplace.

Think it's impossible? Well, I've done this.

Let me tell you just one story.

In the early part of the first decade of the twenty-first century, several right-wing polemicists began a campaign blaming liberals for "stealing Christmas." Some of the more extreme among them pointed to campaigns by civil libertarians and Jews to forbid the placement of Christmas trees in front of city halls and other government facilities, parks, and monuments. They blamed the Jews. I wrote an opinion piece challenging this false charge, and because I was the editor of *Tikkun*, the best-known progressive Jewish magazine, I was invited to debate the issue with Bill O'Reilly, a right-wing pundit on Fox News.

O'Reilly is known for interrupting his guests and dominating the discourse, so many of my friends advised me to say no. I went.

O'Reilly began by talking about the latest attempt by civil libertarians and secularists to take down a Christmas tree and repeated the calumny that these civil libertarians were "stealing Christmas" from the many Christians who look forward to it each year.

My response went something like this: "Bill, you are absolutely right that Christmas is being stolen from Americans, but wrong about who is doing the stealing. Christmas, like Chanukah, has become an orgy of buying and buying and buying, orchestrated by the capitalist market that uses its immense advertising power to convince people that they are failures unless they spend immense amounts of money to give their family and friends expensive gifts as proof of their love. The beautiful spiritual message of both Christmas and Chanukah, that oppression and cruelty can be replaced by love and generosity, has been stolen from us—and all Americans are suffering from this loss."

O'Reilly seemed stunned and stumped. He had expected me to stay on the level of First Amendment rights and I had switched to the level of values and love. And this is precisely what I'm advocating as an important path for liberals and progressives, of course without giving up on rights! After the segment, O'Reilly told me that he agreed with me, that he had never heard a progressive speak this way, and that he was glad to meet me. Millions of Americans watching the show had been exposed to a way of thinking they had never heard before—and certainly never from a progressive kippah/yarmulke-wearing progressive Jewish activist and rabbi.

I wish I could have pointed those viewers right then and there to a movement that embodied that way of thinking, recognizing the deep need for a spiritual dimension in life, and equally welcoming to religious and secular people. The only such group I know of is the Network of Spiritual Progressives started by *Tikkun*. The network has been ignored by much of the Left precisely because we were talking this way rather than simply repeating the rights-based arguments that had already won as much of the U.S. public as they were ever going to win.

Unfortunately, even in the first few decades of the twenty-first century, many in the Left would be shocked at being challenged about this prejudice. When I tell them about the *Nation* and *Mother Jones* having a conference of progressive magazines but not inviting *Tikkun* or *Sojourners* or any of the other progressive religious publications, they shrug their shoulders and wonder whether any religious voice could "really" be considered progressive. Similarly, when seeking diversity in their demonstrations or forums, they look for ethnic or racial diversity but rarely think of religious diversity.

To Change a Society, You Must Respect Its People

Inevitably, this limits their ability to engage the many people who are involved to some degree in progressive religious communities.

Some liberal and progressive groups have come to recognize the importance of religious or spiritual activists but, worrying that they ought not to offend their many religiophobic constituents, these groups make sure that anyone explicitly speaking from a religious perspective should do so by being marginalized into a faith section of the activity, for example, an interfaith service before or after the main march or teach-in or protest, rather than being integrated into the time slots when most participants would still be around and might happen to hear from religious or spiritual progressives.

Most on the Left are either ignorant of or refuse to mention important contributions to progressive thought by religious figures such as Mahatma Gandhi, the Rev. Dr. Martin Luther King, Jr., my mentor Abraham Joshua Heschel, Benedictine Sister Joan Chittister, feminist theologians Rachel Adler, Judith Plaskow, Rosemary Radford Ruether, and Rabbi Rebecca Alpert, Rev. James Cone, Rev. William Sloan Coffin, Rev. James Forbes, Rabbi Arthur Waskow, Rev. Traci Blackmon, Rev. William Barber, or even Pope Francis on the environment, let alone the historically significant liberal activism of the Black Church in the South during the civil rights era, the key role churches and synagogues played in the major national marches against the war in Vietnam, the Liberation Theology movement (particularly in Latin America), the Catholic Worker movement, or the Quaker and Mennonite traditions. The outrageous policies of the Trump administration have bolstered the work of progressive religious organizations such as the National Council of Churches of Christ and the Religious Action Center of Reform Judaism; the social action arms of Reconstructing Judaism, Bend the Arc, and T'ruah; and the social action arms of the Lutheran, Presbyterian, Episcopal, Anglican, the United Methodist Churches, the United Church of

Christ, the Unitarian Universalists, the African Methodist Episcopal Church, the Reformed Church in America, the Disciples of Christ, the American Baptist Church, and the Progressive National Baptist Convention.

Many people on the Left point to the hypocrisy of some religious people whose claims (such as believing in loving their neighbors) are inconsistent with their actions (namely, their unwillingness to love people of color or the United Methodist Church's refusal to ordain gays and lesbians). But inconsistency is human, and is not always reducible to hypocrisy. Some on the Left who are outraged at mass incarceration still give honor to President Bill Clinton, whose administration played a central role in policies that disproportionately incarcerated African Americans. Those who are outraged at attempts to expel immigrants from this country willingly overlook the fact that President Obama's administration expelled over two million undocumented immigrants. When confronted, many of the people involved might answer, "There's more to what Clinton or Obama did than their errors around incarceration or around immigrants." So, too, some religious community members might note, "There's more to our religious life than these parts that you legitimately critique."

Ultimately, many people join religious communities precisely because, apart from families, these are the only organizations they know of that openly proclaim their goal of loving and caring for others. They find in the practices and ideas taught in religious institutions a path to a higher meaning and a powerful alternative to the values embedded in the daily practices of the capitalist marketplace. In my own life, that was a major reason I became a rabbi, to teach that aspect of Jewish religious thought and practice that echoed what had brought me into social change movements and in some cases went even further than those movements were willing to do. (Check out chapter 7 for my call to re-institute in a contemporary way the Sabbatical Year and the wealth-redistributing aspect of the Jubilee.)

To Change a Society, You Must Respect Its People

People are complicated and multidimensional, and it is a huge political and ethical mistake to dismiss them because they ally with groups that participate in cultures of oppression without recognizing other aspects of their consciousness and loving proclivities that might be mobilized to fight oppressive institutions and practices. If we are ever going to have the support we need to take far-reaching action to save the life support system of the planet and pass constitutional amendments like the Environmental and Social Responsibility Amendment to the U.S. Constitution or fund our proposed global Generosity Plan to end poverty, homelessness, hunger, inadequate education, and inadequate health care worldwide, we are going to need to win back many of the religious people who today believe (often based on real interactions with progressives) that people in the social change movements and in the liberal culture look down upon them and think of them as reactionary or stupid. That has to change, quickly!

Although this perspective applies to every part of the country, it is particularly true in regard to winning support for a constitutional amendment from Midwest and Mountain states where rural communities often decide statewide elections. As I discuss in the Introduction to this book, Princeton sociologist Robert Wuthnow's 2018 study, *The Left Behind: Decline and Rage in Rural America,* highlights how a fraying social fabric is fueling fear in small rural communities that their ethos of mutual support and caring, which has provided their sense of security, is being threatened by the larger selfish values of American society. In my view such communities will continue to be resistant to progressive explanations of why this erosion is happening as long as they experience liberal and progressive forces as hostile to one of the most important institutions from which they derive support: their churches.

Here is a constituency that is actually deep in rage, yet unable to hear our solutions until the liberal and progressive world demonstrates real respect for their religious life. No, I'm not calling on social change activists to become religious in order to win votes. But I am suggesting that Democratic Party candidates in state and national elections should openly apologize to religious communities for the way the Left has not recognized that many of the values espoused by religious communities are actually inconsistent with the values of the capitalist marketplace, and that it is time to renounce religiophobia in the Left just as, years ago, it was important to renounce sexism, racism, homophobia, Islamophobia, and anti-Semitism (as the Democratic Party majority in the House of Representatives did again in March 2019).

When rightists are able plausibly to portray progressives as anti-religious, they weaken the credibility of religious progressives who build support for the voices of love and generosity in their religious communities. It would be wise for those who are secular progressives to approach this issue with a bit of humility and nuance and to challenge anti-religious extremism when it appears in liberal and progressive cultural circles.

My point is not to deny the reality of reactionary movements inside some religious communities. Many people who appreciate the joy of loving communities offered by right-wing churches eventually get exposed to a worldview that preaches love but simultaneously teaches that the loving world is being undermined by selfish and materialistic "others" who are destroying what was once good about America. The "others" turn out, as usual, to be women, African Americans and Latinos, undocumented immigrants, refugees, the LGBTQ community, Native Americans, Jews, and Muslims—the list is continually growing. But this is no more grounds for dismissing all religious people than acknowledging that because right-wing extremists have been successful in using democracy to advance their anti-democratic message, this is grounds to dismiss democracy itself. The task for religious progressives is to enter those kinds of religious communities, embrace their love-oriented teachings, and insist that their fellow parishioners recognize that what undermines love is the selfishness and materialism we absorb in the daily operations of our workplaces in the capitalist marketplace.

If we want to build a society based on justice and caring for each other and the planet that is free of all these forms of prejudice, we need to create a movement guided by revolutionary love as defined in chapter 1, a movement that embraces our proposed new bottom line. Such a movement would welcome and honor secular humanists and atheists as well as people from every non-oppressive branch of every world religion. Some of them may prove impossible to reach—the people whose racism, sexism, homophobia, Islamophobia, anti-Semitism, and other forms of hate are so deep that they cannot move beyond them. But there will be tens of millions of others we can attract to the vision of a world of love and the caring society and the new bottom line we spiritual progressives propose.

So here is the stark truth: we can only organize a mass movement if we respect and love people who are not yet part of our movement. Learning to see that every person on this planet deserves care and respect (or in religious language, "is created in the image of God—b'tselem") can often be just as difficult for those who look down on the Right as it is for people on the Right to stop looking down on the groups they've been taught to demean.

Yet both these changes are possible. I know because I've seen it happen in practice. I once had a member of Beyt Tikkun, the synagogue I serve as rabbi, who had been a Klan member and had, as a result of his encounter with empathic members of a Jewish community, rejected his hate-oriented approach, converted to Judaism, and became a wise and caring member of our community. And there are countless stories like this from other rabbis, ministers, priests, and progressive religious communities, as well as from people who have left hate groups or from organizations working with people who want to leave hate groups (e.g., Life After Hate). Demonstrating love and respect in our daily interactions with others goes a long way toward opening many (not all) to the revolutionary love that this manifesto embraces.

OVERCOME DEMEANING VERSIONS
OF IDENTITY POLITICS

What the Right Gets Right

In chapter 3 I explore how people often blame themselves when they don't receive the love or caring they need, respect from their children, or any confirmation that they live in a supportive world. They blame themselves for their failure to have the kind of friendships or family life they imagine others have achieved. And they feel surrounded by people who seem concerned only with their own selfish interests, which dismays them.

Then the political Right comes along and makes two brilliant moves. First, it tells these worried people that they are correct: "You are living in a world filled with selfishness and materialism, and this is not the result of your personal failings. Rather, it is a social reality and you are not to blame." With this message, the Right promises effective relief from rampant self-blaming, speaking to people's actual internalized pain and attempting to alleviate their psychological pain. Second, they create a sense of community that assuages people's sense of loneliness. Thus, by both speaking to people's actual pain and showing them they are not alone in this pain but rather are part of an identity group that is experiencing this pain, they simultaneously relieve people's self-blaming tendencies and meet their needs for belonging to a community that offers them a sense of purpose and higher values than merely the attainment of wealth and power—a community in which they matter and that cares about them and their suffering.

What the Right Gets Wrong

What is immoral about the Right's tactic is that it then goes on to blame the source of people's pain on the "special interests," by which they mean whichever groups are the demeaned "others" in society. In Europe in the first half of the twentieth century, the "special interests" were primarily Jews, who had been blamed throughout Christendom for the past 1,700 years (along with the Roma and later, homosexuals). In parts of Asia the stig-matized groups have been Chinese minorities living outside of China, Bud-dhists and Muslims living in Hindu countries, and Christians and Jews liv-ing in Muslim countries. And in the United States over the past forty years the "special interests" have been feminists, African Americans, Native Americans, Latinos (South and Central Americans), liberals and progres-sives, and even more recently, Muslims and immigrants or refugees. "These are the people who advocate only for themselves," the Right claims, "and your life and your family and your work world would be far better if these groups were no longer part of this society." The idea that some "others" (immigrants, feminist women, people of color, etc.) are the reason they are financially insecure or haven't achieved the success or respect they want is appealing precisely because it alleviates their shame and blame.

This is the moment for liberal and progressive movements to come for-ward and agree that there is a deep spiritual problem in Western societies—and explain that the source of the problem is not those various "demeaned others" of their society but rather, the selfishness, materialism, and extreme individualism built into the current global economic, political, psychologi-cal, and cultural systems produced by the competitive marketplace. Such an approach could dramatically change the psychodynamics of politics in Western societies.

HOW THE LEFT MISSES THE MARK
After my more than fifty-five years in social change movements, I know that most people in them are motivated by high ideals and an intense desire to create a world of justice, equality, democracy, human rights, and environ-mental sanity. And I also know that it's very hard for these activists to hear that they might unintentionally be undermining the support needed to cre-ate the kind of society they want, in part by their religiophobia (discussed in the previous section) and also in part by their shaming and blaming, and

their approaches to identity politics and some versions of what gets known as "political correctness" (discussed below). I hesitate to broach this, because it's all too easy to hear my analysis as a put-down itself, when in fact I love and honor my fellow activists for all the good that they have done and continue to do. Most of them rarely engage in the tactics I'm discussing. But they are part of a much larger liberal or progressive culture in which millions of people do commit these errors. Social media, particularly Facebook and Twitter, are a big part of this dynamic. People give themselves permission to be cruel to each other on these platforms, and words are easily excerpted and taken out of context for rituals of "calling out" and shaming. Late night talk show hosts and shows that ridicule and make fun of people on the Right—as well as sharing memes mocking and teasing people on the Right (even when they seem funny to us)—only build resentment and make things worse.

Shaming and Blaming:
How It Works and Why It's Destructive

Many of the middle income and low income working people I had the privilege of knowing through discussions in the occupational stress groups sponsored by the Institute for Labor and Mental Health and many of the individuals I met through therapy and spiritual counseling in the 1990s and early 2000s eventually wanted to become part of the movement for social change. But when they started going to meetings or otherwise finding ways to participate, they came back to me with upsetting stories of encountering class prejudices from liberal and progressive activists. Ultimately these attitudes discouraged them from being part of the movement. Some even began to resonate with the Right's accusation that the Left is filled with elitism and disdain for ordinary working class Americans. Let's call it classism.

Trying to connect with social change movements, they found themselves in an atmosphere in which they and everyone they knew were being shamed, blamed, or otherwise disrespected and dismissed. Here are some examples I've heard repeated with a thousand different nuances over the course of the past thirty-five years as I've traveled around the United States speaking at bookstores, college campuses, churches, synagogues, mosques, and community centers; in demonstrations for peace, justice, and environmental sanity; in personal conversations with people, and from social media posts after the 2016 election. (I have used pseudonyms and changed some details of their lives to protect people's identities.)

Tom Marconi, 34, assistant manager of a fast food store, Queens, New York:

> I agree with everything that I heard about the need to challenge the inequality and oppressive relations when I went to Occupy Wall Street in New York City in 2011. But then I heard people talking about white men being the oppressors. I'm a white man, and I felt like they saw me and everyone I know as an evil being. Yet they know nothing about my life, my struggles, or that I come from a very poor family.

Samantha Brown, 59, office worker, Chicago, Illinois:

> I'm an African American woman, and I've faced plenty of white racism. But not all whites are racist, and many of those I've met are anti-racist. How do you think this country elected Barack Obama? Twice! I'm not going to be part of a movement that makes white people feel that they have no right to speak or be taken seriously just because they are white or old. Yet I still see this happening in liberal and progressive circles in Chicago.

Leticia Jones, 67, retired nurse, Oakland, California:

> I was active with the Black Panther party for many years, worked serving breakfast for children in East and West Oakland. The Panthers created an alliance with the white students at U.C. Berkeley and I thought that was great. Now it's decades later and these days I hear people talking about white oppression. So I always ask, "What about class oppression?" They never mention it, and actually I don't think they even know what I'm talking about. So now I am active in the social action committee of my Allen Temple

Baptist church where people of all skin colors and racial backgrounds are welcome.

Lois Bernstein, 33, elementary school teacher, Austin, Texas:

One of my friends told me, "Today, it's the liberals who are the establishment, and they make me feel like shit. They are always saying things against whites or against men. I want to support my husband—he has a very difficult job, works hard, respects me and the kids, and I'm supposed to see him as bad because he is white and male. That gets me so angry. I used to be a Democrat, like everyone in my family, but now I'd even consider voting for Trump." I argued against her, but I couldn't convince her. She hates the way people on the Left try to make her feel bad for defending whites and defending men.

Janet Davies, 29, tech worker, Washington, D.C.:

I spent several weeks in my birthplace, a Red state, going door to door to try to convince people to vote for Hillary Clinton. I stayed with an old friend, and I was about to leave to go back home to D.C. I said to her, "Well, it's been hard getting people to talk to me about the issues but I hope you at least will be voting for Hillary." I was shocked when she said, "I haven't decided yet." This was four days before the election! I responded, "If you don't feel safe to say to me that you are voting for Trump, I want you to know that I'll love you all the same." She responded, "I really don't know what to do. I agree with the Democrats so much but I feel like they hate me and everyone like me. I just want you to know one thing: I am not a deplorable." She was referring to that remark of Hillary Clinton's in which she said that half of the Trump voters are "a basket of deplorables." I told my friend that I didn't think she was deplorable at all. Her reaction helped me understand why otherwise bright people could either buy into or accept the outrageous policies of the Republican Party—they weren't voting for the policies, but rather voting against the put-downs they encountered talking to liberals or activists.

A Christian therapy client of mine who I work with on Zoom told me that she felt a totalitarian climate in the liberal circles that surround her life in Manhattan:

Everyone I meet seems to see the world through the framework of a particular ethnic, racial, or gender identity. And woe to those who don't accept the latest orthodoxy. They make using politically correct pronouns their first priority while ignoring the growing gap between the super rich and the struggling working people like me. They never will go to a rally to support asylum seekers. They pooh-pooh the anti-Semitism that I see in parts of the Left and call me a Zionist when I point it out.

A conversation I had with a 29-year-old Lyft driver a few days after the 2018 midterm elections demonstrates just how pervasive this problem really is. The driver told me how very happy he was that the Democrats had won control of the House of Representatives, and said that the reason Republicans had increased their numbers in the Senate "is simple—most Americans are racist and stupid."

If social change movements drive away people who are genuinely committed to social justice and have suffered from oppression and worked to transform it, imagine how many more people are driven away and offended who have not yet tackled, yet alone embraced, the very notion of social change or are not yet capable of seeing the humanity of those who are different from them. Yet this is exactly what we are seeing. And as these anecdotal stories convey, policing, political correctness, and dismissal of those not yet with us (or even those with us but who are not yet "good enough" progressives) are behaviors as prevalent in the Left in 2016 as they were in 2006 and 1996.

While waiting for an airplane in Chicago, I started a conversation with a man from what he called "a shit-filled California blue state." He jumped at the opportunity to tell me the following:

I live in Ohio, and I voted for Trump. I know I'm not as smart as some of the kids from my high school who got into college. I never could figure out those tests you have to take. But I know when people don't like me, don't give a shit about what is happening to my life. All those Obama people who didn't care when I lost my home that I had worked for for twenty-two years, and lots of people I know, the same thing happened to them. They spent billions on the banks, but not a penny for us working stiffs. Obama cared about some tribe of Indians losing their land, but he didn't care about me. I used to be a Democrat, but now all they care about are people who got here illegally. Seems like they want everybody in the world to come here, take our jobs, and destroy our communities. . . . Yeah I know Trump is a jerk, but he's our jerk.

This is what we liberals and progressives are up against and, unless we can build a different kind of progressive movement filled with a compassionate and empathic attitude that affirms the fundamental decency of people, including those who have disappointed us in a variety of ways, our valuable and badly needed programs for social justice, economic equality, and environmental sustainability have little chance of mustering enough support.

If we want to win over those not yet with us, and win back those who have been offended, we need to see their humanity, understand what is motivating them to vote against their own needs and interests, and treat them and speak to them with respect and dignity. Doing this does not require that we simply accept or ignore the genuine vitriol coming from Trump and his ilk. Their use of overtly racist language and racist tropes, over and over again, has emboldened many to give voice publicly to messages that they had previously been willing to say only privately or on social media. As I've said before, there are some we will reach through a more compassionate, empathic approach and others including hard-core racists, sexists, xenophobes, and the like that we will not reach. Nevertheless, to build a mass movement, one that can actually create a radically different society than the one in which we currently live, we need to engage in tactics that embody the kind of society we want to build—namely, tactics that are unfailingly loving, kind, compassionate, generous, and empathic.

The Advent of Identity Politics

Since the 1960s, liberal and progressive social change movements have focused on championing the interests of groups previously denied the privileges granted those who are white and male in a racist and patriarchal world. In many ways this opening of opportunities and perspectives has been a wonderful accomplishment of the Left. A very large sector of the American population (mostly those who have voted for Democrats or the Green Party, or who have been in college during the past sixty years) has been deeply influenced by this mass education. Today there is a more nuanced understanding of racism, sexism, and homophobia than ever before, in the United States and many other countries. And in many areas of life, this deeper understanding has led to significant policy changes. It is no longer legal to discriminate against people of color or women in hiring and firing, publicly funded education, housing, hotel accommodations, or the distribution of many other societal benefits. Gays and lesbians can now legally marry in the United States, a right that is spreading to other countries. People may now lose their jobs and their relationships if others come to see them as sexual abusers. All these changes are terrific and must be protected and extended. Liberal and progressive movements deserve the gratitude of all humanity for having played a significant role in promoting these advances in consciousness!

Nevertheless, de facto discrimination and oppression still exist. Women as well as transgender and queer people still suffer from abuse and discrimination at home, on the streets, and in the workplace. People of color continue to find themselves caricatured and discriminated against in hiring, in mass media, and in the public arena. They are disproportionately the victims of unlawful arrest and police violence, including murder. For many African Americans, just being out in public, walking down the street in a predominantly white neighborhood, sitting down at a table in a coffee shop or a fast food store, or using a barbecue in a public park may lead some white person to call the police. And for the past few years Jews have faced an upsurge of anti-Semitism, desecration of Jewish cemeteries and synagogues, and physical attacks (though some of my rabbinic colleagues from smaller communities outside the areas where a lot of Jews live report that this anti-Semitic harassment has been a fact of life in their communities for many decades). Social change movements must continue to engage in struggles to protect everyone whose human rights are being violated in this society. And we must all open our ears and continue to listen to those who are the victims of oppression, learning to respond with empathy, action, and a real desire to end the oppression that many live with every day. This can be a powerfully positive impact of identity politics.

But there has been a downside to the advent of identity politics: it stopped short of recognizing the forms of class oppression faced by people of every race, gender, and sexual identity. This classism manifests in the huge inequalities of wealth, income, and political power that have been widely demonstrated and reported on in major media (as cited in chapter 1), as well as in the self-blaming described in chapters 2 and 3. Classism is equally implicated in the deprivation of love defined in the first chapter of this book. Although that deprivation is present in every socioeconomic class in painful ways, it has been more difficult to overcome for working class people, who often cannot afford forms of psychotherapeutic and spiritual healing available to the more financially secure. Moreover, classism often dictates the difference between work that gives people opportunities to use their intelligence and creativity on a daily basis and work that carefully constricts those capacities. For a fuller description of this element of classism, please read *Bullshit Jobs: A Theory*, a 2018 book by anthropologist David Graeber. In the United States after World War II, television occasionally depicted the lives of working class men and women, but today's media largely ignore the struggles of most working class people. The result has been the emergence of an American majority whose needs are not only forgotten but sometimes even actively erased by much of the discourse of identity politics.

Democrats as well have too frequently ignored the suffering of working class people even while seeking their votes. The party increasingly embraces identity politics while leaving working class people, of all genders, races, and religions, on the sidelines rather than highlighting the working class as another suffering identity group. In this way, they have played right into the hands of the Right, who have been able to attack Democrats and all liberals as "talking more about gender-neutral toilets than about home repossessions." That is not to say that liberals, Democrats, and progressives should not care about transgender and other identity politics issues—indeed, all of us most certainly should and rightfully do. However, when identity politics are uplifted but the needs of most white working class people, and particularly white working class men, are dismissed as "white privilege or male privilege," don't be surprised if many of them turn to the Right, which acknowledges their pain (while blaming it on the liberals and progressives who instead seek to privilege "the most oppressed"). The Right gives expression to the resentment many people feel at the lack of respect they get in their lives and work with the misplaced nectar that blames various groups of historically demeaned Others.

There is no reason why we cannot have a movement that revives the category of working class Americans as one of the identity groups that deserves respect and support. That has not been what liberal and progressive movements have focused on in the past several decades, but doing so would be an important corrective. All forms of oppression should be taken seriously and can provide a basis for a deeper identification, empathy, and compassion with one another. The development of the transformative consciousness spiritual progressives seek involves learning to be in touch with one's own oppression and suffering, and then learning to recognize and respond with empathy and compassion to the suffering of others—without the need to claim we fully understand each other's unique experience. As our consciousness expands, we can become more fully aware that our own liberation is dependent upon and intrinsically linked to the liberation of all others on Earth. But to get there, the Left must abandon its frequently heard mantra that all men and all whites are "privileged."

INTERSECTIONALITY RE-ENVISIONED

Kimberlé Crenshaw introduced the notion of intersectionality to teach us to recognize that many people can be subject to more than one form of oppression, and hence that the struggle for and experience of liberation require nuanced understanding of how this plays out. For example, the struggle against patriarchy and racism must be inextricably intertwined. I have attended feminist presentations where Crenshaw's idea has been flipped in a very different direction to emphasize that one can be oppressed in some respects and yet also be an oppressor, or someone who benefits from oppression, in other respects. This, in turn, has encouraged some to engage in creating hierarchies of oppression, shaming those who have an identity deemed less oppressed and therefore more "privileged" (mostly whites and men).[2]

When white working class people are blamed for enjoying the "privilege" of not being killed preemptively by racist police, or of not being discriminated against, many feel unrecognized and disrespected. The rates of middle-income white men committing suicide or dying in the opioid/fentanyl epidemic has reached astounding proportions, and at least half of the American population is only one paycheck away from economic devastation. Calling these people privileged drives them to Trumpists or to white nationalist (often fascistic) movements which welcome and honor them.

Rather than blame individuals or even groups of individuals for the suffering and oppression of people of color and other demeaned groups (simply a flip of what the Right does by blaming special interest groups for the suffering of white working class people), we need to place the blame squarely on the system itself. And as one of my interviewees put it, most whites and most men alive today neither participated in setting up the system nor have ever heard of a plausible way to transform it. One of the tasks of a movement for revolutionary love is to provide that possible path to transforming the present system.

Moreover, as many progressives point out to each other (but not often to the larger public), the advantages men and whites get by participating in this system are more than offset by the way ruling elites manipulate them into believing that the system truly works for them. The advantages themselves are the lure to keep them tied to the inequalities and injustices and psycho-spiritual oppression discussed throughout the previous three chapters of this manifesto.

I acknowledge a danger here: some whites insist on class politics instead of identity politics and choose to characterize feminists, LGBTQ people, and/or people of color as selfishly trying to take advantage of white guilt and/or male guilt. They ignore the data that show how even within an oppressive class structure women, African Americans, and Latinos get a worse deal than white men. For example, every indicator shows blacks and Latinos lost much more in the 2008 Great Recession than did whites (and often irreversibly). Some whites and some men use their own suffering as a way of denying the suffering of others. But that is *not* what revolutionary love is about.

Our goal is to help everyone understand that every form of oppression ends up supporting the larger system that hurts almost everyone. To get there, we have to be willing to see that this class-based global capitalist society hurts people in different ways, stop arguing over who suffers most, and open our hearts (and our discourse) to the suffering of everyone.

Let me be emphatic: I am not for overcoming or discarding identity groups! I'm a rabbi, and my life is enriched by my Jewish identity. I love Judaism and its particularity and its spiritual and ethical take on reality. I love its music, its prayers, its rituals, its literature, and its history. I love this part of my identity and will never accept a movement that requires me to abandon it, or to downplay the suffering that we Jews have experienced at the hands of Christians (and in the twentieth and twenty-first centuries from reactionary nationalists and some regimes that labeled themselves communist or socialist as well as, to a considerably lesser extent, from Muslims when significant numbers of Jews lived in near-apartheid-like conditions for centuries). The memory of that suffering is itself part of my identity, and is one of the reasons that I can empathize so much with others who have experienced suffering in their own history or in the present day.

Yet I am also a citizen of the world, a universalist. I know that my well-being as a Jew depends on the well-being of everyone on the planet. And, the reverse is also true: the well-being of everyone on the planet depends on the well-being of the Jews and other minorities that have been victims of oppression. Jewish oppression illuminates interestingly the dangers of failing to recognize the specificity of a group's mistreatment and suffering.

I've noticed a strong reluctance on the part of many on the Left (including many Jews) to recognize Jews as victims of Western imperialism and oppression by Christians. After some 1,500 years of intense oppression in Christian Europe, Western secular societies allowed Jews out of the ghettos and into the capitalist marketplace, where many were allowed to succeed financially. Supposedly, according to some, that was the end of their mistreatment—after all, many on the Left are stuck on the notion that if you are not suffering financially you are not really suffering at all. Yet over and over again in the past two hundred years, when ruling elites in those societies felt threatened by rising discontent, they encouraged nationalist movements to blame Jews as the real source of the nation's problems, deflecting attention from their own power and the systemic sources of economic and psychological pain in capitalist society. And that scapegoating has led time and time again to violence against Jews—just think about Nazi Germany and the Holocaust, in which one out of every three Jews alive in 1939 was murdered by the end of 1945. Economic success in 1920s Germany did not provide protection, just as economic success for some women doesn't protect them from sexist abuse, nor does it protect some economically successful gays and lesbians from homophobic oppression.

The United States and other capitalist countries invented the idea that people who benefited from the economic and political arrangements of Western colonialism and imperialism were "white." They then proceeded to try to convince many groups of Americans that they were white. The term "white" is not an accurate account of the skin colors of most of those who have come to the United States from European societies. Rather, it is used to convey that those described as white are not the victims of Western colonialism and imperialism, but rather its beneficiaries. Whiteness thus became a way of telling immigrants to the United States in the nineteenth and twentieth centuries that they should now identify with the powerful Anglo-Saxon majority who had conquered this country from its indigenous populations and were now enforcing its class structure. I have argued that Jews are *not* white, because far from being beneficiaries of Western colonialism and imperialism, we've been one of the victims of those systems for the past 2,500 years.[3] And yet, at the same time, I acknowledge that on the surface, we may pass as white and thus simultaneously experience the benefits and advantages that passing affords many who may not actually be "white."

Part of the task for social change activists is to problematize the entire concept of white—a concept that was created by the ruling elite so as to divide and conquer the disempowered in society, encouraging them to fight among themselves rather than join together to challenge the ones who actually have power over them, namely, the 1 percent—the richest people in this society and globally. Instead, I think we should be convincing most people in our society to refuse to identify as "white."

The alternative to destructive or polarizing forms of identity politics is not a seamless universalism in which each group subordinates its needs to achieve an ultimate revolutionary transformation. Rather, we need to develop a politics that simultaneously affirms the reality of each identity group's suffering and opens everyone up to learning about the suffering of others. The Left must recognize that suffering is not only based on material lack, but is also based on social, psychological, and spiritual deprivations, and that the best way to alleviate one's own group's suffering is to build alliances with all those who are hurt by the ways we currently organize society—even if they also do have some benefits or advantages that some others do not have in this society. There is little chance of any single identity group actually achieving liberation until all such groups have learned how to respectfully engage with each other and support each other's struggles. And in setting the agenda of the Left, we must reject those who insist that some particular identity group is the most oppressed and hence deserving of special privileges.

Further, we must provide an analysis of the class differences within every identity group. The life of an African American Supreme Court justice or trustee of a large corporation is not the same as the life of an African American mother working two jobs to support her family. Most people in class society are oppressed in some respects but beneficiaries of some forms of privilege in other respects.

Adding nuance to our critiques of oppression with a clear analysis of the role of class would make any identity group hesitate before asserting that everyone in some other group is benefiting from this or that system of oppression. White people and cis men need to be welcomed into the movement, because it is strategic to do so, because they too deserve love and generosity, and because they too would benefit as humans from the destruction of systems that cause deep psychic and spiritual pain even while ostensibly offering them more privilege over others. And one way to help them feel welcomed is to help them see how much whites and men suffer from life in a classist and patriarchal society (as some men's groups are already doing). The first three chapters of this manifesto show how destructive to human relationships this system really is. And that shows up most dramatically in suicide statistics. The American Foundation for Suicide Prevention reported that in 2017, men died by suicide 3.54 times more often than women. On average, there are 129 suicides per day. White males accounted for 77.97 percent of suicide deaths in 2017. Then there are the many whites and many men who try to lessen their suffering through opioids. The Center for Disease Control and Prevention reported that there were more than 70,000 drug overdose deaths in 2017, with a rate of 21.7 per 100,000 population. The rate increased by nearly 10 percent from 2016. The largest absolute increase in death rate is for males age 25 to 44.

None of this should be read to deny that those who are labeled as white or male do in fact receive significant advantages. These advantages are material and economic and include not only greater pay for the same work than women and people of color receive, but also easier access to health care, education, and some other benefits. Whites are also advantaged by being safer in the presence of police. And most men are advantaged by being socialized to voice their opinions and expect them to be taken seriously; they have not been silenced or demeaned or ignored in the ways that many women and people of color are.

Nor am I suggesting that people who have been part of oppressed groups do not have the right to express their feelings, their anger, their outrage, or their suspicion of others who belong to identity groups that have at times been the sources of their oppression.

White people's fear is that when oppressed people become the majority and rule over them, they will simply replicate the same systems of oppression that have been inflicted upon them. This is not an unreasonable fear because all too often history has played out in this way. What we in the liberal and progressive movements must show is that we yearn for a world free of oppressive systems and structures, that we validate and uplift the humanity of all persons, and that we seek to build a world that truly cares for the well-being of all (even those who benefit from the current oppressive and unjust systems). Nelson Mandela understood this fear and reassured the leaders of the apartheid state that they and their followers would not face violence were they to give up power. South Africa's Truth and Reconciliation Commission embodied a new energy in a process by which people who had committed acts of violence on either side of that struggle could confess their sins and regrets without being threatened. Mandela's movement succeeded in creating a democratic society without further bloodshed precisely because it reassured the Afrikaner oppressors rather than demeaned them. Yes, it achieved only a partial victory, securing political rights for all but leaving in place the economic structures of capitalist oppression. But creating a democratic mechanism that can in the future be used to democratize the economy was a major step forward.

Of course, no one outside an oppressed group has the right to demand that the oppressed reassure oppressors that they will be safe when systems and structures of oppression are dismantled and new faces gain power (indeed, those who acted in overtly violent criminal ways or gave the orders for acts of genocide will likely face prosecution). But offering that reassurance to the silent majority of people who benefit materially or in some other respect from class, racist, or sexist oppression would help them feel safe enough to open themselves up to our efforts—rather than continuing to go along with fascistic forces that will only increase the suffering of oppressed groups.

Let me reinforce my main point: we need to both emphasize the impact of oppression and simultaneously do it in a way that will be the most effective path to one's own (and others') liberation. The more liberals and progressives demonstrate their caring for everyone, not just by promoting economic policies that would actually uplift people's lives but also by speaking and acting in respectful ways toward those on the Right or those who are not yet with us, the more we have a chance of achieving our collective liberation. This approach was what made Martin Luther King, Jr.'s "I Have a Dream" speech so powerful and made it possible for the civil rights movement to make impressive gains in the mid and late 1960s. When speaking to hundreds of thousands of people at the 1963 March on Washington, King talked of a world in which whites and blacks together would share the benefits of freedom and mutual caring.

POLITICAL CORRECTNESS

Many white Americans and many men have experienced being denounced, demeaned, silenced, and shamed by some people on the Left. They have felt humiliated in private conversations, in groups at college campus dormitories and social gatherings, and on social media. In response, many have revolted against what some call left-wing fascism, or suppression of free speech, or just plain political correctness.

In simple terms, what "political correctness" means to many people who voted for Trump is this: "All whites and all men bear collective responsibility for the past and present suffering of all women and people of color. If you are white or a man, you talk from privilege and need to renounce your privilege and convince other whites and/or other men to do the same. To question any of this is proof that you yourself are racist, sexist, or otherwise deranged, ethically challenged, or just plain ignorant."

Many people who decided to vote for Trump, and who may continue to support Trump-like politics years after Trump is no longer the president, have felt misunderstood and disrespected by this kind of silencing. Others felt angry at their invisibility. Many poor whites, who are among the lower 80 percent of American income earners or wealth holders, were outraged when told that they are people of privilege when in fact they are struggling financially, often having to take more than one job to keep their family afloat, and constantly worried about how they would pay for health care, child care, elder care, and/or a college education for their children. Among them of course were some true racists and sexists. But others were simply attracted to the candidate Trump and his Republican Party enablers who told them not to blame themselves for failing to meet the Left's criteria for being a decent person. Instead, they should be proud to be Americans and to identify with a politics designed to make America "great again" and place America first!

We need to speak about privilege in a more nuanced way—one that actually reflects the reality of people's lived experiences of oppression and privilege and that includes the unspoken class oppression that leaves people living lives of quiet desperation. We can do this by sharing with them our understanding of the Great Deprivation, the Great Yearning, and the healing that can come from revolutionary love and from creating the caring society, and by fostering a sense of global solidarity through revolutionary love—caring for every person on the planet and doing all we can to alleviate suffering, without denying the variety of forms that suffering takes. The global Generosity (or Marshall) Plan proposed in the second part of this manifesto is one way to manifest this vision, one motivated by love and caring, not guilt and shaming.

Unless a progressive movement can expand its heart to understand the pain and fears of white people and of men, and help them see the source of their suffering in the larger class-based and patriarchal system, despite the victories I expect Democrats to receive in the 2020 and 2024 elections there is a real danger that fascist movements will be powerful shapers of the next decades, in the United States and major European countries.[4]

Prophetic empathy and revolutionary love need to shape our behavior in one-on-one conversations, within our movements, in the liberal media, and on social media. They must be both individual acts and collective acts. We cannot be expected, as individuals, to engage empathically and with love at all times. We do need time for self-nurturance and self-care. But if we are to build a mass movement filled with people who engage in this caring for others, and transform the discourse on the Left, we will eventually get the resources we need to get our message heard and taken seriously.

People sometimes say, "I have relative x or coworker y or neighbor z who is so deeply entrenched in their hatred or so committed to making money as their highest value, so what do you say to them?" When we encounter those on the Right who are so deeply immersed in their racism, sexism, and homophobia, or so committed to the value of accumulating wealth and power, that they seem unlikely to be moved by anything we can do or say in the next decade, we must move on and focus on those who seem more likely to be drawn toward our movement for love and justice. You don't have to take as your first steps convincing those who you are really unlikely to convince. Just speak about the various ways people suffer in a society based on selfishness, materialism, self-blaming, and all the other psychic injuries that these cause to people's ability to find and sustain loving families and communities, and eventually, over the course of many years, you may see people who at first looked impossible to convince slowly beginning to want to hear the kind of analysis put forward in this manifesto! Had we in the movements of the 1960s and 1970s been more attentive to these dimensions of human suffering, we would have been far less blaming of each other and all those who had not yet joined our movement, and hence far more successful in creating sustainable movements. Many of those who became the most oppressive people we encountered in right-wing movements of the past several decades were people who felt demeaned and disrespected during the sixties and seventies.

We must retain a solid commitment to nonviolence. Yet we cannot allow the most violent right-wingers to win because we have been intimidated. The folks who paraded with torches in Charlottesville chanting "the Jews will not replace us" were appropriately confronted and fought by anti-racist and anti-fascist forces. The violence German fascists in the 1920s and early 1930s inflicted against Jews, socialists, gays, and Roma served also to intimidate many decent Germans into silence and fear. Instead, these racists should have been confronted and challenged by an equally militant progressive force in the streets that fascists had succeeded in dominating. I wish there had been people able to stop the murderers of African Americans in their churches or of the eleven Jews at prayer in a synagogue in Pittsburgh in October 2018.

Revolutionary love is committed to nonviolence but the Love and Justice movement we are building will be equally committed to protecting the most vulnerable in our society. We need to challenge the bullies in public in smart ways that stop their violence while simultaneously communicating our message of genuine caring and compassion to those on the Right who can be won to our programs.

There's no abstract formula here that will always be appropriate. It takes practical wisdom, not mechanical formulas, to meet these kinds of threats. And sometimes it takes humor, music, and other forms of creativity. I remember when motorcyclists from the Hells Angels gang confronted us with violence at an antiwar march after our big teach-in on Vietnam in 1965: Allen Ginsberg brilliantly deflected them from their planned attack by chanting Hindu mantras through a powerful loudspeaker. Creative nonviolence, including the use of prayers familiar to Christian rightist white power extremists, can surprise and cut through barriers when rational argument may not.

The revolutionary possibility of love is that it allows the Left to heal itself while healing others and provides the foundation on which a truly loving movement can be birthed. For us love and justice activists—or call us spiritual progressives because revolutionary love is a spiritual, not a material concept—the issue is not how to abandon the struggle against oppression in order to become more popular or win more elections, but how to effectively address and win those anti-oppression struggles. The answer is to build a movement that is based in love, empathy, and generosity, that affirms the deep need for meaning and higher purpose to our lives, and that helps people overcome inappropriate self-blaming and see that their well-being is dependent on the well-being of everyone else on this planet and the well-being of Earth. If we can do this, we have a real chance to win tens of millions more to our vision of the caring society in time to take the dramatic steps needed to avert some of the worst impacts of the deepening environmental crisis.

In this first section, I have presented reasons why we can't expect to stop the destruction of the life support system of the planet and to repair the damage already done simply and solely by rational presentations of the facts. So many people are in so much pain and so deeply believe that any large-scale societal transformation is unrealistic. In addition, many are so reluctant to follow liberal and progressive programs, leaders, and movements because of the elitism and shaming and blaming of those movements. Only a movement that simultaneously presents a rational plan while also addressing all the emotional blocks I've described has a chance to change things. Only a movement that simultaneously addresses the psychological and spiritual crisis created by the ethos of capitalism as it plays out in the workplace and the economy, in the media, and in our personal lives has a chance to win broad enough popular support for the dramatic programs that are needed. In this first section, I have presented some of the dynamics that must be addressed by all of us who want to preserve life on Earth.

In part II, I propose concrete programs and strategies that can move our society gently and compassionately toward revolutionary love and the caring society, which in turn will enable environmental sanity and renewal of the Earth. Though focused on the United States, I present ideas could be useful to others around the world who are similarly seeking to understand what it will take to save life on Earth.

PART II

Strategies for Building the Caring Society

Overcoming the Dictatorship of the Capitalist Marketplace

Martin Luther King, Jr., did not become the major icon of social change by giving a speech to 300,000 people in which his main line, repeated several times, was "I have a . . . complaint." Effective leaders articulate a comprehensive vision of the world they aspire to create, their dream. In these next three chapters, therefore, I want to consider what a movement based on revolutionary love would actually do in the next few decades (chapters 5 and 6) and what the world could look like and what further steps might be taken in the next century if such a movement prevails in the twenty-first century (chapter 7). Let's call that movement the "Love and Justice party."

FIRST STEPS TOWARD BUILDING THE CARING SOCIETY

A significant part of the twentieth century Left, manifested in the Democratic Party and the labor movement, focused its attention on two dimensions: the denial of economic security and the denial of human rights. Both were and remain extremely important. And yet in both realms, the victories were only very partial because they did not address what I've been calling the Great Deprivation of revolutionary love (outlined in chapter 1). Those struggling for material benefits had no categories in which to put ideas like revolutionary love or the caring society. Neither the spiritual critiques by

Martin Luther King, Jr., Abraham Joshua Heschel, and other spiritual leaders, nor the countercultural challenges to the deadening and alienating nature of a society focused on material consumption, nor the ethical challenges to the Vietnam War by millions of the baby boom generation made any sense at all to the Democratic Party leadership, except as problems that needed to be dealt with in order to keep political power. Sadly, in many sections of the labor movement, in the liberal and progressive movements that lobby on the state and local levels, and even among many grassroots activists, these spiritual and "meaning" needs are rarely articulated even though this discourse is so badly needed.

The divorce of the struggle for material needs and political rights from psychological, spiritual, ecological, and meaning needs, or what I've called the need for living in a caring society, is a central manifestation of what I call "the dictatorship of the capitalist marketplace" and its consequent domination of how we are taught to perceive the choices we have in both public and personal life. In separating the struggles for adequate financial well-being from the rich embodiment in revolutionary love, the powerful materialist reductionist discourse of capitalism (and its handmaiden in misusing science by equating it with scientism) estranges us from our own highest aspirations and makes them seem like luxuries or even pure foolishness, to be kept out of the public sphere entirely and marginalized to personal life with no legitimacy to be used to assess our economy, government, legal system, educational system, or public cultural life. Instead, this dictatorship's media, its corporations, its political leadership, and its educational system repeat endlessly that human beings are fundamentally selfish and only care for others to the extent that they can be "useful" to themselves, that there is no alternative possible to the competitive marketplace with its inevitable outcome of winners and losers and a class structure with growing inequalities, and that those who seek alternatives are not only foolish but dangerous. Over the past hundreds of years this way of understanding our world has become

Strategies for Building the Caring Society

so powerful in shaping not only politics but our internal sense of self that it feels like "common sense" and not an imposed worldview. In this chapter I present some of the steps we can take together to free ourselves and others from this internalized dictatorship of the capitalist marketplace through building concrete programs that manifest the values of the caring society and reintegrate them into much of our daily lives.

Sadly, the Democratic Party, the labor movement, and many activists on the Left have often felt the need to fit their own discourse into the acceptable dimensions of a materialist reductionist discourse. They do this partly out of fear that taking on capitalism itself will lessen their own chances of winning minimal advances within the system. What they ignore is that their reforms have been so partial, so unequally distributed, and so tone-deaf to the way the capitalist consciousness undermines love and friendships that they have no clue as to why many of their former constituents in the United States, Europe, and Asia are embracing reactionary nationalism—instead postulating that these people are inherently fascistic, racist, sexist, or stupid. Because they don't understand the yearning for revolutionary love and higher meaning in life, they fall into despair rather than into reconstructing their politics to address spiritual, meaning, and love needs.

The limits of that kind of discourse and politics gave rise in the second half of the twentieth century to movements which, sometimes unconsciously, were seeking a different language and vision. It was this dimension that made the civil rights movement of the 1950s and early 1960s, the New Left of the 1960s, the Paris rebellion of 1968 (which spread momentarily throughout much of the world), and the feminists' powerful critique so exciting. Although all of these movements emerged originally as demands for economic or political rights, they frequently framed their struggles in an embrace of those spiritual and ethical aspirations that the socialist and communist parties of Europe, the Democratic Party in the United States, and the mainstream of the labor movements everywhere found baffling and threatening. The slogans "All Power to the Imagination," "The Personal Is the Political," "Power to the People," as well as the call for participatory democracy and Martin Luther King, Jr.'s statement, "Darkness cannot drive out darkness: Only light can do that. Hate cannot drive out hate: Only love can do that"—all seemed to suggest aspirations that were outside what the guardians of the capitalist marketplace understood as politics. Instead of talking primarily about wages, millions of people began to talk openly about their hunger for a world of higher meaning and purpose, a harbinger of what I've called a "politics of meaning." In so doing, they were liberating themselves from the narrow materialist reductionism that had characterized so much of the liberal and Left way of talking during the previous hundred years and instead re-introduced to Left discourse notions of alienation, love, and celebration.

These outbreaks of hope and joy and revolution in the 1960s and 1970s momentarily transformed the consciousness of millions. Yet except for feminism, which I believe to be the most significant revolution of the past several thousand years, their impact was limited because most of the revolutionaries lacked an explicit understanding of the Great Deprivation, the hunger for higher meaning in life, the need for revolutionary love, the centrality of preserving planet Earth from the destructiveness of unlimited economic growth, and the pernicious impact of the culture of capitalism and its ethos of "me first" selfishness. The anti-capitalist discourse itself had long been taken over by tiny groups of former New Leftists who supported the repressive dictators of the communist parties in eastern Europe and China. Meanwhile, the gut distrust of religion among those activists made it difficult for them to put at the center of their politics the notions of meaning needs or revolutionary love. Moreover, the righteous indignation that so many of these activists felt about the genocidal war in Vietnam, the ongoing repression of people of color, and the growing awareness of sexism and homophobia led many to demand that everyone change themselves immediately on all these fronts or else be considered "the enemy." People began to turn against each other for not having yet transcended any element of racism, sexism, nationalism, homophobia, or even for having an ego! Urged on by undercover agents of the FBI and other "intelligence" branches of the government, activists who had already dismissed their fellow Americans as reactionaries, or even "pigs," began to turn on each other. No wonder so many who had the exhilarating experience of solidarity in a movement committed to transforming the world abandoned their activism when they found so many people lacking compassion or the loving energy that had originally attracted them to these movements. Many of those who became leaders of ultra-conservative movements during the Reagan or Trump years were people who felt battered from the ways they were treated by others in the Left in the 1960s and 1970s. Variants of that same kind of shaming and blaming, manifested in some forms of identity politics which I discuss in chapter 4, could limit the possibilities for progressive politics in the 2020s and 2030s no matter how attractive the Left's economic and political programs become.

Most of those who stayed with some form of activism understood the importance of transitional demands that would show people that there was a way to get from here to there, what Andre Gorz in his 1968 book *Strategy for Labor* called "nonreformist reforms" that would increase democratic control of institutions without yet fully eliminating the capitalist system. Yet, like Gorz, most who stayed involved by the mid 1970s were still not reaching the level of spiritual and psychological needs that are parts of the program the Network of Spiritual Progressives (a.k.a. Love and Justice Movement/Party) present in this and the next chapter. Most who did understand this dimension left political activism and spent much of the following decades in various apolitical, spiritual, or psychological activities, telling themselves that these movements would be sufficient to change the world. Imagine their surprise when changing themselves did not add up to changing the world!

Many of us in the 1960s and 1970s in the United States, Great Britain, France, Germany, and Italy, while excited by the possibilities of liberation, yet having failed to use political instruments like elections to translate our huge popular support into legislative and union victories to change the societies of the West in the years between 1964 and 1976, retreated into what European New Leftists called "the Long March through the institutions of society." Unfortunately, most who took up this challenge lacked the organizational skills and theoretical orientation as well as the psychological or spiritual skills that would help them recognize and resist the co-optive power of the capitalist system. Lacking any larger transformative movement in which they could strategize together, get allies to join them, assess their accomplishments, or analyze their defeats, this became for most a very individualistic enterprise. Seeking power by working within the system to change it took so much energy that it was hard for many to keep their eyes focused on the liberation that had initially inspired that long march. Too many of these young activists ended up being more changed by the institutions they were marching through than changing the core values and practices of those institutions. Still exhilarated by the anarchistic elements of the years of rebellion, they refused to join organizations like the New American Movement that I had helped create in the 1970s, which might have provided a place for them to reflect on the specific challenges and unite their efforts with others in different workplaces that shared their values. Those who recognized the need for organization and coordination often joined Maoist-oriented groups that refused to acknowledge how antidemocratic and suppressive of liberatory creativity Mao's "cultural revolution" had turned out to be in China.

Serving the old bottom line, which was necessary for working in the existing institutions of capitalist society, became the newest idolatry, and even those who had momentarily rebelled against it began to tell themselves that if they just played along with the ethos of the capitalist order, they would someday get into a position where they could change things. Like Clark Kent, they told themselves, when the moment was right they would remove their façade of conformity and become Superman. Yet the mask became the face, and a great many people became the very servants of capitalist self-interest that they had previously sought to escape. Those who did not often ended up in deep depression and isolation.

As you'll see in this chapter, the first step for a liberatory movement is to create love-teams of people who are trained in prophetic empathy and who understand the need to spread a spirit of kindness and generosity, undermining self-blaming while also working together to develop the skills to popularize a new bottom line.

Ever since President Reagan made clear that the goal of Republicans was to dismantle government as much as possible except for those parts that provided support for large corporations and money for defense industries, his political successors have followed that path and tried to undo the reforms of the New Deal, Fair Deal, and Great Society enacted between 1933 and 1968. Their reasons are not hidden: Republicans want to stop government from taxing the rich and from putting environmental, safety, and health or other restrictions on powerful corporations whose interests they unabashedly serve. Their absolute goal is to increase the wealth and power of those who are most wealthy, even while arguing that this wealth will in the long run trickle down to serve the interests of all the rest of us.

The programs proposed below are not only about what government can do. While some of the proposals (for example, universal health care, free education, and a living wage) might sound familiar, what makes this a qualitatively new agenda is that all of these programs are to be implemented in ways that manifest revolutionary love or what in this context I call subjective caring. Together they constitute the outline of a post-capitalist as well as post-socialist society, or if you prefer, a socialism of love, re-envisioning socialism, or what I prefer to call it—the caring society. Its goal is to build a world that has never been tried before, a world in which the ethical, psychological, and spiritual needs of the human race get priority and work together to do *tikkun*, the healing and repair of the world needed to save and protect the life support system of Earth.

The great weakness of the New Deal and subsequent liberal reforms is that they provided "objective" caring in the form of material benefits, but not "subjective" caring in the way that these services were delivered. Idealists who joined government to help implement the New Deal found themselves too busy jumping through bureaucratic hoops to convey effectively the idea that they were seeking to build the caring society. Centrist Democrats were fearful that Republicans would win power by demeaning their objective caring programs and by claiming that recipients were "taking advantage" of the liberal's naïve belief in the goodness of people; instead, Republicans demonstrated that they could be "tough" by putting in place so many restrictions and bureaucratic hoops for government workers that these bureaucrats soon found that they had no time to give a human face to the government they had joined with the best of caring intentions. In our occupational stress groups, I heard many government workers detailing why bureaucratic restrictions made it impossible for them to have the time to show the public the genuine caring that had led them into government in the first place (no, it was not just economic security!) and eventually made them cynical about what government could do.

We propose that government should be the vehicle through which we, the people of our country, demonstrate that we care for each other. If the programs proposed below provide people with the actual experience of being cared for by those who are implementing change, we can all begin to understand government as one of the means by which all of us can manifest our deep compassion for each other and our precious Earth.

In the effort to heal and transform the world there is no way to separate the ends from the means: the path toward the world we want must embody the values of the world we want. Every step, every proposal, must be implemented in the spirit of love and generosity to the best of our capacities. Inevitably we will make some mistakes, and through the democratic process we will seek to correct those mistakes.

This chapter outlines some of the campaigns we can begin now that will manifest and popularize the values needed to build a world of love, generosity, and environmental sanity. These strategic steps are not realistic in ways that will earn them an editorial endorsement from the *New York Times* or the national Democratic Party. Rather, they are initiatives to help people begin to see the possibility of a loving society and imagine concrete programs that would dramatically change the way our current society operates. They aspire to show how very different politics could be. When you begin proposing them to your elected officials and get others to do the same, and when eventually these proposals are put on the ballots as referenda, the public conversations you generate will promote an opening of consciousness in the same way that demands to end patriarchy were dismissed decades ago as unrealistic and yet began to attract people who asked, why not?

The danger in presenting these proposals is that the central idea—namely, that a transformation of consciousness is needed to save our planet and these programs are steps toward building that change—will be skipped over as skeptics critique some of the more technical details. Please keep this in mind: none of the proposals I make, and certainly none of the specifics, are written in stone—this is, after all, just a manifesto, not a detailed blueprint. The programs in these three chapters are put forward to give a sense of what steps *could* be taken to build a different world. Once we gain the will and political power to move the country in a new direction, every idea in the second part of this manifesto can be reformulated and refined as needed. But the core goal remains the same, to create the caring society. Nor is this simply an endorsement of the Bernie Sanders and Elizabeth Warren wing of the Democrats, much as I hope that wing of the Democratic Party will win not only the presidency but majorities in both houses of Congress. That movement, important as it is, is still mostly tone-deaf to the need for the caring society and the revolutionary love that must be at its heart. I don't mean just that they rarely talk about the Great Deprivation or Yearning or about the way that the ethos of capitalist institutions deforms us—for all I know some of these ideas, already previewed in articles in *Tikkun* magazine, may be adopted as smart slogans for purposes of winning more support in the elections of the 2020s. But these ideas are unlikely to actually shape the reality of the Democratic Party when it is in power until a Love and Justice movement, working both within and outside that party, manages to win over enough adherents to the substance of this analysis and the programs below that embody it and make those the real heart of a progressive movement that either reshapes the Democrats or becomes a separate political party.

Can anything that transformative really happen, and especially around ideas like revolutionary love that will be dismissed by the "realists" as flaky or New Agey or utopian or religious? My answer: think of the recent victory for legal same-sex marriage. The shift from a "rights-based" discourse to a discourse of love and care is ultimately what moved both public opinion and the Supreme Court to support same-sex marriage. Rather than try to persuade the Supreme Court that the sole basis for supporting homosexual marriage was because it is a constitutional "right," advocates instead showed the Court (and the public) how important families are to gays and lesbians—the ability to be with one another in emergencies, to attend parent-teacher conferences, and the like. The case centered on the affirmation of love, not the right to marry. This is what won the right for gay and lesbian marriage.

When social change movements dare to put love on the agenda, not to manipulate others but to articulate our greatest yearnings, change can happen very quickly!

Of course, the world we want is not going to be won in a single, big victory. We must seek partial victories along the way (just as happened in the movement for same-sex marriage). Yet those partial victories are only sustainable if we continually affirm that our larger goal is to build a world of love and caring for everyone and that we see the capacity of everyone to move toward such a world.

If newly installed President Obama had campaigned around the country in 2009 for universal free health care (Medicare for everyone), a living wage for every worker, and reparations to every citizen who lost their job or their home during the Great Recession of 2007–2011, he might have failed to get those passed by the Congress in 2009 but could have won an even stronger mandate in the 2010 elections when ordinary people would have been drawn to the liberal worldview that those programs embodied, particularly if he had framed it in terms of a caring society (something we spiritual progressives at Tikkun urged him to do, both in person when I met with him privately in 2006, and in a full page ad we bought in the special issue of the *Washington Post* celebrating Obama's first 100 days in office in late 2009). But liberals projected no unifying theme, much less any commitment to the concept of the caring society, and went on to a smashing defeat in the midterm election of 2010.

In contrast, our strategy today must be to keep the fundamental transformation we seek foremost in our minds and in our public presentations. That is why every program presented in this and the next chapter must be accompanied by and defended in terms of what I call the new bottom line. Let me state it more fully here:

We seek a new bottom line that judges our institutions, our economy, our political lives, our legal system, our cultural institutions, our educational system, and every aspect of our society as productive, efficient, or rational to the extent that they maximize our human capacities to be loving, generous, and caring toward each other and toward the Earth, ethically and environmentally responsible, and committed to social, economic, and environmental justice; and to the extent to which they promote joy, playfulness, compassion and empathy, self-acceptance, humor, and aesthetic creativity, health and thanksgiving for life in all its forms, love of learning science and literature, repentance and forgiveness, treatment of all human beings as embodiments of the sacred and not just instrumentally as means to our own ends, and a response to the universe and our planet Earth that is filled with awe, wonder, and radical amazement (rather than seeing them only as "resources" to fill human needs).

This new bottom line is a vision that can sustain us and can challenge the old bottom line of money and power that is the criterion supporters of the status quo have always relied upon. Many of us who want fundamental change lack the language to challenge existing economic, political, and societal arrangements once the defenders of the status quo bring out their old bottom line, backed by their scientism (which states that everything real must be measurable or empirically verifiable).

The more we use every specific campaign proposed below to popularize the new bottom line, the more effective we will be in changing the public discourse. Remember, the old bottom line is a particular religion which serves the powerful—there is nothing to back it up but the nonexistent consensus that defenders of the status quo claim exists because in their view, "what people really want is money and power."

When I talk about the caring society, what I mean is a society that actually guides itself by this new bottom line. It is the shorthand for the revolutionary love outlined in chapter 1. Help us create a mass culture that affirms and insists upon this new bottom line with intensity, generosity of spirit, urgency, and humor. Don't just accept this in your heart—tell people about this new bottom line. And encourage them also to say something about it to everyone they know or meet!

Say something? you ask.

I'm reminded of a humorous and sad story my father told me about a young man in the 1940s who visited Europe before there were transatlantic phones. He wanted to find the perfect gift for his mother's sixtieth birthday. He searched far and wide till he came to a store that advertised itself as having the most amazing gifts in the world. In he went, searching for that perfect gift. When he came across a parrot that was being sold for $1,600 (remember, in the 1940s that was a lot of money), he asked the owner of the store what would make a parrot worth so much money. The owner explained that this parrot spoke thirty-eight languages. The man bargained the price down to $1,200 and then had the parrot shipped to his mother in Illinois. When he got back to the United States, he called his mother immediately to ask if she had liked his gift. "Like it?" she responded, "I loved it. It was delicious." "Mom," this young man responded, "tell me you didn't eat that parrot! I paid $1,200 for it." His mom was shocked, and responded, "Yes, I ate it and thank you, it was delicious. But why would you pay $1,200 for a parrot?" "Mom," he replied, "that parrot spoke thirty-eight languages!" "Thirty-eight languages?" his mom replied, "So why didn't he say something?"

Don't be like that parrot. If you agree with the new bottom line, start saying something! And quickly. We need a vanguard of folks who reveal themselves as hopeful "love revolutionaries" or spiritual progressives or part of the Love and Justice campaign—and what that means is not that they believe in a god (though some, including me, do) but that they wish to bring about a society based on this specific new bottom line. Atheists and secular humanists of every sort, as well as people from every religious community, are all spiritual progressives or love revolutionaries to the extent that they not only want a world based on the new bottom line, but are willing to spread these ideas to others!

These are the people who can guide liberal and progressive forces to a new kind of movement. They can help every person in our society recognize that they deserve a life surrounded by people who are loving, generous, compassionate, environmentally sensitive, and committed to social and economic justice for all, and that such a world is realizable within the next several decades. The more people realize this, the more social energy will flow toward love and generosity and away from fear and domination. And this is what will enable us to implement the sweeping changes the environmental scientists tell us are necessary in order to save the life support system of Earth. We can together overcome the extinction illness and sadness which paralyzes so many people. Yet it's also important to realize that there is nothing inevitable about the caring society actually happening. It is totally possible to build this kind of a world, but it is also possible that too many people will decide that it is "unrealistic," and that negative attitude will indeed make it unrealistic. So it is up to you and me and many others to take the possibility and make it happen.

A democratic society must be democratically created. The ideas in this chapter and the next two have emerged from the bottom up, rather than the top down, in conversations and conferences that *Tikkun* magazine and the Network of Spiritual Progressives conducted over the course of some twelve years. Moreover, I'm inviting you, your friends, and others to read, refine, critique, and transcend what I'm envisioning here, so please feel invited to send your ideas to me at TheLoveRabbi@tikkun.org.

In a spirit of humility, with whatever guidance the universe provides us and with the recognition that these ideas, developed here in my own language, have been shaped and shared by many throughout history in different forms, let's begin.

All power to the imagination. And please keep out the reality police— namely, those voices in your head that tell you what I'm proposing is not realistic. Just allow yourself to imagine that these programs are possible because in fact, they are. We just need to build the momentum that will make them achievable and that is where you come in!

CREATING PROPHETIC EMPATHY TRIBES

The first step is to create an international prophetic empathy tribe whose mission is to bring forth people's capacity to be empathic, generous, and loving advocates for environmental, economic, and social justice. The prophetic empathy tribe will have as part of its mission the development of many other prophetic empathy tribes.

We call this "prophetic empathy" because our outreach program explicitly seeks both to affirm people's deepest needs and to help people understand that those needs cannot be met fully in a society which is based on promoting and justifying selfishness, materialism, looking out for number one, and domination of others. Empathy as practiced in the West is often only validation of the individual; prophetic empathy affirms each individual, challenges the degree to which they have become attached to the values of the competitive marketplace, and supports them to become involved in building the caring society. As Cat Zavis, executive director of the Network of Spiritual Progressives, describes it:

> In prophetic empathy, we speak to our collective responsibility to care for the well-being of each other and the planet. We speak to and about the suffering of people and humanity's need to restructure our society to address and alleviate that suffering. We say that there is something fundamentally wrong with the way our society is structured and that most people know it but despair about changing it. Prophetic empathy helps us overcome the lessons we've incorporated from this society: that we live in a meritocracy, that there isn't enough, that we are alone and must act to protect ourselves from others who will otherwise use us for their own ends. Prophetic empathy encourages us to tap into the truth that each of us comes into this world with a burning desire to manifest our most loving, kind, generous, just, playful, caring selves. That we want to connect with each other in caring, respectful, loving, and generous ways, and connect to the universe with awe and amazement.[1]

Members of prophetic empathy tribes will be people who teach liberals and progressives how to avoid the shaming and blaming of those not yet our political allies, and how to avoid the classism, elitism, and religiophobia that have facilitated the left-wing demeaning of all men, all whites, and all Americans, who are frequently portrayed as one single group—distorted or stupid, prejudiced, oppressive, and dangerous. Empathic tribe members will teach others about the Great Yearning all people have not just for economic security and social justice (though both are very important to us all) but also for love, respect, generosity, community, and a sense of meaning and purpose in their lives. In addition, they will educate people in prophetic empathy and strategies to help people overcome their own inner blocks that make it hard for them to believe that such a caring world is really possible. And they will foster the development of prophetic empathy tribes around the globe.

Anyone with some degree of sensitivity toward what others are feeling can be trained to be part of this prophetic empathy tribe (that does exclude sociopaths, narcissists, and psychopaths).

We will also draw on people with psychological skills, such as therapists, teachers, health care professionals, mediators, communication specialists, and others to participate in training people in prophetic empathy, meanwhile helping these professionals unlearn any messages they were given about separating their professional skills from social transformation work. Some of those who get this training will become trainers themselves. Eventually, with careful supervision, and over a period of the next twenty years, the empathy tribes could train millions to become agents for global healing. If you have these skills, and feel fully aligned with the ideas in this manifesto, we'll invite you to a training so that you can then become a trainer in this process.

The prophetic empathy tribes will focus on challenging the complex ways in which living within the norms and culture of global capitalism has led people to feel that they alone are responsible for the difficulties and disappointments in their lives. Many intellectually sophisticated activists, teachers, social workers, and even psychotherapists are unaware of how much they blame themselves and equally, they are unskilled in the task of helping others overcome that kind of self-blame generated by the societal teaching that we live in a meritocracy. Few people have been taught about the way this self-blaming aspect of capitalist social reality shapes our personal realities. The feminist movement paved the way by showing millions of women that hurtful aspects of their lives were not their own fault, but the fault of the patriarchal and sexist practices of society. Spiritual progressives can, through prophetic empathy, expand that path in regard to classism, ageism, racism, family dysfunction, and other dimensions of life as well.

Building support for the specific programs described below will be a good way to start the conversation. These discussions might focus on our family support program, our call for a living wage and guaranteed basic income for everyone, the end of the assault on our planet with the Environmental and Social Responsibility Amendment (ESRA), a path to homeland security through generosity, the abolition of student debt and funding free college education, or the many other programs that are outlined below. These conversations will easily flow toward a discussion of the new bottom line and the vision of a world based on revolutionary love. Empathic discourse can help us recognize how to distinguish between our real needs, which should be honored, and the strategies that we've adopted that can sometimes be self- or other-destructive.

In the first part of this book I discuss the ways the Left has missed the mark. Therefore, the first step for members of the prophetic empathy tribes will be to help change the culture of the Left, teaching them how to engage in the correctives needed to be more successful. The prophetic empathy tribes will also teach people in the broad liberal and progressive culture how to be effective in demonstrating respect even for people with whom we strongly disagree, yet without capitulating to an ethically perverse neutrality or avoidance of criticism of behaviors which are oppressive or environmentally destructive. And they will create local prophetic empathy tribes to work in coordination with prophetic empathy trainers who will provide guidance in building the promotional campaigns described below.

The prophetic empathy tribes will then reach out to the masses of Americans who have been discouraged by the elitism and blaming they've experienced from liberals and progressives. We can use as a model what the occupational stress groups developed at the Institute for Labor and Mental Health to accomplish this in the world of work. We will develop family support groups in many neighborhoods to create mutual support and help as people grapple with the inevitable problems of raising children and sustaining loving relationships in a society that privileges selfishness, in the process providing opportunities for people to experience connection and belonging and mutual support. And some might form twelve-step programs for those who have difficulty breaking free from capitalist societal pathologies such as selfishness and materialism and addiction to power over others rather than collaboration and mutual caring and trust.

We will use all forms of media as well as door-to-door outreach to spread a new kind of progressive consciousness that aims to undermine self-blaming and simultaneously challenge the inequalities that have been tolerated in the global capitalist system, insisting that ordinary people (that is, all of us) deserve to be cherished and honored. We will have public lectures, dances, walks, marathons, bicycle rides, and sports activities; summer camps for children, adolescents and adults; and retirement communities for the aging (but connected to communities for people of all ages), all focused on affirming the message of revolutionary love and our shared need to create the caring society.

When we have enough people trained in these skills and enough funding to hire organizers, the prophetic empathy tribes will conduct teach-ins on college campuses and in high schools and union halls and religious institutions to share their empathic skills.[2] We will have weekend retreats and national conferences at which these skills get further refined. And we will encourage members of the empathy tribes to hold a celebratory gathering once a month to refresh our consciousness, share stories of the outreach work we are doing to share the perspective of revolutionary love, create rituals to celebrate the universe and human beings, discuss the current political situation, and nourish each other with loving care.

We will constantly emphasize that our outreach activities and techniques are not designed to manipulate people, but rather to aid each other to outgrow the instrumental/utilitarian way we've all been taught to think about others and about the planet. This process will eventually lead to a fundamental rewiring of our souls, a letting go of past understandings of self, and a growing ability to experience others and ourselves as embodiments of the sacred (or if that word seems too scary to you, too rooted in religion, then substitute the words "deserving of deep respect and dignity").

When we've reached a critical mass of change in the consciousness of the Left, people outside the Left will also be able to feel the difference.

When people attracted to the idea of a new bottom line find a community whose empathic skills make them feel welcome and cared for, a community that respects their lifestyles (including in some cases their religious commitments), they will gradually overcome negative feelings about progressive movements. A significant number will be inspired to be part of what we will call the Love and Justice movement and eventually the Love and Justice Party, which could dramatically change the politics of this country within a decade or two and reverse a significant part of the damage being done to the environment.

As part of this process, we will urge Democratic Party activists to repeatedly apologize for the ways Democrats communicated an elitist message and sometimes supported economic and military policies that served the powerful 1 percent while abandoning the needs of the majority; and we will call upon them to make clear that they no longer accept the notion that those not yet in the liberal and progressive camps are "a basket of deplorables"—even as we continue to challenge racist, sexist, homophobic, and other oppressive behaviors.

Some of the most courageous prophetic empathy tribes will likely try outreach in the red states, especially those Midwest and Mountain states with large rural areas and small populations. Each of these states elects two senators to serve in Washington, D.C., and hence has disproportionate power through its influence in the electoral college and also in voting on the potential constitutional amendments that we are going to need to pass (see below and in chapter 6). The anti-war movement in the 1960s and 1970s created coffeehouses near army bases to attract draftees and present to them some of the movement's ideas. There may be similar possibilities in some parts of those red states. We'll need volunteers who share various forms of Christianity to become part of the churches in red states and present to those communities the ideas of the caring society, revolutionary love (Jesus would certainly have been an advocate of that idea, which derives from the Hebrew Bible), and the new bottom line.

Hopefully some of those involved in our Love and Justice movement will come from or want to work in red states, and will learn how to create outreach programs that are respectful of the nonsexist and nonracist aspects of the culture in those states. They will respect the desire that many have to nurture communities in which people care for one another, opting to counter the selfish and harsh relationships that have developed in the big cities, which they see portrayed in the media. Our empathy tribes will help them recognize that that selfishness is not a product of the values of city dwellers, but rather a product of the same market forces that have shut down factories and workplaces in rural communities—the ethos of the capitalist marketplace. Our domestic and global Generosity (Marshall) Plan will focus on inner cities and rural areas in the United States, bringing back environmentally sustainable jobs for young people who might not need to leave for the big cities if there were enough economic and social opportunities in the rural areas where they were born. Our compassion is not just for those who share our cultural proclivities.

I have no illusion that this is going to be easy work. Some people will be able to donate their time. Others will need to be hired so that this becomes their full-time or part-time work. We will need to find donors who can fund people to do this work. Others will simply volunteer to do it on weekend days or during vacations or in the months just before major elections.

Inevitably, many of us building prophetic empathy tribes and then doing the suggested outreach work will make mistakes, because all of us are imperfect beings. Yet the love that most of us have within will feel liberated by this activity, and that in itself will make sharing prophetic empathy one of the most gorgeous and liberating experiences of our lives.

This outreach by prophetic empathy tribes is the first, critical step. The rest of this chapter is about other programs that will accompany the work of empathy tribes as they seek to promote the new bottom line, and without which these tribes might soon dissolve into a form of self-help, too easily absorbed into (rather than transforming) the dynamics of capitalist society. The importance of ongoing efforts to promote and sustain consciousness transformation cannot be overstated. Too many of us involved in winning legal and legislative victories for civil rights, civil liberties, and other advances for social and economic justice in the 1970s and 1980s thought that winning those battles would be enough. We were sadly mistaken. What was needed was an ongoing consciousness-raising campaign coupled with prophetic empathy and compassion for those who could not overcome their fears and prejudices just because the law required behavioral changes. That is why the prophetic empathy tribes, and their campaign of love and generosity, will serve as the foundation for our movement. There will be many people in our Love and Justice movement who do support various parts of our program and its articulation within the context of the new bottom line but who elect not to be part of an empathy tribe. They too are welcome to be involved in the implementation of the programs described in this and the next chapter as long as they make good-faith efforts to embody the values articulated in the new bottom line and act in generous, caring, and sensitive ways toward others and our Earth.

RE-ENVISIONING WORK AND PROFESSIONS
WITH A NEW BOTTOM LINE

Because most people spend most of their waking weekday hours at work, absorbing the values and ways of seeing the world that the competitive economy assumes as the very meaning of being rational and productive—the focus of the old bottom line—we will focus on bringing our new bottom line into the world of work.

We will seek to create a process through which people everywhere participate in shaping their own workplace according to values of the new bottom line. The process will begin with groups of workers meeting regularly to discuss what their workplace would look like if it embodied those values. What products and services would a new work world produce? Which would it drop or transform to be environmentally sustainable and humanly valuable? The only rule for these groups will be "do not heed the reality police"—those internal and external voices that tell you that the "world we really want will never happen." Those voices have consistently told us that same discouraging story and were frequently mistaken.

Because many owners and managers/supervisors will likely feel threatened, and therefore unwilling to allow these discussions during work hours, these worker groups will meet initially outside of work, in a home or community center, a church/synagogue/mosque, a school, or even the offices of a local social change organization.

I recognize that people are extremely overworked and the thought of adding a discussion group to their plate seems undoable. To make these groups plausible, we need to create environments where workers can gather with their family members, cook meals, and break bread together. These conversations can happen in community, and children can be invited to participate (they usually don't have internal messages that tell them it's not possible and hence are filled with creative ideas and solutions). These can be opportunities to build deeper connections and provide a sense of belonging, meaning, and purpose to people's lives, needs that are often deeply lacking in our workplaces and society. Eventually, the more progressive unions will make these kinds of groups part of what they offer to workers and, in their contract demands, will get management to allow workers the right to create these groups for two hours a week during working hours.

The deeper the discussion of the issues, the more co-workers will be interested in joining a group, and the more group members will develop a productive dissatisfaction with the world as it is. People will become less depressed and more energized to transform their workplace to resemble their ideal world. They will align with people in other workplaces who share a similar intense desire to create change.

Professionals will take an analogous path. They will be invited to reimagine their work as a vocation, an opportunity to serve others and be part of a fundamental transformation of the world. (Many initially entered their professions with this mindset but have become disillusioned by colleagues and even professional organizations prioritizing the pursuit of power, money, or ego.) They will be encouraged to find and join with others in their fields who care about the survival of the planet, about social or economic justice, and about a more caring world to brainstorm together about what their work would look like if it reflected those commitments.[3]

Say that you work in the tech world where new inventions, gadgets, and processes are funded to the extent that they are likely to make a profit. Now try to imagine how amazing it would be for people inside and outside that world to hear that you and a small group of others were promoting a new bottom line that would seek to fund inventions to the extent that they would contribute to a world of love and generosity and environmental sustainability as defined in this manifesto. As word spreads about your approach, others will say, "Hey, if *they* can reach for a different kind of world, so can I, and I don't have to give up my work in tech to do so." Breaking the chains of despair and indifference will encourage others to do the same.

"But wait," you may say, "envisioning is a long way from achieving the changes we want to see. The power relations have not changed, so why isn't all this envisioning a waste of energy?" This was the dilemma faced by Second-Wave feminists who engaged in consciousness-raising groups for several years. Many who participated felt that although it was a moving personal experience, they were not changing the larger world—they were just a few groups of women in places like San Francisco, Los Angeles, Seattle, Madison, Ann Arbor, Boston, New York, and Washington, D.C., who spent a night each week talking about their personal experiences with sexism.

Those who thought they were wasting their time and that their efforts were not "real politics" couldn't have been more mistaken. Those consciousness-raising groups and the writing that came out of them spread like wildfire around the country, putting empowerment of women on the public agenda, and proving that indeed, "Sisterhood Is Powerful." Similarly, these workplace and professional groups could also go viral. The key is to go deep, make it safe for people to think about their actual experiences at work and how that impacts their personal lives, and to express ideas for change. Help people imagine a world governed by the new bottom line. Think big. All power to the imagination! And share what you come up with through *Tikkun* magazine, which will for the moment be a vehicle of communication among love revolutionaries, though eventually many other media will participate.

In addition to encouraging workers to reshape their workplaces and professions, we will find ways to honor all workers. At the Institute for Labor and Mental Health in the early 1980s we created a yearly "Honor the Worker" day. Thousands of workers attended this community event, at which representatives of every kind of work described their jobs and the contributions they make to the well-being of everyone in society. Each worker who attended received acknowledgment and praise for those contributions, including a certificate signed by respected artists, writers, clergy, local sports teams, and government officials expressing appreciation.

We will convince media to promote events honoring workers with all the pomp and festivity that now surround the Oscars or a victorious local sports team. We will encourage media to educate everyone about the ways people around us, while often invisible to us, are actually making our society function. And we will encourage workers to honor their own deep yearnings for a world of love and caring—and educate all about how the values of the capitalist marketplace are obstacles to building that world.

We will also exact a strong commitment from independent labor unions, elected officials, and journalists to take seriously the complaints that working people will be encouraged to voice in these events even as they praise those union leaders and elected officials who have been attentive to their needs. And we will make time for organizing campaigns to increase the well-being of working people.

In the period of transition to an economy enhancing love and justice, we will use these kinds of events to strengthen our resolve to stop the neoliberal assault on the economic well-being of middle income working people, the working poor, and the unemployed. We will resist austerity policies and the cutting of taxes for the super-rich that, working in tandem with each other, enable the transfer of funds to the wealthiest 1 percent, in the process defunding the public sphere and privatizing education, health care, and social services—in essence dismantling all our social support networks.

Finally, although I've put special emphasis on consciousness transformation, we will also foster specific economic and political programs to bring the world of work in line with the caring society. Here are some of those programs which can form a basis for discussions among people who have never or rarely been encouraged to discuss with co-workers what they might want to change in their work world if they had the power to do so:

> We will require that every workplace pay a living wage (not just a minimum wage) to their employees and to any who are hired as

private contractors or part-time workers. A living wage represents the minimum employment earnings necessary to meet a family's basic needs while also maintaining self-sufficiency. The living wage calculator, which draws upon geographically specific expenditure data related to a family's likely minimum food, childcare, health insurance, housing, transportation, and other basic necessities (e.g., clothing and personal care items), as well as the rough effects of income and payroll taxes, was first created in 2004 by Dr. Amy K. Glasmeier at MIT.[4]

We will establish a guaranteed basic income at a level sufficient to ensure families' basic needs for everyone regardless of whether they are employed or unemployed. Decoupling work from filling one's basic needs will give employers a strong incentive to make the work satisfying and enable working people to welcome new technologies that reduce unnecessary labor. And we will create a culture of support for the unemployed by creating endless volunteer activities that provide caring to others (for example, visiting the sick, providing childcare and elder care (with proper training), being trained to be a member of the empathy tribe, gardening for people who can't afford a gardener, painting for those who can't afford a painter, going door to door to spread the message of the caring society, and then honoring those engaged in these activities. Many of those who become unemployed in the coming decades will have useful skills, so we will seek counselors who can creatively suggest how to volunteer those skills as a way of providing societally useful activities rewarded not with money but with deep respect and appreciation. These volunteer activities will be selected with sensitivity to the need of unions to not have their members replaced by these volunteers, undercutting the ability of unions to bargain effectively with the bosses. This will be less of a factor once the ESRA—

Environmental and Social Responsibility Amendment to the Constitution (described in the next chapter)—gets implemented, because it is precisely that kind of reducing of their work force and undercutting of workers' power that will cause the large corporations to lose their corporate charter under the mandates of the ESRA. The campaign we wage for a guaranteed annual income will be brought to the red states as a way of showing people that we actually care about their situation, know that politicians who promised new jobs may be unable to deliver on that promise (if they ever intended to do so), and do want their support for our other programs to strengthen our ability to deliver on a guaranteed income.

We will end discrimination in hiring and in pay. Equal work for equal pay will be a requirement for every workplace. Employers must make visible the amount paid to each worker, and workers must each year affirm that equality has been achieved.

We will campaign for the federal government to develop a massive housing program that keeps up with population growth and provides adequate and high-quality homes for those with lower incomes as well as for the homeless. This program will avoid the shoddy construction and tasteless design that characterized public housing projects after World War II. An added advantage is ensuring high levels of employment. It should be coupled with an ongoing training program to provide skills to the unemployed. Too many working people accept oppressive working conditions for fear that making demands might lead them to unemployment and homelessness. This program coupled with a guaranteed income for everyone will take the teeth out of this worry.

We will support an initiative specifying that any governmental contract of one million dollars or more must include an environmental and social responsibility report. The public will be invited to provide information on the social and environmental record of the corporations applying for the contract, and the city (or county or state) will award the contract to the corporation that has the best history of environmental and social responsibility (of course, selecting from among those that can competently fill the terms of the contract).

We will democratize corporations and institutions so that workers get full and complete access to all decisions made by boards of directors, in language that is accessible to the layperson, and to the financial books of the institution. Workers will be able to choose the majority of persons on the corporate boards of directors, the remaining seats divided between those elected by stockholders (not more than one quarter) and another quarter nominated by the environmental community; they will be able to know exactly how money is spent and who is being paid what, and the justifications given for those decisions. After several years of this, the board should be reconstituted with people who have the skills to be able to conceptualize the major decisions facing that corporation or nonprofit institution, and then put the major alternative paths to the workers for a vote.

We've been taught to think that some work is intrinsically unsatisfying because it involves rote repetition of tasks and little opportunity to use one's intelligence. I believed that too, until I spent months working on a kibbutz, a socialist collective living and work society in Israel. After my daily work assignments, I spent meals and evening time interviewing people who did jobs such as garbage collecting; planting, watering, and later picking fruits and vegetables; cleaning up barns and chicken coops; cutting up vegetables or fruit for eating and then cleaning dishes; cleaning the apartments of kibbutz residents and guest apartments reserved for visitors; and clearing fields of rocks and other impediments to growing vegetables. I sought to penetrate beyond the superficial to find how people really felt about their work. I discovered that, while the work was not fun or challenging, people nevertheless felt proud of it, for one shared reason: they were contributing to the well-being of the larger community of which they were part. That was for many (not all) more than enough to make them feel grateful to have the opportunity to do these tasks. Moreover, everyone else on the kibbutz appreciated the work their fellow members were doing, and saw it not as trivial but as having inherent value deserving of respect.

While kibbutzim were not perfect, these collectives demonstrated that people are more likely to find work worthwhile when they have a fuller sense of how what they are doing serves others and the larger society. As people are allowed, even encouraged, to feel their genuine caring for other people and for the society as a whole, many will develop a desire to do work that serves others even if it is not intrinsically fun or fulfilling or financially rewarding.

In addition, at least in the first few generations of people having that kind of work ethos, employers, aided by government grants, could provide financial incentives so that the garbage collector, the hotel and restaurant workers, the workers on assembly lines, the truck drivers and bus and mass transit drivers, the farmworkers, and others in jobs that are less fulfilling in themselves will make more money than those whose work provides more immediate gratification in the form of opportunities to do creative thinking and/or have personal and deep interactions with people whom they are serving. Since this temporary capitulation to market values could be a slippery slope back toward the materialism we seek to overcome, it must be understood as a form of reparations for generations of underpaid and under-recognized societally important working class jobs and phased out over the first few generations of those receiving this special benefit.

Decoupling work and the basic survival needs of most people will also allow workers to stay with jobs that feel meaningful and valuable for their community, even if the firms they work for can no longer afford to pay them. Corporations today are rapidly trying to reduce their workforce by way of technical advances such as robots. It is estimated that tens of millions of people who are gainfully employed today will be out of work in the next twenty to thirty years. The scope of this potential job loss will go way beyond traditional working class jobs and include many who never imagined it could impact them, in part because they are not taking into account the way dramatic reduction in income will have a rollover impact on who can afford to purchase goods and services in their own town or city and who can afford to pay for various professional services. Job loss will also come as a result of the environmental devastation that will soon wreak havoc with our economy unless we adopt sweeping programs both in the United States and around the world. When tens of millions lose their jobs, there will be an upsurge in emotional depression and suicides, particularly among men who have been taught that their worth is judged by how much money they can make to support their families (women breadwinners are likely to feel the same way). Instead of allowing this dynamic to play out, we need to create for everyone a guaranteed income at the "living wage" level. In so doing we affirm a new ethos in which people see their worth as human beings to be independent from their work status or income level. And to begin to chip away at income inequality, we will seek to pass legislation that matches a living wage with a maximum wage for all income receivers—initially, not more than ten times the median average wage for all workers in the society. In 2018 that median was close to $62,000 (that is, half the population had that much income or less), so the wealthiest income earners, on this plan, could earn up to $620,000 a year. I won't cry for the suffering of those whose income above $620,000 would be taxed away on this plan to help make sure that others are provided an income that in 2018 would be somewhere between $24,000 and $50,000 depending on their local cost of living index. In fact, we should seek to make wage gaps smaller each year.

BUILDING CARING FAMILIES, LOVING RELATIONSHIPS, AND A SOCIETY THAT SUPPORTS THEM

There is only one institution in Western societies whose primary task is to provide love and support to its members—it's called the family. Many families fail dramatically to deliver on this goal, and there is extensive feminist literature exposing the many ways this goal has been used to justify patriarchal domination of women and children. Yet the allure of the goal is so powerful that families remain important in the lives of most people.

Yet as I argue in the first part of this manifesto, the dynamics of the competitive marketplace, internalized and brought home into personal life, increasingly undermine families and weaken loving relationships. Hence, love and justice activists will build a progressive pro-family movement to help people experience what a caring society could be.

In the past several decades, the Right has gained much support by positioning itself as the major pro-family force in our society. Too often this has boiled down to insisting on the right of men to dominate family life, as well as opposing gay and lesbian marriage, birth control, and sex education.

We will expose the absurdity of the Right's analysis of why families are so fragile in capitalist societies. We will defend the importance of women's equality. And we will affirm the value of a wide variety of family forms, including LGBTQ families, single-parent families, blended families from multiple partnerships, traditional families, and whatever other kinds of families emerge in the coming decades.

Recognizing the powerful destabilizing and undermining impact of marketplace values on the intimacy and integrity of families, we will help families free themselves from the poisonous impact of capitalist consciousness.

One possible definition of the family unit we may choose to use could be "any relationship between two or more people who are committed to trying their best to unconditionally accept and cherish each other." This unconditional acceptance includes a commitment to being emotionally available to and supportive of each family member when they are sick, weak, emotionally or financially needy, or unable to take care of themselves. In our definition of family, there is no requirement for a biological tie, but only a caring commitment that extends throughout the lives of the family members, unless the family decides to reconstitute itself and form new family units. Acceptance does not require uncritical approval of what other family members do, but it does require empathic understanding; even family members who are criticized are always welcome and will be given food and shelter to the greatest extent possible when they need that help. Some larger communities that act in these ways, including communes, urban or rural kibbutzim, the Tamera community in Portugal, some co-housing arrangements, and other intentional communities, fit this definition of family to the extent that their commitments to their members are lifelong in intention, though of course divorce or reconstitution of family units must always be available.

We will encourage families to be connected to communities that promote a higher meaning and purpose for life. Those communities can be religious or secular, political or cultural, as long as they counter the ethos of individualism and selfishness fostered by the capitalist marketplace. Communities of meaning are healthy and contribute to a world of love to the extent that they affirm and respect the value of every human being on the planet, not just their own members.

We will also build family support networks in every community. These networks will teach empathy, generosity, and techniques for overcoming problems that often emerge as people try to build families in the class society in which we now live. They will draw on shared experiences and the solutions some have found along the way. These family support efforts will have a radically different perspective on loving relationships than does the capitalist marketplace.

Because our movement values adequate time for participating in family matters, as well as joy, reflection, engagement in community, and contribution to the well-being of all on this planet, we will reduce the normal work week to twenty-eight hours over four days as an important component of our pro-family agenda. That kind of schedule will allow adequate time to be with children when they come home from school, share housework across gender lines, and nurture friendships. It will give working people more time to develop their intellectual, spiritual, and political interests, as well as time to exercise and care for their physical well-being. The reduced workweek may also be an incentive for some corporations to hire those who are unemployed or partially employed.

One reason we believe it is immediately possible to dramatically reduce the average work week from forty to twenty-eight hours is that much of the labor expended today is dedicated to the production and delivery of goods and services that are unnecessary. Further, much that is produced today depletes the Earth's resources for future generations and/or contributes to the destruction of Earth's life support system (e.g., by polluting the air, ground, waterways, or oceans). These harmful goods and services could gradually be eliminated.

When justifying the production of such goods, defenders of the extreme form of market society in the United States will often say, "Hey, we are just producing what people want—the market is democratic." But the market doesn't work on the basis of one person, one vote, but of one dollar, one vote. For instance, a family living on $70,000 a year may find that they can cover their rent or mortgage, food, clothing, transportation to work, and basic energy needs, perhaps leaving only $3,000 a year for non-essential purposes. A family making $280,000 a year might spend more on food, clothing, housing, and some of these other basics, but still have $60,000 left to pay for items of choice like expensive vacations, luxury items, or the newest electronic gadgets. Even though the higher-income family has only four times as much income as the middle-income family, their discretionary income gives them twenty times the vote about which non-essential items are desirable. It is deeply misleading to say that the market responds to consumer choices. The market responds to money, and those who have more of it have way more votes than those with fewer dollars. In addition, we are well aware of how marketing specialists can sell people goods and convince them they need them, even when such items literally kill them (such as cigarettes) or destroy the environment (such as gas guzzling large trucks or plastic goods).

In addition, women or men who work in the home doing the necessary support work for a family (cleaning, cooking, childcare, and so on) will be paid the median income in the society and will receive the same social security retirement benefits that other working people receive. Payment for housework is a part of transforming hierarchical gender relations to help build families that move us from what feminist theorist and economist Riane Eisler, author of *The Chalice and the Blade*, calls domination societies to partnership societies.[5] As she puts it, "If children grow up in cultures or subcultures where economic injustice and even violence in families are accepted as normal and moral, they learn basic lessons that support domination systems." She points to the severe consequences of not making this transformation: "Along with the subordination and devaluation of the female half of humanity came a gendered system of values in which anything associated with women or the 'feminine'—like the essential work of caring for people and keeping a clean and healthy environment—was also subordinated and devalued. *And as long as caring is devalued, we cannot realistically expect more caring policies.*"[6]

We will build the psychological foundation for a partnership society by building families that are respectful and caring to all its members, including children, completely nonviolent, and freed from hierarchical relationships between parents. When children grow up in the domination-oriented inequalities of hierarchical family relationships, it is far easier for them to accept inequalities not only in the home but in their economic and political lives as well.

We cannot have a caring society where some people receive more caring because of their gender, sexual orientation, race, religion, physical appearance, or physical abilities. In the name of family, we will fight patriarchy, sexism, racism, classism, homophobia, Islamophobia, anti-Semitism, ageism, prejudice against those with disabilities, or other oppressions that still have a large hold on the individual and collective consciousness of the human race. We have a long way to go before we can say honestly that these inequities have been dealt with. We will raise children to understand and reject these bigoted systems.

Finally, to support families, we will immediately confront the vast and growing economic inequality in the Western world, particularly in the United States. As I write, the top 20 percent of the wealthy own 85 percent of the wealth, and the bottom 80 percent own just 15 percent of the wealth. What's more, the top 1 percent of the wealthiest in the U.S. population own 40 percent of the wealth. (The inequality gap grows each year, so, when you are reading this manifesto, be sure to check the latest figures.) These inequalities quickly translate into inequalities in health, longevity, and opportunities to enjoy retirement without financial worries. Obviously, these economic disparities have a major impact on families.

We will gradually decrease this income and wealth inequality by establishing income taxes at close to confiscatory rates on the portion of anyone's annual household income above ten times the median household income in this society (in the United States the median income in 2018 was approximately $62,000, so if we were implementing this gauge then, the heaviest tax would begin to fall on people with household incomes above $610,000 per year). And we will create tax breaks for renters to help them survive the surging costs of rentals.

We will honor the option of living alone or in some non-family connection with others. We reject the notion that there is something wrong with being single and recognize that healthy and happy people sometimes choose not to be in a partnered relationship or any variant form of family.

On the other hand, we will provide safe and enjoyable ways for people who do not want to be single to meet each other without the pressure of speed dating or the exploitative potentials of computer dating or the bar scene. Many people looking for relationships today find that they are encountering people who are more interested in using them for sex, entertainment, or connections than they are in building the foundation for a lasting friendship or something more. Religious, spiritual, political, social change, and community-building groups should plan hikes in nature, movie nights, dinner parties, concerts, and other events in which the explicit goal is to help people make new friendships, potentially romantic but not necessarily. We will encourage people who are in satisfying relationships to go out of their way to bring acquaintances together to meet one another, in situations not charged with expectation. We seek safe ways for people to meet but oppose any societal pressure to choose a partner, much less having one assigned to them.

We reject unequivocally the assumption that there is something lacking about people who are single and don't want to be. We will communicate clearly and repeatedly that if someone is single and doesn't want to be, it's not their fault. We explicitly reject the self-blaming attitude that the reason someone hasn't found the right person is because there is something not okay about them. We all currently live in a capitalist society that rewards selfishness and materialism. Too many people have lost the capacity to see each other as embodiments of the sacred. We encourage everyone not to settle for a partner who has been shaped more by the ethos of the capitalist marketplace than by the values that make loving, long-term commitments work.

Strategies for Building the Caring Society

To maximize our capacities to be loving, generous, and caring for each other, the caring society must reshape every institution and economic or social practice that encourages us to see others as instruments for our own advancement rather than as embodiments of the sacred. Whenever possible, we will challenge the remnants of cynical attempts to reduce life to self-interest and power over others. And, without demeaning the value of pleasure-seeking as one part of a multidimensional life, we will oppose the cheapening of sexuality that regularly occurs in advertising and mass media and reduces love to narcissistic self-gratification.

TRANSITIONING TOWARD A CARING ECONOMY

We will institute national and global economic planning to ensure that all production contributes to saving and repairing the environment at a rapid enough pace to avert the destruction of Earth's life support system and at the same time ensures the well-being of all people.

Nonetheless, the transition toward a new kind of society based on caring and revolutionary love—never yet created—will be a gradual process. We will ensure that the caring society democratically shapes itself, unlike state-run socialist economies that have often resulted in a centralized economic authority, ecological insensitivity, and ultimately a decrease in democratic participation in shaping the society.

We will be guided in this transition by the new bottom line that asks how each element of society contributes to a loving and just whole. We will abandon measures (such as the GDP and GNP) that allow for evaluating material goods harmful to human health as "productive." We will seek new kinds of measures that count the work of caring for people in households as productive. We will avoid measures that subtract from society's total value those externalities such as the cost of natural disasters resulting from climate change. For example, Eisler's Center for Partnership Studies has developed social wealth economic indicators that measure "the state of a nation's *human capacity development,* as shown by data such as child poverty rates, enrollment in early childhood education, gender and racial equity, educational attainment, and ecological deficit/returns" and also "a nation's *care investment;* for example, public spending on family benefits, funding for childcare and education, and government and business investment in environmental protection."

We will preserve the Commons, those aspects of our physical environment such as air, water, land, and natural resources, which are the shared inheritance of the human race and all other life forms. We will make it illegal for corporations or wealthy individuals to own any part of the Commons. And by extension, people will not be able to buy property in outer space.

We will bring prices in line so they reflect the actual cost of current consumption to the planet and to our future. By building the full environmental costs into the price of goods, and redistributing money so that vast inequalities are dramatically reduced, we will create a market that discourages consumption of the Commons. A fuller discussion of this approach can be found in Charles Eisenstein's *Sacred Economics.*[7]

We will develop everyone's capacity to let go of consumerism and the capitalist addiction to endless growth. We will encourage communities to follow any religious or non-religious path that increases the ability to distance oneself from the misplaced desire to increase one's possessions. Meditation, artistic creativity, dance, playing musical instruments, community singing, prayer, walks, and camping in beautiful natural settings have all proved helpful to many. For some, the celebration of a weekly Sabbath day of rest can help move attention away from the world of "getting and spending" or otherwise exercising domination over nature; in my own life, the Sabbath has been one of the greatest gifts for overcoming workaholism and a constant need to have a "practical" outcome to every activity.

We will not tolerate the production of wasteful products or services. To monitor that, we may ultimately need an amendment to the Constitution to enforce environmental and social responsibility (a proposal for this is presented in chapter 6), but we will immediately seek new ways to control the production of goods that deplete the resources of the planet or generate waste that cannot be recycled effectively or otherwise are harmful to the environment. We are already destroying our oceans and wiping out many species of fish, polluting the air (which in turn raises the level of lung and other forms of cancer), and reducing the capacity of our farmlands to supply healthy food.

In his article "The Pluralistic Commonwealth," Gar Alperovitz provides a possible model for how to ensure democratic participation to control the production of goods that deplete the resources of the planet. Alperovitz suggests that "development should begin at the community and neighborhood level, moving up to higher state, regional and national levels only when absolutely necessary. Among the primary local institutions considered are: cooperatives, neighborhood corporations, worker-owned companies, social enterprises, land trusts, and municipal utilities—along with, of course, small scale private businesses and innovative high tech firms, and in many areas, traditional non-profit institutions."[8]

Imagine, for example, a workplace that chooses its leadership based not only on their ability to build a financially successful business, but also on their ability to treat their employees with care, kindness, and respect. Imagine a workplace that promotes employee cooperation, shows respect and care for actual and potential customers, comes up with ideas that enhance the capacity of that enterprise to serve the common good and repair the environment, and actively promotes participation in democratic decision-making about all aspects of how that enterprise operates in the world. There are some small businesses that have made significant steps in this direction.

We will work toward an economy that promotes and helps build worker-owned enterprises, cooperatives, social ventures, and local sustainable economies, an economy that democratizes banks and investment companies, builds legal arrangements making it easier for people to cooperate rather than compete with each other, and facilitates the sharing of the world's resources and consumer goods that are already widely available. Such workplaces would soon be supporting people's capacities to care for each other. If these values and experiences were brought home from one's daily work instead of the "looking out for number one" ethos of the capitalist marketplace, families and loving relationships would be dramatically strengthened within the course of a few short decades!

While the economic system we are describing incorporates many elements that are commonly called socialist, we will provide a better alternative to a top-down, fully controlled marketplace. The Next System Project is a think tank working on the details of how to build worker ownership and democratize society.[9] Revolutionary love activists may modify some of what we are saying here in light of future successes by this project. And we will go far beyond socialism as practiced in social democratic countries in Europe. Like them, we still see some value in a marketplace and in the free operation of small businesses and small-level entrepreneurs and inventors as one part of the economy, but it must be governed by the following restrictions:

Huge disparities in wealth must be eliminated.

The operations of large corporations will be required to meet standards of environmental and social responsibility.

The people in each community will have democratic rights to impose environmental, safety, health, and ethical requirements on the operations of the marketplace such that they can, for example, ban the production of goods and services that promote or enable violence, domination, or hate, or that are environmentally destructive or involve poor use of the resources of the Earth.

Individuals will have the right to seek court injunctions against the production of goods and the offering of services that they find to be hurtful to the environment or the well-being of their communities. Within the court system, judges and juries shall be composed of people who have demonstrated deep understanding of the environmental and ethical needs of a caring society.

But what will most distinguish our approach from most currently discussed progressive visions for an economic system is our insistence on the underlying vision of a loving, generous, and caring world. We will focus at all times on three goals governing our economic system:

Fostering our ability to see others as ends in themselves rather than as a means to our own ends, so that we can regain access to the core yearning of our souls.

Fostering our ability to find deeper satisfactions in our own inner lives, our connection with and caring for other human beings and animals, and our connection to the transcendent elements of existence.

Helping us see the Earth and the universe not merely as resources to satisfy human needs, but also as amazing living realities of which we are a part, deserving of care and eliciting joy, thanksgiving, awe, and radical amazement.

These revolutionary love values will help build stronger and more fulfilling human relationships in both the workplace and our family lives. Over time more and more children will be raised with values that predict success in their human relationships and their ability to sustain love in their lives, and many, many people will be happier and more joyous. We realize that sustaining family support, building a caring society, and re-creating our economic system are inextricably bound together in real life. And all the ideas in this chapter are part of what we mean when we say that ours is a post-socialist or revolutionary love-oriented socialism.

AN EDUCATION SYSTEM RE-ORIENTED TO LOVE AND JUSTICE

We will reshape our education system so that it teaches values of love, caring, generosity, intellectual curiosity, tolerance, social and economic justice, nonviolence, gratitude, wonder, democratic participation, and environmental responsibility without abandoning necessary skills in reading, writing, and scientific analysis. In fact, we understand both reading and writing as practices that often foster the development of empathy by helping students to consider other viewpoints and learn about the needs of people from different communities. And we see good science education as a way to foster awe and wonder, as well as develop strategies for how to better care for our planet.

We will resist the corporate control of childhood as manifested in child-oriented media, branding, advertising, publishing, and corporate shaping of school curricula. And we will insist that schools foster and support our children's capacities to be playful, spontaneous, joyous, loving, excited by ideas, emotionally and spiritually mature, creative, environmentally literate, and compassionate.

We will undermine and ultimately dismantle the racism and classism built into our educational system by eliminating the disparities between poorly funded urban and rural schools and wealthier suburban and private schools. We will insist that all schools be adequately funded, and we will create an education tax on wealthy parents to ensure that all children have access to the benefits now available primarily in higher-income public school districts and in private schools. We will advocate for higher salaries for teachers in communities with below average incomes to ensure that all schools have highly qualified teachers.

In addition, we will develop ways to teach children to recognize all of the distortions of a domination society (including racism, classism, sexism, anti-Semitism, ageism, xenophobia, and homophobia) and empower them to struggle against these wherever they pop up in childhood, adolescence, and adult life. For pre-teens and teens, education will include:

Empathic communication skills based on the premise that every person deserves to be respected and cared for, and prophetic empathy that teaches students how to be respectful while at the same time challenging injustice with the passion that the biblical prophets embodied.

The history of societal distortions, and how to recognize and effectively challenge racism, sexism and sexual abuse, homophobia, Islamophobia, anti-Semitism, put-downs of transgender people, ageism, and all other forms of oppression. Students will learn how Western societies systematically undermined the capacity of the global South and East to develop economically, and then used that failure to claim that our societies and economic systems were superior. At every grade level from sixth grade through high school, students will learn the details of the genocide against Native Americans, Jews, Roma, and more; the brutal enslavement of African Americans; the realities of the Jim Crow South and ongoing assaults on blacks well into the twenty-first century; the prejudices that greeted Italians, Irish, Eastern Europeans, and Latinos who came to the United States as immigrants; racism against Chinese, Japanese, and other Asian immigrants; and the violence directed at gays and lesbians and transgender people. They will also learn about how white working people were exploited by the wealthy and manipulated into adopting the pseudo-compensation of racism. They will learn how to build effective alliances without demonizing and blaming all members of dominant identity groups for economic, political, and social arrangements that they did not create and have not yet understood how to transform.

Teaching about class structure in American society and the lies about meritocracy. Students will learn to honor all working people and to discern the kinds of work needed to keep a society functioning from those that could be eliminated if caring for the planet were a high priority.

Methods for resisting the sexist consciousness that transmits the message that girls' fundamental worth is based on their attractiveness and sexual availability to boys. Girls will be taught to challenge media-generated social pressures to increasingly sexualize their bodies as a way of achieving social recognition in their peer groups. They will learn how to resist any kind of sexual abuse.

Teaching about the destructive impact of patriarchal forms of masculinity. We will challenge the demand that boys suppress their feelings and look down upon their own nurturing instincts; we will refuse the notion that "real men" are those who know how to dominate and control others. Instead, we will affirm a masculinity of gentleness, caring for others, and valuing love. Boys will learn that the burden of ending sexual abuse and sexualizing girls must rest with them, not on girls—who are the victims of these distorted sexist behaviors and conditioning. We will undo sex-stereotyped behavior for both girls and boys to give them a wide variety of choices about how to be a caring and loving person. And both boys and girls will be taught how to have compassion for those who have not yet fully transcended the sex-stereotyped conditioning that has been handed down in families and societies for millennia.

Teaching students from fourth grade on how to mentor students in grades behind them (supervised by skilled teachers of empathy and generosity). Activism and democratic participation will be taught not only as a school subject, but also as a lifelong practicum for students.

Helping students develop a sense of awe and wonder at the miraculous Earth we live on. Science classes will no longer focus solely on understanding the technicalities of physics, chemistry, biology, and math, but will also foster the ability to appreciate and celebrate the beauty and grandeur of the universe as well as skills to reduce our environmental footprint and protect the Earth from pollutants. Children in earlier grades will be given free playtime for at least three hours each day at school to foster creativity and the exploration of nature—which will also help students become more positive about their time in school.

In addition to what I've outlined above, there are a number of other important skills and talents that we will foster in our new education system that will support the new caring society. What those are will be developed through the creating of the caring education system.

As important as gun control is for school safety (and safety in our churches, mosques, and synagogues, our sports and concert arenas, and our shopping centers), the truth is that the distorted consciousness of the haters who enter public places with high-powered guns can and have also used bombs in other locations or set fires when guns were not available. Safety from terrorists requires public education, both in the media and in our schools at every grade level to undo the messages of hate that are so available and so useful to the powerful who seek to set us against each other. Couple that with efforts to find and then give counseling and emotional healing for those who are not yet able to see the humanity of those who have been demeaned by perverted politicians and hate movements. Along with the environmental crisis, this is another real societal crisis which manifests in hurtful policies toward the most powerless as well as in individual acts of violence.

To make this strategy work, college admission will depend in part on evidence of a student's ability to care both for the planet and for other human beings, including the well-being of those who have been left behind in the competitive marketplace. College accreditation will depend in part on how many graduates become involved in some aspect of building the caring society not only immediately upon graduation but in decades to come.

College, graduate, and professional school will be free except to those whose family incomes exceed five times the median income of the society. Graduate and professional students will receive a cost-of-living stipend so that they do not have to simultaneously work or borrow from predatory banks to finance the learning of skills and wisdom that our society badly needs.

In return, upon graduation all students will be required to serve three years in a national service corps in which they are paid a living wage. The programs of the national service corps could include childcare and pre-school education; elder care in private homes or retirement communities and nursing homes; assistance in construction of housing for the homeless; rebuilding the infrastructure of cities in the United States and around the world; assistance to small scale farmers; medical, dental, and mental health services in rural communities; community art, music, and theatre programs; teaching computer skills to the public; recycling waste; preserving forests; providing free accounting services to small businesses; working in publicly funded development of tech innovations that are designed to protect the environment; or serving in an international group to support security through generosity (see chapter 6 for specific plans on engendering domestic and international peace and generosity).

Free education for all will thus be not an entitlement but an empowerment of people to better serve the common good in creating a world of love and kindness that actualizes the new bottom line.

The rebellion against school taxes in the United States today is based on the complaint about having to pay for "others" to get an education with the result that they make more money. It will be a major step toward creating the caring society when students receive the kind of education that inclines them—not through force or crude indoctrination—to use their knowledge and talents for the well-being of everyone, not just themselves. When this altruism is perceived to be the actual outcome of schooling, public support for education will be much more generous than it has been in the past decades.

CREATING A HEALTH CARE SYSTEM THAT HEALS

A health care system based on revolutionary love will be about caring for the whole person, not a mechanistic treatment of the body disconnected from its inner life. This system will address the spiritual, psychological, and physical dimensions of human beings and the impact of social and environmental influences on well-being.

We will campaign for universal coverage for all aspects of medicine and health care, moving away from the profit motive. This will mean initiatives like Medicare for All, a single-payer system that ensures complete health care for everyone.[10]

But, recognizing that human health cannot be reduced to our physical mechanics, nor divorced from environmental, social, spiritual, and psychological realities, we will also reshape the entire medical system to focus on health maintenance and well-being. Practitioners will have multiple levels of knowledge, and teams of health care workers will bring a broad interdisciplinary approach to education, prevention, diagnosis, and treatment.

To successfully integrate health care in this way, we will transform our medical training to ensure that practitioners see their patients in all their beautiful complexity—not ailing bodies but human beings who deserve all the love and caring their community can muster.

We will support the construction of many more training schools in nursing, medicine, psychology, nutrition, dentistry, chiropractic, and other health modalities to increase the number of practitioners in these fields. Trainees in all fields will receive free tuition with fully subsidized postgraduate training and living expenses. Hospitals will be required to compensate interns and medical residents reasonably and limit on-call hours to provide adequate opportunities for rest, sleep, and emotional and spiritual nourishment. In exchange for this free education and training, practitioners in all health modalities will commit to work at least five years in underserved areas.

No medical or health care professionals will earn greater than five times the society's median average income. Such a restriction will discourage those whose primary interest in health care is potentially high remuneration, while still making it attractive to those who truly want to practice healing arts. We will decrease the cost of comprehensive medical care by monitoring and discouraging the lucrative practice of ordering unnecessary procedures.

Research on pharmaceuticals, preventive care, and treatment strategies will be funded by the government and separated from any profit motive. Pharmaceutical companies and medical instrument developers and suppliers will be required to offer medications and new technologies at affordable costs. If they are unable to do so, the government will fund the production of affordable drugs and will entirely replace any pharmaceutical company that cannot find a way to develop new health-promoting medications and offer them to the public at an affordable cost.

We will seek to permit those suffering from incurable disease, such as Alzheimer's or Parkinson's, terminal cancer, ALS, and the like, to end their lives or receive medical assistance in doing so without fear of punitive legal or financial consequences. Psychological and spiritual care must be offered to any person considering suicide. And, to prevent the decision from being influenced by a fear of burdening loved ones, we must create retirement and hospice communities that allow people to spend their declining years in ways that do not tax the emotional or financial capacities of their families, who will be encouraged to give as much love and caring as they possibly can. While in today's world, it is usually the upper 20 percent of income earners who can afford to live in retirement communities that provide truly high-quality food, medical care, and activities for those able to use them, in a caring society these facilities would be located in the larger community and served by staff and volunteers who are seeking to share their talents and skills to make the life of the aging less oppressive than it is for many in today's class-stratified societies.

The more vulnerable people are in their lives, the more they need the revolutionary love we seek to share. The more we build mechanisms to communicate this love to others at their most vulnerable moments, the more recipients of this loving energy will come to believe in the possibility of building the caring society.

CHALLENGING RACISM

We will challenge and undo the ongoing institutional racism that permeates our society at all levels.

In addition to creating the anti-racist educational system described above, we will transform media and the legal system and make the undermining of racist ideas and practices a central goal of government. We will provide material support to help people understand that countering racism actually serves their interests and values. This involves acting in solidarity with black and brown peoples, Asians, Native Americans, Jews, and all other groups who have been targets of violence, systematically excluded, and/or marginalized in Western societies—and if you live in other societies, you probably can name more groups that have been similarly oppressed.

In Western societies, everyone will be taught about the racism embedded in educational, legal, economic, and other institutions. Instruction will be offered in how racism diminishes everyone's humanity, how to expose and undo white supremacy, and how racism has been used to pit less powerful groups against each other.

We refuse to perpetuate divisions based on race, class, gender, or ethnicity and recognize that unity among all peoples can only be achieved by dismantling racism. Even in critiquing harmful policies, we will be maximally inclusive in our language. For instance, policies that impact negatively on middle income and poor people of all races are best described as classist, without ignoring their special burden on people of color. By being precise about the groups these policies affect, we can show care equally for all and build a cross-race and cross-class alliance to change those policies.

Economic equality alone will not achieve the transformation needed to end racism. We will also eliminate multiple assumptions built into the culture and educational system of our society. Here are some steps we will take in the United States to undo and transcend racism, in addition to those sprinkled elsewhere throughout this chapter:

Create a highly visible, homegrown Truth and Reconciliation
Commission to allow our country to fully face and heal the legacy of slavery, the mistreatment and slaughter of Native Americans, the history of Western society's role in undermining the economic development of the global South and East, and present-day, ongoing discrimination.

Grant reparations for the enslavement of African Americans and the destruction of Native American populations.

Equally fund all public and private childcare centers, preschools, schools, and retirement communities without regard to their location.

Mandate media that use the public airwaves to dedicate at least one-fifth of their prime time to shows that aim to creatively challenge racist practices, prejudice, and biases.

Adopt restorative justice as a primary form of response to wrongdoing in schools and in the criminal justice system as a whole. This will ensure that schools become learning environments for all children rather than school-to-prison pipelines for some.

Fund education, jobs, and housing for people released from prison.

Gradually dismantle police forces and replace them with neighborhood security committees, trained in de-escalation and empathic intervention. These committees will be backed up in emergency situations by local community forces (neighbors trained to meet violence effectively).

Eliminate or radically reconstruct prisons based on the principle that the time in prison should provide opportunities to learn skills to make a living after release and to receive therapy or counseling to help repair the damage done to their psyches that led prisoners to become violent or act in hurtful ways toward others. Those incarcerated and previously convicted felons will retain their right to vote in all elections. It will be the obligation of the justice system (which will be adequately staffed with social workers and others) to find meaningful employment and emotional support networks for those about to be released.

Guarantee full access and protections of the right to vote through universal voter registration at birth, same-day voter registration, and mandated holidays for voting so that most people do not have to work on those days.

If these steps are implemented along with all the other proposals in this chapter, we will soon see a dramatic improvement in the well-being of people previously targeted by racism in the United States.

SEPARATING CHURCH, STATE, AND SCIENCE

We will be vigorous in our separation of any specific religion from state power, and protect all people from fundamentalist attempts to impose a particular faith. Yet we will not fall into a First Amendment fundamentalism that attempts to keep all spiritual values out of the public sphere, but will encourage the integration of spiritual insights and practices into public life to the extent that they contribute to building a society based on the new bottom line.

Therefore, we will not disqualify an idea that derives from religious tradition from the public arena. Nor will we exclude values from the public sphere simply because they have their origins in a particular religion. But we will insist that people make arguments for their political positions on some other basis than what their religion or religious teacher teaches them.

For example, some religious people believe that the ideal of treating every human being as essentially valuable and deserving of respect and human rights derives from the Abrahamic religions. Yet many atheists and secular humanists share this value too and can articulate why. These kinds of ideas should not be banned from the public sphere as "religious": they can be supported on non-religious grounds.

We will separate scientism, the belief that only what can be empirically measured is true (see chapter 1), from true science.

We will defend science from pressure by the state, corporations, or religious communities to reach conclusions contrary to evidence.

We will advocate for scientific research directed toward human needs, not the accumulation of wealth for individuals and corporations or the development of powerful weapons, both tools to dominate others. While we

Strategies for Building the Caring Society

will not ask scientists to tailor their research to support particular beliefs, we will demand that their research be evaluated according to the new bottom line, for instance by contributing to people's health, environmental sustainability, cooperation, and mutual caring.

We will promote independent scientific institutes with adequate public funding and independence from corporate, university, or government pressures.

We will encourage the exploration of different approaches to the physical, biological, and social sciences that may contradict contemporary dominant paradigms in each field.

And we will support some percentage of research that has no plausible human or environmental value, because we will also value accumulating knowledge for its own sake.

Teachers in public schools, health care providers, and other innovators in the public arena may worry that introducing the values we champion in the new bottom line (love, generosity, empathy, celebration of the universe) will put them on a slippery slope toward religion. They are mistaken. The success of twelve-step programs like Alcoholics Anonymous and Narcotics Anonymous that insist on a spiritual dimension to the recovery process demonstrate the value of some forms (not all forms) of spirituality for improving human health. Grade school educators who report greater academic progress when children are given lots of time and opportunity to experience wonder in nature during school hours are not recruiting children to worship some god but rather giving children the opportunity to connect with the awe and inspiration of nature. Value-based approaches to learning and to healing should be explored, not ruled out because the values of love and caring are not scientifically derived—though in fact it is possible to study scientifically whether any specific technique or approach yields people who are more or less caring or loving.

RECONSTRUCTING FOURTH OF JULY
AS GLOBAL INTERDEPENDENCE DAY

We will transform the nationalist holiday, the Fourth of July, into a day that balances celebration of what is good in our country with critical reflection on the oppressive practices in our past and present and an affirmation that in the twenty-first century our individual well-being depends on the well-being of everyone else in the world and on the well-being of the planet itself.

Was there ever a nation that came into existence without horrific acts of violence, theft, and domination? The genocide of indigenous peoples, and the sexism, racism, homophobia, and xenophobia that exist today in many countries are a legacy from thousands of years of oppressive practices. Unfortunately, nationalist celebrations tend to obliterate the memory of these brutal histories and the way they continue to shape present-day culture.

The United States is no exception. Its process of creation included wiping out Native Americans and enslaving Africans, and in the nineteenth and early twentieth centuries it obtained through wars of conquest parts of Mexico and other "territories" including Alaska, Hawaii, and Puerto Rico. For the past 110 years, U.S. elites serving the corporate interests of the rich and powerful have aspired to expand the American Empire by penetrating other countries and subsidizing their governments to support U.S. economic and political interests (argued in detail in recently published books by Victor Bulmer-Thomas, *Empire in Retreat,* and David C. Hendrickson, *Republic in Peril*—both cited in Jackson Lears's February 7, 2019, article "Imperial Exceptionalism" in the *New York Review of Books*).

Yet in many countries in the world, including the United States, there has also been important progress that deserves to be celebrated. Nationalist celebrations can be positive if they are done in ways that affirm the particularity of a given people while also affirming and fostering appreciation of all other people on the planet.

We will use the Fourth of July to appreciate the good in the people of the United States and what we have been able to accomplish to make this country more democratic and more humane, even as we resist ongoing efforts of the political Right to dismantle some of what is most praiseworthy in America, instead promoting a reactionary nationalism that demeans non-Americans or non-whites or non-Western societies or validates violence and militarism as a means of achieving security. And we will encourage a similar consciousness to shape nationalist celebrations around the world. We will call this holiday Interdependence Day to emphasize our connection with all people on this planet.

Reactionary nationalism sets some people into one privileged group, usually the dominant ethnic or religious group in any given country, while demeaning all others as somehow "less than" the dominant group. We will challenge that kind of nationalism by using our U.S. celebration to honor all subgroups and all countries and peoples around the world, recognizing that our lives are inextricably intertwined.

We will especially highlight the way that in the past the United States welcomed immigrants, while acknowledging how too many of them were demonized upon arrival (particularly African, Italian, Irish, Polish, Chinese, Japanese, Latino, and Jewish immigrants in the nineteenth and early twentieth centuries; and in the twenty-first century, Muslims, Arabs, Mexicans, and . . . well, the list keeps growing) and exploited thereafter. We will also acknowledge the willingness in the past several decades of other countries to similarly welcome immigrants from around the world.

We will repudiate the vile causes to which American nationalism has sometimes been tied. For instance, the Trump/Pence regime has used nationalism to bully people seeking asylum in our country. I believe that this shameful moment in U.S. history will require that many future generations repent and grieve how horrendously these asylum seekers were treated, their children often separated and warehoused in for-profit prison-like facilities, some of whom were treated so poorly that they died in custody. I was part of a group of hundreds of clergy who went to the U.S. border with Mexico to bring public attention to the horrendous conditions that the Trump administration inflicted on asylum seekers. This is an example of what social change activism would look like in building a caring society—directly confronting injustice using nonviolence tactics and without demonizing the border guards.

In the aftermath of the Trump/Pence years, we are going to need powerful rituals and healing to overcome the destructive impact of popularizing the America First ideology, which, in conjunction with racist immigration policies, is really de facto a White People First worldview. We will create stories, rituals, songs, and conversations at these celebrations that reject white supremacy while carefully ensuring that we are not blaming all white people for being white or for being the inheritors of privileges in a society that they did not construct and which they and we have not yet been able to fully transform. (We at Tikkun have written a guidebook to celebrating the Fourth of July in this spirit.)

Instead of cheering "bombs bursting in air" and the militarism that is often associated with the Fourth of July, let's invite our friends and neighbors and others to a celebration that acknowledges the good that has happened here, but also emphasizes the need to overcome chauvinistic nationalism and racism, and embraces our interdependence with all beings. Just as identity politics need to be balanced with a celebration and respect for all the various non-oppressive forms of identity besides one's own, so nationalism must always be linked to an internationalism which affirms the equal value of all nations and peoples on the planet, without diminishing our critiques of social and environmental justice in those nations that are oppressive to their own people and/or contributing to the destruction of the life support system of Earth.

The activities and programs described in this chapter, if linked in each particular to a vision of a world based on revolutionary love and the new bottom line, could attract millions of people to a new paradigm for societal transformation—but if and only if those who advance these ideas are themselves embodiments of revolutionary love and prophetic empathy, and joyously celebrate with awe and radical amazement other human beings and the Earth. By building on generations of progressive ideas, yet contextualizing them within a framework that highlights our commitment to a world of love and generosity, nonviolence and the caring society, informed by the psychological and spiritual wisdom of past millennia, this approach can be the foundation for a Love and Justice movement and eventually a Love and Justice Party, whose structural transformation ideas I turn to in the next chapter.

Major Institutional Changes for Building a Love and Justice Movement

I outline below three examples of major institutions and approaches that embody and promote an empathic and generous spirit and move toward a fundamental transformation of the class structure and the racist and patriarchal practices that bolster it. These ideas and programs will at first be dismissed as outlandish and impossible. Yet if promoted in a spirit of kindness and generosity and continual attention to the new bottom line that reminds people of the values that guide us, even if they never come to fruition in the forms suggested below, the political struggle for them will have a huge impact. The struggle for the Equal Rights Amendment (ERA) failed to get the support needed to make it an amendment to the Constitution, but the education campaign about sexism and patriarchy that was a central part of the campaign for the ERA galvanized many women and turned what at first was dismissed as a fantasy into a huge and powerful movement that accomplished much more than the amendment itself might have achieved. The proposals below have a similar potential for getting deep support for the new bottom line and a world of love, kindness, generosity, and environmental sanity!

POLITICAL AND ECONOMIC DEMOCRACY VIA THE ENVIRONMENTAL AND SOCIAL RESPONSIBILITY AMENDMENT

The Environmental and Social Responsibility Amendment (ESRA) to the Constitution is designed to link the U.S. government and economy together as strong allies in enacting all steps necessary to save the life support system of the planet and achieve the goals specified in the report by environmental scientists cited in the Introduction to this manifesto.

Climate activist Bill McKibben, in a November 26, 2018, article in the *New Yorker*, has done his best to remind us of one dimension of the environmental crisis: "We have already managed to kill off sixty percent of the world's wildlife since 1970 by destroying their habitats . . . coral reefs, rich in biodiversity, may soon be a tenth of their current size . . . By 2050, if temperature rises by two degrees, a quarter of the earth will experience serious droughts and desertification. . . . We are on a path to self-destruction, and yet there is nothing inevitable about our fate." Or as David Wallace-Wells, author of *The Uninhabitable Earth: Life After Warming*, put it in a February 16, 2019, *New York Times* opinion piece entitled "Time to Panic": "It is O.K., finally, to freak out. Even reasonable. *This, to me, is progress.* Panic might seem counterproductive, but we're at a point where alarmism and catastrophic thinking are valuable."

In the introduction to this book I feature the Green New Deal advanced by Congresswoman Alexandria Ocasio-Cortez. The proposal was greeted derisively by the Democratic Party leadership and neo-liberal intellectuals, who likely will be even more dismissive of the ESRA. Thomas Friedman, a weekly columnist for the *New York Times*, on January 9, 2019, opined that the only solution likely to get enough Republicans to pass it in Congress would be a green new deal shaped in a way that would win support from the capitalist marketplace. As he boldly put it, "There is only one thing as big as Mother Nature and that is Father Greed," a.k.a. the market.

What Friedman ignores is the report by 15,000-plus climate scientists, also cited in the Introduction to this book, who warn: "Humanity is jeopardizing our future by not reining in our intense material consumption." Their report goes on to point the finger in part at "the role of an economy rooted in growth," that is, the central tenets of the capitalist market with its ethos of selfishness and materialism cheered on by mainstream liberal thinkers like Thomas Friedman and a critical factor restraining any fundamental change in the economic and political system. The capitalist system is fundamentally about growth, and the competition it rewards is about who can make the most money fastest, not about any other social goal. As many have said, "The Market knows the cost of everything but the value of nothing."

The survival of the human race depends on a different kind of competition within and between countries, a competition about who can be most generous and caring for other human beings and animals everywhere and the most dedicated to protecting the life support system of Earth. That, of course, would quickly lead us away from competition and toward a higher ethos of global cooperation. And the most immediate cooperation needed is to reverse the process by which the capitalist system has shaped a consciousness that privileges selfishness, looking out for number one, and the belief that endless consumption is the indispensable element of "the good life."

No matter what country you live in, you can find others who will join with you to develop specific strategies to move the public consciousness in this new direction. In the United States, the Constitution will need to be amended to achieve a fuller democratic society and to undermine the ability of the super-rich and American corporations to interfere with the goals specified in the environmental scientists' report. The first part of the ESRA enunciates changes to increase democracy, and the second and subsequent parts are concerned with economic and educational goals aimed at creating a public that is fully empowered to ensure that our economy and political institutions are doing as much as possible to enhance social and environmental responsibility.

As long as the super-rich are allowed to donate a significant portion of their wealth to shape the outcome of elections, and corporations are able to threaten to move their assets and employment out of any region that imposes significant environmental and social responsibility on their operations, most politicians will continue to serve the interests of those who fund their campaigns. Even the most progressive elected officials, who refuse to take money from the super-rich and the corporations, understandably feel a responsibility to their electorate to do what it takes to keep corporations and the jobs they provide inside their electoral district. If they don't, and significant levels of unemployment result from a corporation reducing its number of employees or moving to another area of the country or the world, this will in most cases cause those officials to lose their next election.

Corporate power subverting democracy cannot be stopped by elected officials alone. Nor can simply winning a congressional majority solve this. For the foreseeable future, the Supreme Court is likely to strike down any legislation that significantly threatens the power of corporations and the super-rich. There are many well-intentioned organizations seeking to get money out of politics, but none of their strategies seems to address the multiple ways in which corporations and the super-rich are able to make the system work in their favor, including forcing even well-intentioned elected social-justice-oriented Democrats to respond to corporate needs more than to the needs of the environment. Even a Congress and White House filled with principled, environmentally and social justice-oriented progressives would not be able to enact the kind of strong measures needed to save our planet's life support system and empower the American people without passing the Environmental and Social Responsibility Amendment or something very close to it. And that failure will intensify "extinction illness"—the global psychological depression that increasingly saps the life energy out of the human race as we together sense the approaching extinction of all human and animal life on the planet—and drive increasing numbers of people to the populist Right and many others into not bothering to vote at all.

The ESRA will reestablish political democracy and help move our society toward economic democracy, and use that democratic power to enact policies and empower all of us to take the necessary steps to slow climate change and reverse the worst damage already done to Earth.

Because the ESRA will be modified in a variety of ways as more and more people and organizations become involved in supporting it, the most recent update to the text of the ESRA will be available on the website www.tikkun. org/esra. What follows is a summary of some of its major parts. When you read and discuss it, please be aware that the U.S. Constitution does not specify a form or length of an amendment, so we've written the ESRA as something that resembles legislation because we are aware that should we ever get to a point where a strong majority of the Congress supports its planks, the Supreme Court that we would likely be facing in the next twenty years, a majority of whose members are champions of the super-rich and their corporations, could declare the ESRA unconstitutional were its component parts merely passed by Congress and signed by the President. Therefore we need an amendment with enough specificity to make it harder for a future Supreme Court to pretend to be interpreting it by turning point A or B or C into not-A, not-B, and not-C as the Court did when it interpreted the 14th Amendment (which was originally written to grant equal rights as citizens to former slaves after the Civil War) in the late nineteenth century by applying these same rights to corporations, and then in the twenty-first century by deciding that corporations were "persons" with the same rights to shape public discourse and policies as human beings.

While the ESRA could be proposed as two separate amendments, one focused on democracy and the other on environmental and social responsibility, for the moment they are joined together because together they present a coherent program for saving the life support system of the planet and restoring democracy, which is a prerequisite to stopping the corporate forces and defeating the worldview that underlies corporate power.

The preface of the ESRA states that every citizen of the United States, every branch of the U.S. government, the government of the separate states, the county and local city governments, and every organization chartered by the United States or operating within the United States or promoting its products, services, or ideas in the United States or any of its several states shall have a positive legal responsibility to promote the ethical, environmental, and social well-being of all life on the planet Earth and on any other planet or place in space with which humans come into contact.

The ESRA has four main components:

Money is not speech. Corporations are not people and have no rights except those given to them by Congress, and these can be taken back by Congress. Public funding of all national and state elections is required; monies from any other source is prohibited. The president shall be elected by popular vote; the Electoral College is abolished. Congress and the several state legislatures shall take all necessary steps to ensure that the electorate may place ballot initiatives at the city, state, and national levels, that all citizens shall be permanently registered to vote automatically at birth, and that no one including Congress or the state legislatures shall put any impediments or stumbling blocks to discourage or prevent those citizens seeking to vote from doing so.

Corporations with incomes over fifty million dollars per year must have 50 percent of their board elected by their employees and 25 percent of their board selected by those national environmental organizations that have had a history for at least twenty years of challenging corporate environmental irresponsibility, opposing fracking, and supporting the speedy elimination of fossil fuels and other pollutants. In addition, corporations with incomes above fifty million dollars a year must get a new corporate charter every five years, which would only be granted to those that prove a satisfactory history of environmental and social responsibility to a panel of ordinary citizens who would receive testimony from people all around the world who have been impacted by the policies, products, and services or the environmental, financial, or advertising practices of the corporation. This panel would be assisted by environmental scientists and social justice activists who have shown in their lives that they actively support the goals and processes of the ESRA.

Environmental sustainability, peace and nonviolence skills, empathy and compassion, and civic engagement education shall be required at all grade levels from kindergarten through college, postgraduate, or professional schools.

Guaranteed annual income for all adults is a key element in social responsibility. A major way that corporations and the rich succeed in preventing environmental legislation is to claim that environmental provisions will eliminate jobs. To take the teeth out of that threat, and to show that caring for the Earth and caring for each other are intrinsically tied, the amendment will ensure that people can support environmental change without fear of being left destitute.

I elaborate on these four main components below, but to read the entire amendment please go to the Tikkun website where the latest version resides (www.tikkun.org/esra).

The first clause reverses the disastrous 2010 Citizens United decision of the Supreme Court declaring that corporations are people and their money is speech, thereby opening the door for massive campaign contributions. We have to explicitly overturn that decision and then make all elections publicly funded. Many current proposals by various groups to address money in politics give Congress the power to legislate the amount of campaign contributions that congressional candidates may accept. That is like asking the fox to guard the hen house! Even if we muster the support needed to pass such a narrow constitutional amendment, we would then have to spend all our time and energy ensuring Congress passes comprehensive campaign finance laws every few years, and we will have to get a majority of Supreme Court justices to uphold the legislation. As long as we are going to use our energy and resources to pass a constitutional amendment, let's make sure we get an amendment that actually does what we want and need, not one that still allows disproportionate power to the wealthy and their corporations.

The proposed amendment includes language to ensure that candidates who receive public funding have significant public support before receiving that funding and allows those that do not have that support to receive very limited campaign donations until they have reached the minimum threshold needed to obtain public funding.

It also includes language to ensure that all eligible voters actually are registered to vote, that election days are national holidays, and that workers are protected so they can have the time they need to vote without being penalized by their employers. It abolishes the Electoral College as well. And it mandates that all communication sources (including radio, television, daily and weekly newspapers and magazines, internet-related sources of information, or any other source of mass communication) give free prime time in the month before statewide and/or national elections for debates on the major issues facing the society with representatives of a wide variety of positions presented (except those that promote discrimination against any particular religion, gender, race, ethnicity, or sexual preference).

The second clause defines which corporations fall under the auspices of this amendment and includes those operating outside of, but selling their goods and services, within the United States. The panel can hear testimony from people throughout the entire world as to the social, environmental, and economic practices of any corporation to assess whether it has met the required environmental and social responsibility tenets to maintain its corporate charter. Panel members and their expert environmental consultants are ensured a sufficient income during the time that they serve and are provided the resources, ability to subpoena individuals and corporate records, and whatever else is needed to conduct their service professionally and ethically. The panel could mandate changes in the operation of the corporation it is evaluating, and if those changes have not been made to the satisfaction of the panel, it could assign the charter and assets of the corporation to a different board composed of environmentalists and representatives of the public and of the corporation's employees.

The panel will receive guidance from environmental and social justice activists as well as other experts to help guide its decision and will have the ability to require changes to the corporation, including turning over the corporation to the workers or to a group of qualified people, such as environmentalists, who will run the corporation in ways that are in alignment with social, economic, and environmental responsibilities.

This amendment spells out numerous factors for the panel to consider in making its assessment: the impact of the corporation's products and services on human, animal, and planetary health; the societal and environmental value of its services and products; how the corporation treats its employees, including whether it pays a living wage, encourages employees to operate in accord with our "new bottom line," and includes workers in the decision-making processes; and the extent to which it contributes to the well-being of the communities in which it is located and fosters caring for everyone in the society.

Special factors are the assessment of businesses such as banks and investment houses. Panels assessing the environmental and social responsibilities of these financial institutions would also assess the degree to which they direct the flow of money loaned or invested to socially and/or environmentally useful activities, including nonprofits serving the most disadvantaged of the society, the financing of local business cooperatives and local community banks, and the support for housing with affordable mortgages for low and middle income workers. If financial institutions are investing in environmentally destructive projects such as oil or gas extraction, refinement or delivery, or other earth-destroying activities, or are refusing to finance housing for the homeless or for low-income people, they are unlikely to retain their corporate charter.

This part of the amendment is needed to enable those many corporate leaders and employees who do care about the environment and social responsibility, but, because of their fiduciary responsibilities to investors, cannot make the fiscal changes needed to also be environmentally and socially responsible. To change these dynamics, more will be needed than a change in consciousness—let alone mindfulness training and meditation (though all that can and will be useful)—or even promises by corporate leaders to commit to a "triple bottom line" that includes environmental responsibility, because the capitalist marketplace will always force corporate leaders to give higher priority to profits over people or the environment.[1] Only a fundamental change in the structure of the marketplace will enable people in these corporations to prioritize environmental protection and social responsibility.

The ESRA will enable ethically and environmentally responsible employees and corporate management to tell their investors that they had no choice but to become much more responsive in their specific corporate decisions to environmental concerns about the well-being of the planet, their employees, and the community because without doing that they would violate the ESRA and potentially lose their investors' investments. Worker ownership of the corporations that cannot demonstrate social and environmental responsibility is a next step, and if that isn't sufficient to achieve serious environmentally friendly and democracy-promoting changes in the corporation, then the next step will be public ownership and the election of the boards of directors by the public every five years. In cases like energy and transportation or other environmentally strategic industries, the ESRA will also mandate the nationalization of energy and transportation companies by 2040, which will thereafter be governed by a board half of whom are elected by the public in elections governed by the "no money in elections" of the first clause of the ESRA, and half of whom are selected by environmental organizations that supported the ESRA years prior to its passage.

An additional section under the second clause addresses the concern that large corporations would simply move their businesses elsewhere to avoid complying with the ESRA. Before they can move or dramatically reduce the number of their employees, the amendment imposes requirements on corporations with over 200 employees to provide reparations to employees, the city, and the state for the individual and societal damage their move or reduction in employment will cause.

The amendment also includes language to reduce in stages and then ban the use of fossil fuels by 2040, to prohibit the release of carbons and other environmentally destructive products, and to promote and fund the development and use of alternative and environmentally friendly sources of energy while phasing out vehicles and severely reducing the use of other means of transportation that emit carbons.

The third clause addresses the need for all students at all grade levels to receive an education that provides the skills, talents, and information needed for them to work for the well-being of the planet and its inhabitants. (This is described in detail in chapter 5.)

For the past forty years, many politicians and even some key labor unions have opposed environmental regulations because of their potentially detrimental consequences for working people. This opposition to critical environmental progress can be reduced through the implementation of a universal basic income at a level to provide a living wage and through a societal recognition that the unemployed are making a real contribution to the society by not insisting on military spending or other societally and environmentally destructive employment.

Worker control doesn't guarantee that corporations will act in the best interest of the larger society and the environment. It could take time to overcome the ethos of materialism and selfishness instilled in many of us. Workers and even environmental experts put on a corporate board might develop a loyalty to their particular corporation or solidarity with the short-term interests of their own fellow workers to the detriment of the larger environmental and ethical concerns that we hope they will prioritize. That's one reason why the ESRA institutes an outside panel to review even worker-controlled corporations on behalf of the needs of the life support system of Earth, the development of the caring society, and the enhancement of social and economic justice.

To ensure that conservative courts more beholden to the interests of the ruling class than the well-being of the American people and planet do not prevent the implementation of the ESRA by ruling parts or all of it unconstitutional or in violation of whatever they come up with, there is a final clause that allows this amendment to override prior court opinions, laws, U.S. treaties and international agreements, and even the Constitution to the extent that any of them are in conflict with this particular path toward the survivability of the planet and the well-being of its inhabitants—economically, environmentally, and socially.

The ESRA will guarantee a major expansion of democratic power and will increase the likelihood of even greater steps toward economic democratization. Though likely to be initially dismissed as unrealistic, just as was the movement for same-sex marriage, the ESRA could actually become a major item for public debate by the mid-2020s.

Don't be "realistic"! Don't let all the columnists, talking heads, political scientists, and other "experts" convince you that the changes we actually need for our own environmental sustainability are either impossible or else unnecessary because scientists will come up with a miracle cure. Environmental scientists have already told us that what is needed is a dramatic transformation in our society and economy. By expanding the public's sense of what might be possible, the political struggle for the ESRA takes a step beyond the Green New Deal and will help liberate the creativity and innovation of the growing environmental movement.

NATIONAL AND GLOBAL SECURITY THROUGH GENEROSITY: THE GLOBAL GENEROSITY PLAN

Efforts to push the public discourse about what is possible are also needed in the area of homeland security. Mis-educated by the media and many politicians, many Americans accept the notion that the world is fundamentally unsafe and that the goal of American policy should be to dominate other countries, either militarily or through one-sided global economic arrangements, cultural penetration, and diplomacy. Democrats and Republicans differ on the relative balance between military and "soft power," but many in both parties share the mistaken assumption that the only way to achieve security for the United States—frequently defined in terms of what serves the interest of American corporations and investments of the wealthy and powerful—is to build a world in which we get our way. We end up spending vastly more on the military than on any other programs or services, including education, health care, protecting the environment, and helping those most negatively impacted by the normal operations of the capitalist marketplace.

The Love and Justice movement will support instead a path of generosity to resolve the global refugee crisis that will achieve true homeland security. This path will be embodied in a global Generosity (or Marshall) Plan.

I recognize that some will resist using the words "Marshall Plan" (and even some of the plan's tenets) because of the critique that the post–World War II Marshall Plan was covertly designed to advance U.S. and global capitalist interests, even though many at the time saw it differently. Yet there are older generations who have a favorable association with the Marshall Plan, so I will use Marshall Plan and Global Generosity Plan interchangeably.

Here are the essential elements of our version of the plan:

> We will provide enough funding to eliminate U.S. domestic and foreign poverty, homelessness, hunger, inadequate education, and inadequate healthcare, and to repair the global environment. The most modest cost projections of this are 5 percent of the annual governmental budgets of the world's developed nations each year for the next twenty years. The United States should take the lead because we are one of the countries that contribute most to the world's pollution and environmental destruction. To do this, we will dedicate 10 percent of our budget to local communities both in the United States and abroad that are working to address their local pressing needs, including eliminating poverty, providing health care and education for all, promoting personal and environmental well-being, and the like. We are aware that China is already involved in reaching out to countries around the world to help them with some of their financial needs, although the Chinese initiative does not do so in the way that I propose below. Nevertheless, we should use the 2020s as an opportunity to join China in this kind of venture, rather than automatically assuming that we should allow our militarists and imperialists to define China as a permanent enemy, thereby strengthening the need for endless expenditures on armaments and ongoing acts of hostility toward China.

> The aid in our plan should go directly to local communities so that they have the power to make and implement decisions in alignment with

their community's needs. The goal must be to achieve ongoing buy-in and involvement by all stakeholders—except for those who seek to divert the funds to local elites, military and police agencies, or to powerful but environmentally and societally irresponsible corporations and their infrastructure needs.

We will establish an international non-governmental agency that will receive the funds from all participating nations and distribute them in a way that is environmentally sensitive, respectful of indigenous cultures, safeguarded against corruption, protected from manipulation by elite interests, and empowering of the people in each region and each village. This agency or mechanism will be governed by a board of ethicists, religious leaders, artists, writers, social theorists, philosophers, economists, environmental scientists, social change activists, indigenous groups, and local community members from various locations, all of whom have demonstrated that they give higher priority to the well-being of others than to the well-being of corporations or wealthy elites, and who reject all forms of neoliberal economics or other trickle-down theories of how best to serve the poor.

We will revise U.S. trade agreements so that they serve the poor, the economically struggling, and the refugees of the world rather than the most powerful and economically successful. Global trade must be both multilateral and equitable. New agreements will provide support and encouragement for working people to organize, earn a living wage, and establish adequate safety and health conditions and environmental safeguards. They will also protect farmers at home and abroad by encouraging land use that is environmentally sustainable, and food prices that both enable farmers to make a living and ensure that food is distributed to all who need it regardless of ability to pay.

Forgive national and international loans to foreign countries that could only afford to pay them back by imposing severe austerity measures on their own people.

Fund trained, unarmed civilian peace teams to intervene in areas of conflict. Retrain the armies of nations around the world to become experts in nonviolence, as well as implementors of ecologically sensitive designs for agriculture, health care, housing, infrastructure, education and computers, and other technologies.

Ensure the empowerment of girls through literacy, education, and skills training programs and jobs.

Make environmental goals central to qualifying for funding.

The programs of this plan must be delivered in a way that manifests respect and genuine caring by all those who implement it, and by the countries that fund it. Otherwise we fall back into the "objective caring without subjective caring" pattern that ultimately makes recipients feel that the caring is more to serve interests of the wealthy than to manifest the caring society.[2]

Within a few years of fully implementing the global Generosity/Marshall Plan or a similar program, we will see the economic refugee problem decline. And if this plan and the ESRA are implemented with adequate funding from both the United States and other wealthy countries of the world, there could be a comfortable resettlement of the hundreds of millions who are at risk of homelessness, currently or in the foreseeable future, because of environmental destruction, economic insecurity, and/or violent gangs (either private or governmental).

One of the important issues raised by scientists is the threat to the environment caused by growing populations. There is now considerable evidence that as poverty declines, so do birth rates. Thus the global Generosity

Plan could be an important adjunct to any environmentally sensitive plan for the future.

I already hear a fearful response. "Generosity? What about terrorism? Will terrorists be stopped through generosity?"

Terrorism is most frequently provoked by a nationalist, imperialist, or colonial arrogance that demeans the lives, values, and traditional customs of other people around the world. While in the West we tell ourselves that our globalized corporate culture, our sex-and-money-crazed media, and our political domination of others are bringing enlightenment and rationality to a so-called backward world, many people around the globe experience the West quite differently. They see its extreme individualism and materialism, high rates of divorce and addiction, and decline of some religious behavior as a sickness that, through force or media indoctrination, threaten to over-power the values and communities upon which they have built their identi-ties and cultures. These assaults, coupled with the imposition of global eco-nomic arrangements that impoverish most while enriching only a wealthy local elite, threaten to reduce or destroy allegiance in other cultures to their own sources of meaning and higher purpose in life.

Through the global Generosity/Marshall Plan we will commit to culti-vating trust and hope among the peoples of the world. To the extent that the plan is implemented in a spirit of generosity, so that it reflects both objective and subjective caring, and manifests real respect for those who are recipients of assistance, this approach will in fact make it much harder for terrorists to recruit and sustain the loyalty of people who are witnessing on a daily basis the actual caring that we show through this program. Ter-rorists will find that people no longer believe that they are serving anyone but themselves or working for any reasonable or religiously sanctified goal. But this will only happen if we do in fact build a societal commitment to generosity rather than see this plan as a crude way to buy allies for ourselves.

And it is important to remember that most acts of terror committed in the United States are carried out by white U.S. male nationalists and right-wing U.S. male extremists, not terrorists from other countries or different religions.

Now to address skeptics about how the global Generosity/Marshall Plan impacts homeland security. We will maintain a strong national defense, while reaching out to others around the world to demonstrate that we respect and care for them and understand their anger at Western societies. Combined with generous funding and other help to provide for the economic well-being of other national groups, this strategy of generosity and respect will be more likely to make us secure.

Moreover, the global Generosity/Marshall Plan, especially if implemented in cooperation with other advanced economies, will dramatically reduce global migration. Few people leave their countries because they think that the United States (or Great Britain, France, or Germany) has nicer mountains or prairies or oceans "white with foam." The most significant causes of mass immigration to the United States are our own economic policies, trade agreements, and military actions that have destabilized or devastated foreign countries and made them unsustainable financially and unsafe politically and personally. In the not too distant future another main cause will be environmental chaos unless the United States and other countries quickly implement the kinds of programs embodied in the ESRA as well as some of the steps suggested by Pope Francis in his environmental encyclical *Laudato Si*. Ensuring the genuine well-being of people throughout the world without trying to advance the economic interests of our own corporation or our military power will be a much more effective and morally coherent approach to global safety, peace, and environmentally sustainable development.

The global Generosity/Marshall Plan also addresses the question of currently undocumented workers, students, and others by offering full and equal citizenship to all current residents of the United States, including those here without official documentation of approval from previous administrations and those who are called Dreamers (people brought to the United States as children by parents who were undocumented).

We will judge our program not only by its economic effects but to the degree that people feel safe and cared for, less alone, more trusting, and more willing to engage in acts of caring and generosity toward others. This spiritual outcome is our bottom line: we aim to nourish and excite the souls of everyone alive on the planet, so that they burn with passionate intensity for life and embody a new level of inner calm and gentleness that can help repair the planet.

We will maintain a military in the short term for the following two reasons. First, in this historical moment, a global Generosity/Marshall Plan will only win mass approval if it is seen as part of a two-pronged strategy in which the other prong, military defense, is still intact and powerful. We will withdraw U.S. forces to our own borders, close our military bases around the world, and strengthen international institutions that provide nonviolent interventions. Our military will protect our borders from terrorist attacks while also retraining army personnel to become experts in assisting efforts to reduce and eliminate poverty, hunger, and homelessness in the United States. Second, we will use our military in the case of clear and present danger of genocide (or ethnic cleansing)—but only through an international force that is not led by the United States or NATO.

Dramatically reducing our military budget or redirecting it to implement the global Generosity/Marshall Plan will provide the money needed to implement this plan. After all, it is a plan for national defense through global peace and generosity! Because additional resources will be needed, we will place a tax of 1 percent on international financial transactions of one million dollars or more, and we can increase taxes on world trade, carbon emissions, and corporations in years that they have large profits or in years that they pay their corporate boards and top management salaries above ten times the median income of the society in that given year.

These new taxes will not add to the economic burden of middle income people because they will not impact them. More important, the values of solidarity and caring for others that the global Generosity/Marshall Plan will foster are precisely what is needed to stabilize the world economy and purge it of the striking irrationality that happens when a society rewards selfishness and the practice of looking out for number one.

Although we believe that nonviolence is the only path for the future of the human race, we understand that convincing Americans of the viability of a nonviolent defense will take many decades. A rational defense policy coupled with the global Generosity/Marshall Plan will provide far better security than the United States has been able to muster by depending primarily on military interventions around the world. The success of the plan will prove that generosity can actually work to increase security. While that process proceeds, we will ask our allies in the liberal and progressive think tanks to devise a generous plan to create jobs to fit the skills of those who will lose their employment in the military-industrial complex once we implement massive cuts to the military budget. For instance, many of those currently employed in the military-industrial sector could be gainfully employed in retooling military-based corporations to become the suppliers for the goods that we will be delivering to other countries as we implement the global Generosity/Marshall Plan. We can use these retooled facilities to provide housing, food, and other necessities to those who are homeless or hungry both in the United States and around the world in ways that are not environmentally destructive. Meanwhile, the plan for universal basic income will help.

We must avoid the arrogance with which previous aid programs were implemented, on the one hand mostly aimed at the elites of the countries, their corporations, armies, and police forces that repressed dissent rather than addressing the needs of their people, and on the other hand offered with the subtle attitude that because we have money to give away we are superior to them. On the contrary, in implementing the global Generosity/Marshall Plan we must approach the world with a deep humility and a spirit of repentance and offering of reparations for the ways in which the West has maintained its dominance of the planet through wars, environmental degradation, economic policies, and a growing materialism and selfishness. We have much to learn from the peoples of the world, their cultures, their spiritual and intellectual heritages, and their ways of dealing with human relationships. And it is in our own interest as humans to recognize that our individual and societal well-being depend on the well-being of everyone else on the planet.

Equally important, all humans have a deep need to care for each other as momentary embodiments of God (or whatever name you use for the goodness, love, and generosity of the universe at its current stage of evolutionary development). We will support this ethos of caring for each other because it is ethically and spiritually right to do so, not just because instrumentally it is the only sane policy for saving the planet and with it the lives of future generations (including our children and grandchildren, for those blessed to have them).

Domestic support for the global Generosity/Marshall Plan will grow to the extent that people perceive it as a manifestation of genuine caring rather than primarily as a savvy way to protect the United States (which it also is) or as a way for some smart liberal and progressive politicians to gain greater public support (which it also is). In fact, the plan has a particular potential to speak to that section of Christian Evangelicals who have not totally forgotten the biblical imperative to care for the poor and the downtrodden. We can use the campaign for the plan to help people understand what the new bottom line is really about—providing the foundation for us to become a Caring Society—Caring for Each Other and Caring for the Earth. This ethical and spiritual goal may seem counterintuitive at first but our campaign will eventually attract many who have previously suppressed their deep desire to live in such a world.

Though, again, while it's likely to take a long time before the United States and other world governments adopt the Love and Justice version of the global Generosity/Marshall Plan, our campaign for it is valuable because it will place into public discourse fundamental human needs that have been too long ignored and will challenge notions of what is realistic that have constricted our imaginations and crippled our politics. Meanwhile, the plan will prove the most appropriate weapon for the war on terror: it will replace the failed strategies of military interventions with a strategy of generosity that addresses the root causes of terrorism in our world. The advanced industrial societies of the world can't afford anything less than the global Generosity/Marshall Plan.

A COOPERATIVE AND CARING LEGAL SYSTEM

Now imagine yourself in a society in which the Environmental and Social Responsibility Amendment and the global Generosity/Marshall Plan have been implemented and in which democratic control of the economy and generosity toward others have become the accepted practices of our society for at least thirty years. People have happily embraced the new bottom line and feel themselves committed to the caring society. Objective caring is matched with subjective caring so that increasingly people recognize that the society is filled with caring people. A living wage has become the norm for everyone employed and comparable benefits are given to everyone so that no one has to worry about whether they will have a roof over their head, adequate food, health care, and other life necessities. When this becomes the daily reality for everyone, we likely will be most successful in seeking to promote a cooperative and caring legal system—though we should start now to promote these ideas in colleges, law schools, and media so that public debate about them can begin.

The Anglo-American legal system was developed to reform feudal and monarchical societies whose religious and political leaders arbitrarily exercised huge amounts of power to enhance their wealth, maintain the patriarchal and sexually abusive order that served them, and protect themselves against popular discontent. The solution proposed by the theorists of the emerging capitalist societies of the twelfth to the twentieth centuries was to create individual legal rights as protections against the claims and abuses of the monarch, church, or other potentially powerful societal forces.

This new approach offered many advantages. However, its designers were responding in part to the needs of an emerging class of traders, shopkeepers, bankers, independent artisans, large scale farmers, and independent professionals who together constituted what became known as the bourgeoisie and more generally, capitalists; their motivations were not purely to help all of humankind. Most members of this emerging class were resentful of legal constraints on their ability to accumulate wealth imposed by the Christian feudal religious system, which required them to pay the Catholic Church's version of "a fair wage" to workers and charge "a fair price" for consumer goods. First through the Protestant revolution, and later through political revolutions, this new class reshaped public discourse, convincing people that the best way to achieve fairness was through a capitalist marketplace in which each person could sell their labor power to whom they chose and purchase goods at a price they chose to pay. They neglected to mention that the vast inequalities of wealth that already existed in feudal societies would grow ever vaster in capitalist societies. Most people's choices would remain severely constrained, only now the constraints would be blamed on the individual for failing to have the money or the skills needed to succeed in a (supposedly) free and competitive marketplace.

The legal systems that emerged were charged with protecting the individual from the ever-present reality of governmental overreach. But in large part, the individual worker was left to fend for himself (these rights were not extended to women in the first few hundred years of the capitalist experiment). Those who succeeded in the competitive marketplace were seen either as more meritorious than the rest or as specially blessed by God for reasons that humans could not comprehend. The legal system was not supposed to interfere with the marketplace but only to ensure that each individual was protected from interference in the "free" pursuit of his own self-interest. Some twentieth century political theorists have called this legal system "negative freedom."

The caring society will need a different kind of legal system, one whose goal is to enhance people's capacities to achieve a world of love, generosity, environmental sanity, social and economic justice, and awe and wonder at the miraculous universe in which we live. We will reform our legal system to promote peacemaking, understanding, empathy, and respectful problem-solving with the overarching aim of restoring people's dignity, respect, caring for each other, and connection with community. This is a kind of "positive freedom," a system that promotes the fulfillment of our most basic human needs.

We will foster the obligation to care for others as a societal ethos. While in our current society there is no such obligation, meaning you can turn your back on the homeless, the hungry, or even someone who is drowning or being assaulted by others, in the caring society children will be raised knowing how to intervene appropriately on behalf of those in need. However, we will not create a legal obligation to care for others, particularly in the early stages of the caring society. Given the tendency of Americans to insist on instant gratification, well-intentioned people might bring legal charges against those individuals or groups they judged to be "not caring adequately." Think of this kind of dynamics as political correctness run wild, which I've witnessed in the Left. We are going to have to educate people carefully in the guiding principles of action in a caring society: gentleness, compassion, and affirmation of each other, no matter how reactionary and outrageous are those who seek to return to the patriarchal and capitalist consciousness of each man for himself. It is only through love and gentleness that the caring society can obtain and then retain the allegiance of a large majority of Americans, not through emotional or intellectual bullying and certainly not by using the courts to enforce caring! To say it again: our path to the world we want must embody the values of the society we seek to create. On the other hand, as discussed above in the section on the ESRA, we will create a legal obligation to care for the Earth—this is an immediate survival necessity for life on this planet.

While redistribution of wealth and a guaranteed income for everyone will reduce dramatically the amount of theft and scarcity-related crimes, and support for women and school courses teaching empathy will decrease family violence and physical assaults, there will still remain pathologies that lead to some crime. We will handle these incidents with compassion. When someone is charged with a crime, they will be asked to participate in a restorative justice process. They will meet with the people who have been hurt by their actions, and learn to understand fully the damage they have caused, not only to the individuals directly involved but also to the surrounding community. The restorative justice process will give priority to four goals:

Repairing the social damage done to our capacity to trust others and restoring a sense of security for victims.

Repairing personal damage inflicted by individual and corporate criminals.

Fostering reconciliation and forgiveness.

Seeking rehabilitation and transformation of those in prison rather than prioritizing punishment.

In the courtrooms, we will replace an adversarial system with a system in which lawyers have an obligation both to their clients and to the larger society. This duty will bind lawyers to find the truth of what has been done by their client, what healing that client needs, and what protections the rest of the society needs. These are often complex psychological and ethical questions, so lawyers will be trained in ethical thinking, compassionate and empathic ways of understanding human behavior, and psychological sophistication as prerequisites to being licensed to practice law. Similarly, district attorneys and their assistants will be required to demonstrate that their handling of each case embodies a true commitment to healing the society rather than simply punishing perpetrators or improving their conviction rates. When judges, lawyers, and prosecutors consider themselves to be agents committed to the promotion of love and caring, restorative justice will be more likely to lead to results that are best for everyone involved. In many cases, this will mean that we seek to repair not only the distortions in our society and the damage done to the crime victim but also the damaged perpetrators, so that everyone involved can live healthy and safe lives.

We will deliver justice in ways that embody our highest values of love and caring for both crime victims and offenders. Whenever possible, we will avoid sending people to prison. We will seek to heal and repair the damaged psyches of the perpetrators so that they never engage in hurtful acts again. However, in some cases prison will remain an option so that we can protect society from those convicted of violent crimes who might revert to violence. Because our goal at every step will be to treat the accused or convicted with respect for their humanity and our deep desire will be to assist them in healing the traumas that led them to criminal acts, we will in every case attempt to have them confront the full damage caused by their criminal behavior. If a victim is not willing or not available to participate in a restorative justice process, we will find other ways to ensure the perpetrator is held accountable and restorative mechanisms are implemented, including strategies to heal the perpetrator as well.

We will seek a transformation of the penal system. Where prison is unavoidable, the values we seek to establish in a caring society will be built into a prison's physical arrangements, food, provisions for learning, and opportunities for genuine repentance and transformation. Guards will be trained in compassion and rewarded when they show caring to inmates. Management of prisons will be supervised by panels of psychologists and clergy who are empowered to hire and fire all prison personnel through an assessment of their capacity to demonstrate compassion toward prisoners daily. Prisons will train inmates in employable skills and upon completion of their sentence, individuals will be connected with halfway houses and services that will provide financial, emotional, spiritual, psychological, and community support to help ensure their successful reentry. Those who have been released from prison will be given full voting rights and the same free education available to everyone else.

We will decriminalize personal behavior that does not hurt other human beings, including the use of recreational drugs. We will draw on successful programs in other countries to determine how best to implement these changes to adequately address drug addiction so that people can obtain the services and support they need. We will seek to protect people from abuse of potentially addictive drugs but simultaneously trust that as our society provides more opportunities for people's needs for meaning and purpose to be met, the use of drugs and other strategies to drown their sorrows will be significantly diminished.

The more a society embodies the values of revolutionary love in its child-rearing, family practices, economic arrangements, and cultural proclivities, including the sharing of our resources and providing for everyone's basic material and emotional needs, the less crime and violence there will be. In the meantime, we will still need a police force to provide protection from criminal behaviors. But we will also establish guards against the misuse of the power police have historically exercised against the poor, working people, and people of color. Our long-term goal will be to abolish the police and replace them with neighborhood security committees, as discussed in chapter 5. People in communities and neighborhoods will care for each other.

HOW YOU CAN HELP TO CREATE THE LOVE AND JUSTICE PARTY

The Love and Justice Party is not yet a political party. Rather, it is an idea for creating a framework within which we can together build a movement committed to revolutionary love and the caring society. Yet it is possible in the coming years that this movement will evolve in ways that make it necessary to function as a political party.

You, dear reader, are crucial to establishing the Love and Justice Party. Think of it as the "Tea Party of the Left," seeking to push public discourse toward the worldview of revolutionary love and the vision of a caring society. And let's make it a joyous community. If you agree with the analysis in this manifesto, help us popularize our ideas. And join the Love and Justice movement at www.tikkun.org/lj.

First step: invite friends, neighbors, fellow students if you are in an educational institution, co-workers, co-retirees, or members of your civic or political or religious organization to join a study group with you to read this book, discuss it, and try to implement some of its ideas. That group could meet weekly, biweekly, or monthly. And on the Tikkun website and in *Tikkun* magazine, available on that website, we will continue to print articles that give you opportunities to discuss ideas, and in some cases, critique them. Then turn the study group into a local chapter of the Love and Justice movement, get the training for being a part of the empathy tribe, organize a group of co-workers or students to re-envision your work place, or get training to run an occupational stress group or a family support group. We have already begun to build this movement with our Network of Spiritual

Progressives, which envisions a path to a world of love and justice. We have already trained potential empathy tribe activists, and have begun to build chapters which are trying to share these ideas. What they and we need are more people who are inspired to join these efforts. If you are interested in doing so, please sign up for our next training at www.spiritualprogressives. org/training.

There are other steps you can take now. Take any ideas from this book that you like and send them out to your Facebook, Twitter, or other social media connections. Write opinion pieces to local and national media incorporating the new bottom line and using our perspective to critique what is happening in national and local politics. Create a public gathering to celebrate Interdependence Day on the Fourth of July and invite everyone you know (we have materials you can print out to help you shape the event). And insist that any candidate who asks for your support in local or national elections publicly endorse the new bottom line.

You or others in your local chapter of the Love and Justice movement could take these ideas, and others based on revolutionary love, and turn them into a platform to bring into the electoral arena. Run for local school boards. Run for city council, state legislature, or a congressional seat by espousing the new bottom line and applying it concretely to specific issues facing your community. Present any part of the ideas in this book—they will stir controversy and get people talking.

If your reaction to this idea is "I'd never win," don't be so sure. Winning an election is not the only way to win. The short-term goal is to widen the kinds of issues that get discussed in the public sphere, and to do so by affirming the humanity of all, including those who do not yet agree with liberal or progressive ideas. Do not avoid talking about the revolutionary possibility of love or about the caring society. Don't let others convince you that it would be better to downplay the new bottom line, the Environmental and Social Responsibility Amendment, the global Generosity/Marshall Plan, or other of our ideas until you win office. This timidity is the slippery slope that led to the current weakness of the Democratic Party. So many of its leaders started out principled and conscientious, wanting to make a difference, but then became convinced that they had to hide those parts of their idealism that might get them dismissed (by the media and other politicians) as ideological, or utopian, or just plain naïve. Instead, they became "realistic," and settled for contributing to a party that doesn't really have a coherent worldview.

As the U.S. electoral system is currently set up, the Democratic Party primaries are the only place that progressive ideas can be directly presented to tens of millions of working people. This allows the mass media to continue to ignore those ideas or ridicule them. So a first step is to create a Love and Justice presence in the Democratic Party and the Greens and any other political party, while also pushing activists outside and inside electoral politics to embrace the new bottom line and emphasize it in all their public actions.

Some will say it's too late for these fundamental changes—the environmental crisis won't wait until we can achieve them. Well, yes, it won't. But when 2032 comes around, you will be sorry we didn't start building a Love and Justice movement now. Consider the implications of more years of a progressive politics that does not address the hunger for recognition, respect, love, community, and higher meaning to life; does not overcome the religiophobia, and the shaming and blaming, and the toxic forms of identity politics (as discussed in chapter 4); and does not build popular support for the replacement of the globalization of selfishness with a coherent vision of a love-infused socialism. After all that, if people in the 2030s turn once again, as they did in 2016, to a reactionary nationalism, one even more humanly destructive than Trumpism and the current Republican versions of hate-driven-politics, you will wish the infrastructure and mass support for our movement had already been built.

CHAPTER SEVEN

The Caring Society in the Twenty-Second Century

In this chapter I want to imagine a society in the mid twenty-second century that had really taken seriously the ideas and proposals in this manifesto and had already implemented all the programs described in chapters 5 and 6. Although I and most of those who read this manifesto in the next twenty years will not be there to witness the next century, it may be helpful to imagine some of the possibilities that could emerge. They are offered as much to stimulate others to engage in similar reflections on the world you may want to hope for, once revolutionary love becomes the dominant ethos of all our societies.

Of course, the thinking here is the opposite of what has been common among futurists in Western societies, many of whom are celebrated in the media and by the technological and financial elites of the twenty-first century. Because these futurists don't want to envision a society in which patriarchy and classism, domination and manipulation, and an instrumental response to others and to the planet have been transcended, they are only going to embrace visions of revolutionary love which are translatable solely into personal transformations that do not touch, much less overcome, the capitalist system at its essence.

Mainstream futurists often depict technology bringing more comforts or more challenges to the existing patriarchal and class-dominated world. For example, Yuval Noah Harari's best seller, *Homo Deus: A Brief History of Tomorrow,* describes a world in which we have become new kinds of beings, with our bodies and minds altered in ways to enable us to live considerably longer—possibly to age 150 for people born in the twenty-second century as more and more of our body parts are replaced by sophisticated mechanical devices. But what lies ahead is for homo sapiens to be replaced by smart robots who have learned to program themselves and see human beings as inefficient for running whatever is left of planet Earth.

Actually, it's hard to argue with Harari's scenario and other such dystopian visions for the future, even if it unfolds in two or three centuries rather than sooner, unless humanity has embraced some version of the kind of revolutionary love that fosters the caring society articulated in this book. The only protection for the future of the human race is for us to become the kind of loving and caring, generous and awe-filled beings that our prophets and poets, our spiritual leaders, and our own inner voices have been calling us to become, despite the powerful voices of the reality police with their combination of gadgets and allures and their pessimism about humans ever being capable of creating a world aligned with the highest ethical and spiritual values of the human race. Indeed, though many ethical scientists will privately oppose it, from the standpoint of a scientistic worldview, there are no scientific grounds to stop the replacement of human beings with robots. Instead, it would take ethical considerations, the kind of thinking the newest technologies cannot compute and the newest technologists shun as irrelevant to the accumulation of money and power, as their comrades in other branches of industry have been doing for centuries.

While I have been arguing for the alternative possibility—a world of love and caring and awe and wonder and recognition of the sacred, there is nothing inevitable about the vision of revolutionary love actually getting adopted by the human race. Nor is there anything inevitable about the dystopian visions of our future—though they are a bit easier to achieve, because their ascendance requires only that most of us sit back, wallowing in powerless-ness and despair, and passively watch as the dynamics of a materialist and selfishness-oriented domination society work themselves out. But ulti-mately, such a dystopic future depends on decisions made by you and other readers of this book to work actively to create the caring society, instead of just observing what the people seeking money and power come up with, in coming decades.

In this chapter I invite you to imagine a society in which love, caring, kindness, and generosity prevail and transform the unconscious assump-tions of how people should treat each other and the Earth. Imagine a society in which the focus on individualism, selfishness, and materialism had been largely transcended and most people celebrate each other and avoid instru-mental thinking about others, and in which those who work have jobs that contribute to the well-being of all and are honored for that. In such a world, those who do not work—in large part because the total amount of work has been dramatically reduced in order to avoid artificially creating desires for gadgets that waste the resources of the planet, and to allow the mechaniza-tion of tasks that can be given to robots—will receive a sufficient guaranteed income to live comfortably. And imagine that environmental destruction has been stayed and climate change and toxic pollution are no longer a threat.

At that point, the programs I suggest here could be the next phase of implementing revolutionary love. But only then—they are not meant to be part of the program of the Love and Justice Party until at least forty years after both the Environmental and Social Responsibility Amendment and global Generosity/Marshall Plan, as well as universal health care and much of the rest of the programs outlined in chapters 5 and 6, have been imple-mented and accomplished one of their most important goals: to revive hope and empower imagination. To make it clear that I do not want readers to think that I'm asking you to agree with the imaginings in this chapter, in the presentation below I describe the ideas as though they were being told to us by someone in 2140 who is looking back at the progress made so far and discussing the new steps being tried out now that patriarchy and class society have been overcome.

A REPORT FROM THE NEXT CENTURY
Government
In the first thirty to fifty years of our Love and Justice movement, we formed regional environmental districts to determine how to use the resources of the planet in a way that serves everyone. We also figured out, in a loving and respectful way, how to achieve a decline in population sufficient to enable the human race to live within Earth's resource limitations.

Now, we seek to refine our political system in line with our values of living nonviolently, replacing relationships of domination with cooperative relationships, and promoting the well-being of everyone on the planet rather than just the well-being of our own country. Within the government, hiring, promotion, and salary levels are shaped in part by the degree to which the people being served report satisfaction with the way they have been treated, and whether they experience government itself as a vehicle through which all of us manifest our caring. With this approach, people feel far less upset about paying taxes.

We guard each person's absolute right to make decisions in their own private life, without fear of intimidation either by government, corporations, or other economic entities or by "politically correct" majorities. And since democracy cannot protect against democratically chosen forms of mass coercion, we have checks and balances, in particular an independent judiciary to which ordinary people are automatically assumed to have standing and can appeal for relief from such perceived coercion.

Major decisions are made through direct democracy, locally, nationally, and internationally. Revolutionary love has not ended all disagreements: there are still choices that reflect different assessments of the best way to serve humanity, animals, and the sanctity of the Earth. The latest techno-logical developments make it possible for people to vote at home several times a year on the major issues. The task of the state legislatures and Congress is to frame the issues by highlighting the major philosophical and ideological differences that characterize the alternatives. The only requirement for voters is that they listen to several hour-long presentations detailing all perspectives on the issues under consideration—including minority views not yet found among those in elected office—before weighing in.

There is a story in the Talmud about the conflict between two different approaches to Jewish law, which is still taught to children of every religious and secular perspective in our schools. The story goes that after years of intense disagreements between the School of Hillel and the School of Shamai, both schools were able to agree to call upon God to resolve their dispute. They prayed to God for guidance about which approach God would sanction. Suddenly, everyone heard a booming voice from heaven saying, "Both of these are the words of the Living God." Commenting on this story, generations of rabbis have explained how this seemingly contradictory position could be held by saying that this dispute was a "dispute for the sake of heaven."

Now that our society has incorporated most of the Love and Justice Party proposals and the new bottom line is taken as a matter of course, disputes are similarly "for the sake of heaven," that is, aimed at finding the best way to protect the Earth and promote each other's well-being. These disputes take place in a framework of love, generosity, and a genuine desire to find a path that will fill the needs of others and not just oneself—though this path is not always easy to find and in some cases, simply impossible—but what is wonderful is that almost everyone accepts the process as legitimate and no one wants to go back to the self-interested decision making that led to those aspects of environmental destruction that took place before revolutionary love and the caring society managed to win fundamental change ninety years ago.

Jubilee—Redistribution of Wealth

In the twenty-second century, we returned to a brilliant biblical idea: the Jubilee. This injunction for an equal redistribution of wealth, articulated in the Torah, was radical when proposed some 2,200 or more years ago—and so scary to ruling elites ever since that they used their influence in every Bible-oriented community to ensure that most people in them never heard of this idea, or if they did, heard it contextualized as something they didn't really have to take seriously until the messiah came (whether for the first time or returning being a dispute between Jews and Christians that Jews settled by saying "when s/he comes to Earth and the weapons of war have been melted into ploughshares and nations have long since abandoned wars, we'll ask if s/he has been here before"). In an ancient agrarian society, wealth took the form of land ownership; the injunction was that every fifty years each person returned to the original, basically equal, distribution that God had allocated to each tribe.

The Torah portrays God as worried that people would not be able to embrace the practice of radical redistribution: God reminds people that they don't have a right to more wealth than others. "The whole earth is mine," God says, "and you are just temporary sojourners on this planet." It's a hard message to take in fully, but none of us lives much beyond 120 years, if even close to that. God's point, as portrayed by the Torah, is that ownership is something people invented, not something God necessarily approves of, but only tolerates as long as people are willing to redistribute every fifty years, and as long as in the meantime they follow God's command to "love your neighbor" and also the most frequently repeated command in the Torah in various forms to "love the stranger/the Other!"

This radical redistribution ensured that unequal accumulation of wealth did not get passed on forever. Now, in the twenty-second century, we have a comparable practice: every fifty years we create a new money system, which is distributed to everyone equally. All money in banks, stocks, investment companies, gold, silver, and precious metals—even cash under your pillow—is declared null and void. Anyone attempting to use the old money is liable to criminal charges. The playing field is leveled, eliminating many of the inequalities that characterized the world's societies previously.

Our Jubilee does not affect all material resources. Everyone still gets to keep their houses, cars, computers, cell phones, and other valuables. And by the way, our government now prioritizes environmentally sustainable and aesthetically beautiful apartment buildings and cities. But it makes a significant step toward equality in purchasing power, hence making the section of the economy that still retains marketplace freedom a more equitable arrangement. After this redistribution every fifty years, consumer purchases more closely represent what people actually want, rather than being heavily tilted toward what the richest people want. And since we've managed to make the actual difference in income and wealth much smaller than it was in the twentieth and early twenty-first century, those differences are largely inconsequential in terms of how we live our lives or shape our public decisions.

It took a good eighty years of this transition for most people to recognize that the very notion of owning land or houses or consumer goods is a product of a distorted relationship to planet Earth. Although it may take another century for this new consciousness to persuade everyone around the globe, more and more people see this concept of ownership as outdated, to be transcended as were sexism and racism in the past.

Environmental Responsibility

In addition to questioning the concept of ownership, many people champion voluntary simplicity and ethical consumption, now that they do not have to choose between the economic well-being of their families, on the one hand, and environmentally sustainable behaviors, on the other. Neighborhoods share resources such as housing, energy, and consumer goods. Moreover, spiritual practices and wisdom have helped us renounce the belief that what we own or consume could ever be the measure of our worth.

Another spiritual advance is the transformation of our relationship with the environment: most people now respond to the universe with awe and wonder, seeing nature both as a resource and as fundamentally valuable. Many people voluntarily observe a regular sabbatical or Sabbath day each week, dedicating it to celebrating the universe and doing no work-related activities, nor using money or in any other way being involved in the "getting and spending" that once led to humans' domination over the Earth.

Even more dramatic, we now have a Sabbatical Year once every seven years, geared toward creating a year of rest from work for at least 85 percent of the population. During this year, most of the selling of goods and services is suspended. Most businesses are shut. Factories that produce anything not essential for life are closed. People have a full year to choose how they want to spend their time.

Essential enterprises that cannot be suspended for a year, such as medical services and hospitals, energy and mass transportation, plumbing and electrical work, and many others, are provided by about 15 percent of our population. Those people, though unable to fully participate in the general Sabbatical Year, are compensated with one and a half years of sabbatical every seven years on a different schedule, such that they take their Sabbatical when the rest of the society is working. To make this work we have trained more people to perform essential skills.

To connect students in elementary and high school to the Earth, part of their Sabbatical Year is assigned to working on the land, including planting, caring for, and harvesting the population's food supplies under guidance from skilled farmers. This allows most other farmworkers a year off. These pre-college students spend another part of the Sabbatical Year learning the important skills of childcare and elder care, again under the supervision of experts in these important fields.

For the rest of the population, the Sabbatical Year offers opportunities to participate in democratically choosing societal priorities for the next six years; to learn new skills in case they wish to change their occupation; to play, celebrate, relax, or read; or to undertake studies and develop skills or talents for which there has never been enough free time. Those who have those skills and wish to share them (at no charge) to the rest of the population are invited to do so.

And we have created a new line of work during the six years between general Sabbatical Years—preparing the society for the next Sabbatical Year. These government jobs include purchasing, accumulating, and storing food and supplies for distribution during the Sabbatical Year and organizing the courses volunteer teachers will offer, in everything from computer skills, history, and science to exercise, economic planning, music appreciation, and childrearing to foreign languages and cross-cultural dance. The government purchases the equipment and supplies needed for these courses.

In the Sabbatical Year, all normal money transactions are banned. Every person is given an equal amount of a Sabbatical Year currency, which is the only means of purchasing necessary goods, food, and services. Thus people experience living in a society where whatever is available for purchase is equally available to everyone. But since all stores, other than those supplying food or pharmaceuticals, are closed for the year, everyone also experiences a year in which consumption of items is severely curtailed. As a result of this, people focus on new, non-consumerist ways of finding meaning and satisfaction. Some might write poetry, some might learn healing skills, some might spend much of their time talking to friends and neighbors or playing sports or making videos or just plain finding their own best way of being in the world.

This intentional decrease in production and consumption gives the Earth a year of rest once every seven years, and underlines the advantages of living a life of voluntary simplicity. To spend more time in our local part of the

Earth heightens our appreciation of it and reminds us of our need to manage the world's resources for the needs of future generations.

International Solidarity, Goodbye to All Borders, and Unity of All Being
In the early years of the twenty-second century, many of the colonial and imperial powers that played a role in underdeveloping the global South and East began to acknowledge this role, repent, and provide reparations for the damage they had done to the peoples of the world. Since that time, China, Russia, the United States, the European countries, and the Islamic countries have all been working together to repair the damage of the past and to ensure that there are no more hot wars, trade wars, or diplomatic struggles. Israel and Palestine are living as friendly neighbors and together launched a Near East version of the Global Generosity Plan. Open borders are the norm, and even the concept of a national border is beginning to disappear.

After having spent most of the second half of the twenty-first century repairing the damage done to the environment, we still are mourning the suffering and massive deaths caused by environmental irresponsibility. Yet the process of repair that continued in the first decades of the twenty-second century helped nearly everyone on Earth to develop a global caring consciousness, facilitated in part by all of the countries of the planet implementing the Global Generosity Plan. Proposed by the Love and Justice movement, this plan was embraced by the children and grandchildren of those whose policies and economic selfishness had massively contributed to the destruction of large parts of Earth.

Unexpectedly, that crisis has also led to a near-universal embrace of rituals that facilitate awareness of the unity of all being. I myself and most people on the planet now testify to being overwhelmed with awe, wonder, and radical amazement at the grandeur and mystery of life, consciousness, and the universe that has evolved us into being. Some of this takes religious form. Most of us who do not believe in any traditional notion of a god nevertheless cannot deny the powerful impact of these beliefs that are based on daily experiences that almost everyone has of the beauty, magnificence, and mystery of life in this universe, and our determination to cherish and celebrate it. We no longer raise animals for slaughter and consumption—we eat only vegan food and experiment endlessly with delicious new and old recipes. The whole earth seems eroticized and filled with joy, or at least that is how most of us now experience it in daily life. Now that most countries have reduced time at work by implementing the twenty-eight-hour work week, we spend a major part of our lives enjoying play and joyful celebration, art and music, love and ecstasy, sports and exercise, community gatherings to shape our future and just to sing and dance together, quiet reflection, reading, making amateur scientific discoveries, listening to engaging lectures or giving them, writing fiction or poetry, meditating and praying, gardening, taking long and short walks in nature, and energy-renewing rest.

WITH HUMILITY AND EXCITEMENT

Switching back to the present day, I offer a final reflection on the path ahead. To build the caring society with revolutionary love requires a spirit of humility. *Tikkun olam*, the healing and transformation of our world, will take many generations. The ideas put forward in this manifesto may seem utopian today, but in a few generations they will seem overly cautious and not imaginative enough! Revolutionary love activists must always be open to transformation as we move from the narrow consciousness imposed upon us by growing up in a racist, sexist, classist society to an awareness of the immense possibilities available to the human race once we overcome our fears of each other and move social energy from domination to generosity.

We unequivocally know that all life is to be cherished, that every human being is infinitely precious, that the path to transformation must be as holy as our goals, and that every human being is wounded to various degrees by growing up in a social order that privileges aggression, power over others, material possessions, and selfishness. We must have compassion for everyone, including ourselves, and yet that compassion must be used proactively and forcefully to change the systems of oppression and to protect those who are suffering.

To sustain our efforts to change the world in the ways envisioned in this manifesto is going to require rigorous attention. Thankfully, there are many different religions and many non-religious spiritual paths that have developed considerable wisdom in how to keep us focused on the states of consciousness we seek to embody.

I've benefited greatly from the Jewish practice of *teshuva* (returning to one's own highest vision of the good) that is the central goal of the ten days of repentance that go from Rosh Hashanah through Yom Kippur each year—a time when the Jewish tradition calls upon us to really take stock of the ways we may have strayed from our highest values. You certainly don't have to be Jewish or even religious to get something out of this process. And I've also learned much about getting back on the right path from the Buddhist teacher David Loy, the Benedictine Sister Joan Chittister, and from my personal contacts with the Dalai Lama.

Jews conduct a ritual Seder once a year to celebrate our liberation. I'd like to see love revolutionaries adopting and transforming that ancient ritual into an evening community meal once a year on a national holiday in which we retell the various stories of the liberation struggles of all humanity. With song, dance, dramatic performances, teachings, and delicious vegan food! In the United States, I propose using President's Day, since it is the one national holiday which none of the previously oppressed groups have claimed as the day for focusing on their own suffering. Those who wish could always include references to past U.S. presidents that they feel in some important way contributed to liberation. In other countries the local history and culture would have to shape choices of time, place, and manner for such a yearly celebration.

On the other hand, there is also a wisdom in "not knowing"—that is, in recognizing that we don't fully know how to find the right balance in every situation, that we are likely to make mistakes. Even our purest intentions can sometimes be subverted by our own inner confusions and conflicts, or by not fully understanding the complexities of another human being. The path we seek requires a recognition of the limits of our abilities to fully know the consequences of our actions, combined with a fierce determination to promote as much caring, generosity, social and economic fairness and justice, care of the Earth, and love for each other as possible—all the while maintaining an absolute commitment to never reconciling ourselves to a society that causes severe suffering to others and to the Earth.

Just as we remind each other to not be "realistic" in our goals, and constantly retell each other the stories of the victories of past and present social change movements, so too we remind each other that a balanced life as an agent of social change must include time for being alone and outside of the claims on us of any movement. This should include time to celebrate and rejoice at the grandeur and mystery of the universe, time for introspection and love-making, and time to introduce playfulness, art, music, dance, ritual, altered states of consciousness, and humor into our social change movements. Let our movement for transformation toward a world of love and justice become known for how much joy and fun it is to be part of, and we will achieve the world we seek all the more quickly.

Afterword

I am hoping that you'll take a month after finishing this book to immerse yourself in the feelings of hope that come when you allow yourself to imagine you and the people you love living in the caring society governed by revolutionary love and implemented by the Love and Justice Party.

Of course, while trying to imagine this you will be constantly confronted by the reality police, in your own head and among your friends and family who have not yet been swayed by the ideas in this book. Encourage them to read it, but also recognize that it's going to take a lot of energy to stay hopeful amid the cynicism of those around you.

And yet, you can take some concrete steps to keep these ideas alive! Start a study group with friends to read and discuss these ideas. Join the Love and Justice community at www.tikkun.org or the Network of Spiritual Progressives at www.spiritualprogressives.org and enroll in the training offered by Cat Zavis and others. Subscribe to *Tikkun* online at www.tikkun.org. Donations to Tikkun and to the Network of Spiritual Progressives are tax-deductible. Stay in touch with me at TheLoveRabbi@tikkun.org. Send me your email so I can invite you to the first regional and national gatherings of the Love and Justice movement sometime in 2020 or 2021. The Love and Justice movement can soon become real. But not without your help.

Please help your friends and family to resist the knockoffs, namely, the phony versions of this message, propelled by people who recognize the need for a world based on love and justice but who think that we can get there without overcoming the economic, political, and cultural institutions of our current society that are so deeply linked to an ethos of selfishness and materialism. Real change cannot be achieved without nonviolently replacing those institutions that count on our passivity, self-blaming, and attachment to tradeoffs that seek to make us content with inequality of power and wealth and an ethos of endless growth that, together with racism, sexism, and classism, constitute today's capitalist societies.

There are tens of millions of people who would join you if they knew they weren't alone. Help us find donors to provide the start-up monies needed to train an empathy tribe and convene regional, national, and international conferences focused on turning these ideas into reality. Help us find the thousands of local volunteer organizers we will need to get this project into motion. Help us find the movie makers, TV writers and producers, novelists, poets, experts in social media and mass technology, the wealthy donors who want their money to go to something transformative rather than solely to repair the damage being done to our planet daily and to so many people's ability to sustain hope for a different world. This is a movement that needs funding at every level, from those tens of millions who could give a hundred dollars a year to those few who could give lots more.

If enough of the readers of this book are inspired, and if a community of people wills it, change can and will happen. Please use this book as a vehicle to spread the ideas, and use your own imagination and energy to start the process, find the funding, and reach out to others. Don't wait for me or others to make it happen—take the initiative locally to build groups to join our Love and Justice movement or our Network of Spiritual Progressives, which will be part of the organizational foundation for the caring society.

But what if you can't hold on to the vision presented here? What if your fear and cynicism about others—or theirs about you or about us—stymy any attempt to build a movement with enough power to propel the United States out of its current alternation between a politics of hope, love, and caring and a politics of fear, control over others, and domination? What if the progressives who win in 2020 or 2024 are able to implement their programs rooted in revolutionary love but only with an attitude of objective caring that doesn't really touch the heart or speak to the despair that lead people to reactionary politics? What if by their failures they produce more cynicism and humiliation among people who believed that this time they would create a different kind of world?

It is certainly possible to imagine fear winning out during the next few decades. Among other things, we are up against an extremely undemocratic institution created by the Founding Fathers: the U.S. Senate. As Paul Krugman points out in a November 9, 2018, *New York Times* opinion piece, representation in the Senate is based on each state having the same number of seats—two—regardless of population; this means that the fewer than 600,000 people in Wyoming have the same representation as almost forty million in California—which "drastically overweights those rural areas and underweights" the majority of Americans living in urban and suburban areas. This arrangement was created in large part to prevent the abolition of slavery.

If we can't overcome the challenges to gaining the political ground for the kind of psychologically, ethically, and spiritually sophisticated movement I have proposed, we may need to create a two-country solution. For the past thirty to forty years we've had an endless tug of war between conservative social policies and more liberal ideas that still fall far short of the message of revolutionary love. In each election we move a few inches to the Left or a few inches to the Right, but nobody really gets the society they want. If this continues to be the case, perhaps, at least in the short run, we will need to create a loving divorce, so that both sides can be winners, and each can create a society based on its own highest principles.

The technology exists to create two separate countries in what is now the United States. Let's imagine this for a minute. For convenience let us call them the Progressive States of America (PSA) and the Conservative States of America (CSA).

Each of the current states could decide by referendum which of the two countries it wanted to join, and each state should have the option to change that decision regularly—say, every twenty years. Both countries might get to vote every thirty years on the option to go back to being one unified nation.

Given advances in communication technology, the states in each country would not have to be physically contiguous. So, the PSA would likely include many states on the East and West Coasts, and the CSA might have most but not all of the states in the south and middle of the current United States. We can even imagine some of the largest current states breaking themselves into more than one state, each of which could affiliate with either the CSA or the PSA; for instance, California might become two or three separate states based on what its large and politically diverse population wanted.

Such an "Amerexit" could solve much of the tension between the two worldviews in our society. These two countries would enter into a peace agreement, committing to never use violence against each other. Any official of either country who promoted violence would automatically lose their job and be sent to prison. Both countries would agree to share their electric grid and maintain their major highways and means of transportation so that people would have easy and free access to other states in their own country even if that required travel through the other country. The peace agreement could also specify ways to ensure that the pollution generated by one country did not end up undermining the environment of the other, and a mechanism for correction and compensation if this happened unintentionally.

Each country would develop its own foreign and defense policies, but both would contribute to the maintenance of a protective force on the borders of the states neighboring the Atlantic and Pacific Oceans and Mexico and Canada, though the Progressive States of America would most likely want to open its doors to more who are seeking asylum than would the Conservative States of America. There is already a movement in California to drop out of the Union, and with an economic motor that makes it the fifth largest economy in the world, California might be able to succeed on its own. But that would be a selfish solution unless it offered the opportunity for other progressive states to join with it to create a new reality.

I truly hope that this two-country solution is never needed and that people quickly begin to join the Love and Justice movement, embrace revolutionary love and build the caring society. But if all else fails, the two-country plan is better than spending the rest of our lives in a society that alternates between a mild liberalism that lacks the courage to address the transformations needed to save the planet, and a reactionary mindset that seeks community and sense of meaning in oppressive and destructive ways. If you don't want to spend the rest of your life watching increasing degradation of the environment and power grabs by the super-wealthy to create enclaves of safety for themselves and their most loyal employees, police, and armies, all blessed by a reactionary Supreme Court and enough Senate seats to block the Environmental and Social Responsibility Amendment and the global Generosity/Marshall Plan, then either join us in remaking America into the caring society that I've outlined above, or work toward a two-country solution.

The inconveniences of the two-country option would be a small price to pay for most people feeling liberated to live by their values and ideas. And if the PSA embraces significant pro-environmental regulations that the CSA does not, that might still prove more advantageous for the environment than our current reality in which serious environmental legislation doesn't get off the ground at all.

I realize that this is a thin picture of what a two-country solution would look like. If this possibility intrigues you, fill in the details, and send them to me at *Tikkun* magazine. I hope that even this sketchy outline wakens you to the need for an urgent transcendence of politics as it has been in the United States and other Western countries for the past seventy-five years.

Before retreating to the two-country solution, let's try to advance change rapidly in the next two decades through a movement that becomes the Love and Justice Party. Please don't give up too quickly. You can help others get in touch with their own inner yearning for revolutionary love and the caring society. Even as the political world grows darker, the hunger for this kind of alternative moves closer to the surface. This is a wonderful moment to be alive, because together we can bring into actuality dreams that the human race has been nurturing for thousands of years. We are at the moment where the alternative to the successful implementation of the ideas of revolutionary love and a caring society, based on the new bottom line, would be a disaster for humanity and for all life on the planet. Choose life! Choose Love! #Love&JusticeParty

I rejoice and thank God for the opportunity I have been given to share these ideas and to stand in awe of the unfolding of the love that permeates the universe! And I invite you to use your energy, your creativity, your capacity for caring and appreciating this amazing humanity of which we are part and this planet which nurtured the evolution of the human race to create the Love and Justice Party along the lines discussed here, and to go beyond all that I have suggested and make a world of love and justice the central project of your life, thereby making it actually possible to save the life support system of Earth. When you read this book, I'll be 76 years old or older, and I have no desire to be "the leader" or anything of the sort. I want you to be one of the leaders, or at least one of the local organizers of this effort, and while I'm still alive I want to join with you and others to make it all happen. It really can! What a blessing to be alive while it is all still possible. Join me and embrace the revolutionary possibility of love as the path to global healing and transformation.

You can reach Rabbi Michael Lerner via email at TheLoveRabbi@tikkun.org. Or you can write to him at 2342 Shattuck Ave., Suite 1200, Berkeley, CA 94704 USA.

INTRODUCTION

Epigraph. Michelle Alexander, "This is the last post that I intend to . . . ," Facebook, February 18, 2016.

1. William J. Ripple, Christopher Wolf, Thomas M. Newsome, Mauro Galetti, and Mohammed Alamgir, "World Scientists' Warning to Humanity: A Second Notice," *BioScience* 67, no. 12 (December 1, 2017): 1026–28, available at https://doi.org/10.1093/biosci/bix125.

2. The Intergovernmental Panel on Climate Change (IPCC) is the United Nations body for assessing the science related to climate change. It was established by the UN's Environment Programme and the World Meteorological Organization in 1988 to provide policymakers with regular scientific assessments concerning climate change and its implications and potential future risks, as well as to put forward adaptation and mitigation strategies. The IPCC has 195 member states.

3. Editorial, "Midterm Climate Report: Partly Cloudy," *New York Times,* November 10, 2018.

4. When I use the term "the Right" I mean those who believe that the problems of the capitalist market can be solved by that market without any outside or governmental interference, while "the Left" refers to all those, both liberals and progressives, who believe that the market is not self-correcting and that there is

an important role that must be played by government, nonprofits, and the people to forbid, restrain, or transform the practices and behaviors of the capitalist market and repair the damages it inflicts on our world and on the life support system of the Earth.

5. Thomas Frank, *Listen, Liberal: Or, What Ever Happened to the Party of the People?* (Metropolitan Books/Henry Holt, 2016).

6. Arlie Russell Hochschild, *Strangers in Their Own Land* (The New Press, 2016).

7. Keeanga-Yamahtta Taylor, "Trump Was Repudiated," Jacobin website, November 7, 2018, available at https://jacobinmag.com/2018/11/2018-midterms-voter-suppression-democrats-voting-trump.

8. Robert Wuthnow, *The Left Behind: Decline and Rage in Rural America* (Princeton University Press, 2018).

CHAPTER ONE. A WORLD OF PAIN, A HUNGER FOR LOVE

1. You can keep in touch with the latest on economic inequality by reading the website inequality.org, which provides reports from Chuck Collins and others at the Institute for Policy Studies.

2. Keeanga-Yamahtta Taylor, *From #BlackLivesMatter to Black Liberation* (Haymarket Books, 2016), p. 216.

3. Ibid.

4. The Seattle Seven indictment and trial by President Richard Nixon's Justice Department was in response to an antiwar demonstration I helped organize in 1970 while serving as an assistant professor of philosophy at the University of Washington in Seattle. When hundreds of police charged the nonviolent (until that point) demonstrators, swinging their clubs and tossing tear gas at us, some of the demonstrators threw paint on the federal courthouse outside of which we were assembled and others threw rocks. The charges against us were "conspiracy to destroy federal property" ("conspiracy" because none of us had actually destroyed anything) and "using the facilities of interstate commerce with the intent to incite to riot" ("intent" because none of us had actually incited anybody to riot). During the trial the major undercover agent who had infiltrated our organization, the Seattle Liberation Front, admitted under cross-examination that the U.S. government had bought and then had brought both the paint that

had been thrown and the rocks to the site of the demonstration. With the U.S. attorney's case fallen apart, the judge declared a mistrial, and when we mounted a protest—because obviously we were going to be acquitted, as jurors confirmed in conversations with the press once the trial was declared over—the judge found a pretext to send us to prison after all, for "contempt of court." I was sent to Terminal Island Federal Penitentiary in Southern California which held many Nazis and right-wing extremists, hence the need for the protection that the Black Panthers supplied in prisons.

5. Ron Purser and David Loy, "Beyond McMindfulness," available at https://www.huffingtonpost.com/ron-purser/beyond-mcmindfulness_b_3519289 .html (published July 1, 2013). See also Ron Purser and David Loy's updated "Beyond McMindfulness" in *Tikkun*, July 27, 2017, at https://www.tikkun.org/newsite /beyond mcmindfulness.

6. Diana Butler Bass, *Grateful: The Transformative Power of Giving Thanks* (Harper One, 2018).

7. In chapter 4, I present the testimony of some people whose experience with progressive movements led them to develop negative attitudes about liberal and progressive movements and their put-downs of men and whites.

8. Carol Gilligan, *In A Different Voice* (Harvard University Press, 1982). Gilligan's books are fundamental to a revolutionary love perspective on healing our world. See especially *Joining the Resistance, The Birth of Pleasure, Why Does Patriarchy Persist?* and her foreword to Judy Y. Chu's *When Boys Become Boys.*

9. Nel Noddings, *Caring: A Relational Approach to Ethics and Moral Education* (University of California Press, 2013).

CHAPTER TWO. FEAR AND DOMINATION, OR LOVE AND GENEROSITY?

1. See Antonio Gramsci, *Selections from the Prison Notebooks* (International Publishers, 1971). Gramsci saw elites exercising their power in two overlapping systems: the overt power of economic and political institutions of the state (including armies, police, control of the economy and of most people's incomes) on the one hand, and cultural power shaping what ideas and ways of thinking were validated as legitimate through what he called "hegemony"—the cultural shaping of shared consciousness.

2. See Richard Dawkins, *The Selfish Gene* (Oxford University Press, 1976). Dawkins's ideas were given huge attention by the mainstream press and the explicators of pro-capitalist scientism. He went on to greater fame with his crusade against religion in his 2006 book *The God Delusion*.

3. See Erich Fromm, *The Anatomy of Human Destructiveness* (Holt, Rinehart & Winston, 1973). In my view, this is one of the most significant studies challenging scientism and its conservatizing influence.

4. D. W. Winnicott, *The Child, the Family and the Outside World* (Perseus Books, 1987; originally published in 1964).

5. Though most of us involved in seeking to build social transformation have long been aware of the many factors that influence the extent to which people move more toward hope or more toward fear, it was Peter Gabel who first talked about the rotation of energy from one person to another and around a whole society.

CHAPTER THREE. TOXIC SELF-BLAMING AND POWERLESSNESS

1. Michael D. Carr and Emily E. Wiemers's 2016 report for Center for Equitable Growth available at https://equitablegrowth.org/working-papers/the-decline-in-lifetime-earnings-mobility-in-the-u-s-evidence-from-survey-linked-administrative-data.

2. For details of some of the quantitative research, see my book *Surplus Powerlessness: The Psychodynamics of Everyday Life . . . and the Psychology of Individual and Social Transformation* (Humanities Press International, 1991).

3. Richard Sennett and Jonathan Cobb, *The Hidden Injuries of Class* (W. W. Norton, 1973).

CHAPTER FOUR. TO CHANGE A SOCIETY, YOU MUST RESPECT ITS PEOPLE

1. After Rosh Hashanah services in 2016, my congregation marched to the nearest Wells Fargo bank to protest its funding of the Dakota pipeline, and *Tikkun* magazine sent out a list of all other banks funding that environmental disaster.

2. Kimberlé Crenshaw's work is built on a conversation initiated by the Combahee River Collection, and her insight has been expanded by Patricia Hill Collins.

3. Read more about this in my book *The Socialism of Fools: Anti-Semitism on the Left* (Tikkun Books, 1991).

4. To understand those fascist tendencies, and how they grow even when liberal Democrats are in power, see Henry Giroux's article on the Tikkun website at https://www.tikkun.org/nextgen/the-politics-of-neoliberal-fascism, as well as his book *American Nightmare: Facing the Challenge of Fascism* (City Lights Books, 2018) and Jason Stanley's *How Fascism Works* (Random House, 2018).

CHAPTER FIVE. OVERCOMING THE DICTATORSHIP OF THE CAPITALIST MARKETPLACE

1. From verbal statements to author by Cat Zavis.

2. The Network of Spiritual Progressives has an online training program, which you can learn about at www.spiritualprogressives.org/training.

3. At Tikkun's Network of Spiritual Progressives, www.spiritualprogressives.org, we have sample leaflets that can be modified to fit a specific profession. Email me for sample leaflets, at rabbilerner.tikkun@gmail.com.

4. The living wage calculator is updated at http://livingwage.mit.edu/pages/about.

5. It is worth studying the work of Riane Eisler and attending her seminars or trainings at the Center for Partnership Studies.

6. This quote from Riane Eisler appears in her article "Partnerism," *Tikkun* 33:3 (Summer 2018), emphasis added. Among her many important contributions to the program of revolutionary love presented in this manifesto are *Tomorrow's Children*, *The Power of Partnership*, and *The Real Wealth of Nations*.

7. Charles Eisenstein, *Sacred Economics* (North Atlantic Books, 2011).

8. For more of Gar Alperovitz's approach to the new economy, see "Democratizing the Economy for a New Progressive Era," *Tikkun* 27:4 (2012): 47–48. Quote is from Alperovitz's website, http://www.pluralistcommonwealth.org/democratized-ownership-forms.html.

9. Information about the Next System Project is available at https://thenextsystem.org.

10. Physicians for a National Health Plan delineates such a plan at pnhp.org.

CHAPTER SIX. MAJOR INSTITUTIONAL CHANGES FOR
BUILDING A LOVE AND JUSTICE MOVEMENT

1. To understand why this is so, I recommend reading the important books by Michael Edwards, *Small Change: Why Business Won't Save the World;* Jerry Mander, *The Capitalism Papers;* and Michael Sandel, *What Money Can't Buy.*

2. For more on the global Generosity/Marshall Plan, go to www .spiritualprogressives.org.gmp.

Bass, Diana Butler. *Grateful: The Transformative Power of Giving Thanks*. Harper One, 2018.

Bauman, Zygmunt. *Wasted Lives: Modernity and its Outcasts*. Polity Press, 2004.

Bauman, Zygmunt, and Carlo Bordoni. *Liquid Love: On the Frailty of Human Bonds*. Polity Press, 2003.

———. *State of Crisis*. Polity Press, 2014.

Becker, Ernest. *The Denial of Death*. Simon and Schuster, 1973.

Benhabib, Seyla. *Exile, Statelessness, and Migration*. Princeton University Press, 2018.

Benjamin, Jessica. *Beyond Doer and Done To: Recognition Theory, Intersubjectivity and the Third*. Routledge, 2017.

———. *The Bonds of Love*. Penguin Random House, 1988.

Brueggemann, John. *Rich, Free, and Miserable: The Failure of Success in America*. Rowman and Littlefield, 2010.

Brueggemann, Walter. *Celebrating Abundance*. Westminster John Knox Press, 2017.

———. *Sabbath as Resistance: Saying No to the Culture of Now*. Westminster John Knox Press, 2014.

———. *The Word Militant: Preaching a Decentering World*. Fortress Press, 2007.

Chu, Judy Y. *When Boys Become Boys: Development, Relationships, and Masculinity*. New York University Press, 2014.

Coates, Ta-Nehisi. *We Were Eight Years in Power*. Penguin Random House, 2017.

Collins, Chuck. *Born on Third Base*. Chelsea Green Publishing, 2016.

Cone, James H. *The Cross and the Lynching Tree*. Orbis Books, 2011.

Cox, Harvey. *The Market as God*. Harvard University Press, 2016.

Crenshaw, Kimberlé, Luke Charles Harris, and George Lipsitz. *The Race Track: Understanding and Challenging Structural Racism*. The New Press, 2018.

Crenshaw, Kimberlé, Cornel West, Neil Gotanda, Gary Peller, and Kendall Thomas, eds. *Critical Race Theory: The Key Writings That Formed the Movement*. The New Press, 1995.

Dawkins, Richard. *The God Delusion*. Bantam Press, 2006.

———. *The Selfish Gene*. Oxford University Press, 1976.

Dear, John. *Living Peace: A Spirituality of Contemplation and Action*. Doubleday, 2001.

Dorrien, Gary. *Breaking White Supremacy*. Yale University Press, 2018.

Duhm, Dieter. *The Sacred Matrix*. Verlag Meiga Publishers, 2007.

Dyson, Michael Eric. *Tears We Cannot Stop: A Sermon to White America*. St. Martin's Press, 2017.

Edwards, Michael. *Small Change: Why Business Won't Save the World*. Berrett-Koehler Publishers, 2010.

Edwards, Michael A., and Stephen G. Post, eds. *Spiritual Activism in Dialogue with Social Science*. Unlimited Love Press, 2008.

Eisenstein, Charles. *Sacred Economics*. North Atlantic Books, 2011.

Eisler, Riane. *The Power of Partnership*. New World Library, 2002.

———. *The Real Wealth of Nations*. Berrett-Koehler Publishers, 2007.

———. *Tomorrow's Children: A Blueprint for Partnership Education for the 21st Century*. Westview Press, 2000.

Essed, Philomena, and David Theo Goldberg, eds. *Race Critical Theories*. Blackwell Publishers, 2002.

Frank, Robert H. *Success and Luck: Good Fortune and the Myth of Meritocracy*. Princeton University Press, 2016.

Frank, Thomas. *Listen, Liberal: Or, What Ever Happened to the Party of the People?* Metropolitan Books/Henry Holt, 2016.

Fraser, Steve. *Class Matters*. Yale University Press, 2018.

Fromm, Erich. *The Anatomy of Human Destructiveness*. Holt, Rinehart and Winston, 1973.

Gabel, Peter. *Another Way of Seeing: Essays on Transforming Law, Politics and Culture*. Quid Pro LLC, 2013.

———. *The Desire for Mutual Recognition*. Routledge, 2018.

Gilligan, Carol. *The Birth of Pleasure: A New Map of Love*. Penguin Random House, 2003.

———. *In a Different Voice*. Harvard University Press, 1982.

———. *Joining the Resistance*. Polity Books, 2011.

Gilligan, Carol, and Naomi Snider. *Why Does Patriarchy Persist?* Polity Books, 2018.

Giroux, Henry. *American Nightmare: Facing the Challenge of Fascism*. City Lights Books, 2018.

———. *Neoliberalism's War on Higher Education*. Haymarket Books, 2013.

———. *On Critical Pedagogy*. Continuum, 2011.

Gopin, Marc. *Healing the Heart of Conflict*. Rodale, 2004.

Gorz, Andre. *Strategy for Labor: A Radical Proposal*. Beacon, 1968.

Graeber, David. *Bullshit Jobs: A Theory*. Simon and Schuster, 2018.

Gramsci, Antonio. *Selections from the Prison Notebooks*. International Publishers, 1971.

Harari, Yuval Noah. *Homo Deus: A Brief History of Tomorrow*. Harper, 2016.

Haught, John F. *The New Cosmic Story*. Yale University Press, 2017.

Heschel, Abraham Joshua. *The Prophets*. Harper and Row, 1962.

———. *The Sabbath*. FSG Classics, 2005.

———. *Who Is Man?* Stanford University Press, 1965.

Hochschild, Arlie Russell. "Male Trouble." *The New York Review of Books*, December 20, 2018, pp. 13–15.

———. *Strangers in Their Own Land*. The New Press, 2016.

King, Martin Luther, Jr. *The Essential Writings of Martin Luther King, Jr*. Harper and Row, 1986.

Klein, Naomi. *No Is Not Enough*. Haymarket Books, 2017.

Lamont, Anne. *Almost Everything: Notes on Hope*. Riverhead Books, 2018.

Lerner, Michael. *The Left Hand of God*. HarperSanFrancisco, 2006.

———. *The Socialism of Fools: Anti-Semitism on the Left*. Tikkun Books, 1991.

———. *Surplus Powerlessness: The Psychodynamics of Everyday Life . . . and the Psychology of Individual and Social Transformation*. Humanities Press International, 1991.

Lichtman, Richard. *The Production of Desire: The Integration of Psychoanalysis into Marxist Theory*. The Free Press, 1982.

Mander, Jerry. *The Capitalism Papers*. Counterpoint Press, 2012.

May, Rollo. *Love and Will*. W. W. Norton, 1969.

Noddings, Nel. *Caring: A Relational Approach to Ethics and Moral Education*. University of California Press, 2013.

Palast, Greg. *The Best Democracy Money Can Buy: A Tale of Billionaires & Ballot Bandits*. Seven Stories Press, 2016.

Polakow-Suransky, Sasha. *Go Back Where You Came From: The Backlash against Immigration and the Fate of Western Democracy*. Nation Books, 2017.

Pope Francis, *Laudato Si* (On Care for Our Common Home), Our Sunday Visitor, 2015.

Ripple, William J., Christopher Wolf, Thomas M. Newsome, Mauro Galetti, and Mohammed Alamgir. "World Scientists' Warning to Humanity: A Second Notice," *BioScience* 67: 12 (December 1, 2017).

Rosenberg, Marshall B. *Speak Peace in a World of Conflict*. PuddleDancer Press, 2005.

Saade, Chris. *Second Wave Spirituality*. North Atlantic Books, 2014.

Safi, Omid. *Radical Love: Teachings from the Islamic Mystical Tradition*. Yale University Press, 2018.

Sandel, Michael J. *What Money Can't Buy*. Farrar, Straus and Giroux (reprint), 2013.

Sennett, Richard. *Together: The Rituals, Pleasures and Politics of Cooperation*. Yale University Press, 2012.

Sennett, Richard, and Jonathan Cobb. *The Hidden Injuries of Class*. W. W. Norton, 1973.

Solnit, Rebecca. *Hope in the Dark*. Haymarket Books, 2016.

Stanley, Jason. *How Fascism Works*. Random House, 2018.

Tarnas, Richard. *Cosmos and Psyche*. Viking, 2006.

Taylor, Charles. *A Secular Age*. Harvard University Press, 2007.

Taylor, Keeanga-Yamahtta. *From #BlackLivesMatter To Black Liberation*. Haymarket Books, 2016.

Wallace-Wells, David. *The Uninhabitable Earth: Life After Warming*. Penguin Random House, 2019.

Wallach, Michael A., and Lise Wallach. *Psychology's Sanction for Selfishness*. W. H. Freeman, 1983.

Winnicott, D. W. *The Child, the Family and the Outside World*. Perseus Books, 1987.

Wuthnow, Robert. *The Left Behind: Decline and Rage in Rural America*. Princeton University Press, 2018.

Bibliography

Adler, Rachel, 112
affirmative action programs, 10–11, 37
African Americans: affirmative action
    and, 37; assaults on and murders of,
    14, 37, 38, 124, 137, 183; #BlackLives-
    Matter, 37; class differences among,
    131; discrimination against, 124; and
    Jim Crow, 183; and mass incarcera-
    tion, 113; as Others in right-wing
    churches, 115; and the police, 37, 124,
    132, 224–25; reparations for, 190; and
    slavery, 35–36, 183, 190, 194, 243; as
    "special interest" in right-wing
    discourse, 118. *See also* Black Church;
    civil rights movement; people of
    color; racism
African Methodist Episcopal Church, 113
ageism: education and dismantling of,
    183; Love and Justice movement as
    undermining, 28, 175; percentage of
    voters who are deeply ageist, 100;
    prophetic empathy tribes teaching
    the systemic nature of, 157
aging, care for the, 189

agriculture, 86, 233, 235
Alexander, Michelle, 1
Allende, Salvador, 74–75
"All Power to the Imagination," 144, 154,
    164
Alperovitz, Gar, "The Pluralistic
    Commonwealth," 179
altruism, 63, 187
America First ideology, 196
American Baptist Church, 113
Anglican Church, 112
anti-Semitism: current-day violence and
    murder, 38, 124–25, 137; dismantling
    of, 28, 175, 183, 189–90; fascist
    demonstrations of, 136; the Holo-
    caust, 22, 23, 129–30, 136–37, 183;
    immigrants and, 195; percentage of
    voters who are deeply anti-Semitic,
    100; in religious communities and
    secular movements, 109; in
    right-wing discourse, 101, 115,
    117–18; of right-wing voters, as
    assumed by the Left, 10; "stealing
    Christmas," 110. *See also* Jews

antiwar movements: coffeehouses near military bases, 160; creative nonviolence in, 137; Democratic Party and lack of understanding of, 142; and fear of being perceived as "weak," 60; key role of churches and synagogues in, 112; and Seattle Seven trial, 38, 250–51n4

Arabs, as immigrants, 195

Arendt, Hannah, 23

Asians: acting in solidarity with, 189–90; as immigrants, prejudice against, 183

asylum seekers, Trump administration policy of abuse of, 44, 73–74, 195–96. *See also* immigration and immigrants; refugees

atheists, 59, 153

attachment theory, 69–70

Barber, William, 112

Bass, Diana Butler, 57

Beauvoir, Simone de, 71

Bend the Arc, 112

Benjamin, Medea, 7

bigotry. *See* discrimination and bigotry; respect for the shared humanity of all people

birth control, 171

Black Church, 38, 112

#BlackLivesMatter, 37

Blackmon, Traci, 112

Black Panther party, 38, 120, 250–51n4

blaming. *See* identity politics—blaming and shaming; self-blame

blended families, 171

"Blue wave" (2018 midterms), 12–13, 25, 122

Bonhoeffer, Dietrich, 57

bourgeoisie, 220

British Labour Party, 16

Buddhist mindfulness, 55

Buddhists, as Others, 118

capitalism: overview, 28; Anglo-American legal system designed to protect, 220–21; bourgeoisie, 220; "common sense" of, 26, 45, 80, 142–43; co-optive power of, 146–47; "dictatorship of the capitalist marketplace," 142–43; disaster capitalism, 42; economic growth, belief in, 14, 200; funding by the Left and perpetuation of, 8–10; meritocracy as myth in, 80–81, 83–85, 93, 156–57, 221; neoliberalism, 54–55, 86, 159, 165, 199–200; as not self-regulating, 87; old bottom line, 49–50, 51, 146–47, 152; selfishness as ethos of, 50–51, 53–54, 59, 89–90, 94, 98, 200; values of, as hated by the Right, 110–11, 115–16, 118. *See also* economic inequality; fear and domination worldview; materialist reductionist view; post-socialism (socialism of the heart/spiritual socialism); scientism

—COMPETITIVE MARKETPLACE: and blaming of "special interests"/Others, 118; and Christmas as "stolen," 110–11; as "common sense," 142–43; and fear vs. love worldview, 73; Great Deprivation and, 34–39, 54, 61, 125, 144; as replacing social solidarity, 82; self-blame as produced by system of, 96, 104; systemic practices of elites to divide the workforce in, 24; top income earners and illusion of resistance to, 54; viewed as preexisting human condition, 67

—CONSUMERISM: as capitalist indoctrination, 53; futurist imagining of, 234, 235–37; income inequality and market forces, 173–74; and mid-twentieth-century period of wealth expansion, 84; paths to distancing oneself from, 178; self-fulfillment in consumption as message of, 80

—"REALISTIC" IDEAS AND POLICIES OF: change in the world as dependent on challenges to, 23–24, 25, 154; as de facto continuation of path towards destruction, 26, 29; the ESRA and, 199–200, 209–10; liberal funders not creating systematic challenge to, 10; mocking of ethical choices, 98; reminders to each other not to be swayed by, 239; social conditioning to adhere to, 50, 104

carbon emissions, 7–8, 216–17

care investment, 178

Caring Society—Caring for Each Other and Caring for the Earth: framing of social values for, 105–6; as goal of revolutionary love, 2, 42–43; and hope for the future, 14–15, 229, 241; inner blocks to belief in possibility of, 156; two-country solution as alternative to, 243–46; what can be done now to bring about, 241–47. *See also* Love and Justice movement; new bottom line; program proposals for the caring society; prophetic empathy; revolutionary love

Catholic Church, 112, 220

Catholic Worker movement, 112

Center for Equitable Growth, 84, 85

Chanukah, 110–11

Charlottesville, VA fascist demonstration, 136

childbirth rates, reduction of, 4

childrearing: adults turning to children for their missing emotional connection, 90–93; and a partnership society, 174–75, 253nn5–6; attachment theory, 69; and bigoted religious communities, 109; and bigoted systems, rejection of, 175; and democratization of the economy, 181; and fear vs. love worldviews, 69–70, 71–72, 174–75; feminism and, 62; and intervening appropriately on behalf of those in need, 221; revolutionary love and, 63; and self-blame, development of, 92–94, 104; slaveholders and, 36; and workweek reductions, 173; yearning for respect from children, 96. *See also* education; families

China, 56, 118, 146, 183, 195, 211

Chittister, Joan, 112, 239

choice: constrained, and self-blame, 95–96, 220; and "dictatorship of the capitalist marketplace," 142; taking personal responsibility for, 98

Christians: Evangelicals, 29, 109, 218–19; the global Generosity Plan and appeal to, 218–19; as Others in Muslim countries, 118; and prophetic empathy tribe outreach to red states, 160. *See also* religion

Christmas, as "stolen," 110–11

Citizens United decision, 86, 202, 204–5

civil rights movement: and external vs. internal change, 36–37; meritocracy myth and, 81; psychological and spiritual meaning needs and, 143; as reawakening sense of need for collective struggles, 80; and unity of

civil rights movement *(continued)*
    black and white people together, 134.
    See also King, Martin Luther Jr.
class action suits, denied to employees, 86
classism: and cross-race alliances, 190; as
    cultural system, 38–39; education
    and dismantling of, 182, 183, 184;
    failure of the Democratic Party to
    address, 11; hidden injuries of, 94;
    Love and Justice movement as
    undermining, 28, 175; and meritoc-
    racy as fantasy, 80–81, 83–85, 93,
    156–57, 221; percentage of voters who
    are deeply classist, 100; prophetic
    empathy tribes teaching about, 157;
    self-blaming and, 99; universalist
    vision in solidarity against, 38–39.
    See also economic inequality; identity
    politics— and class oppression;
    ruling elites; self-blame
class societies: pessimism as intrinsic to,
    15; systemic practices and conscious-
    ness fostered by, 24; violence as
    intrinsic to, 34, 35. *See also* middle
    income people; patriarchal societies;
    upper middle class people; working
    class people
Clean Air Act, 6
climate change. *See under* environmental
    crisis
Clinton, Bill: dismantling of financial
    institution regulations, 87; failure to
    address economic inequality, 11–12;
    and mass incarceration, 113; and
    materialist reductionist view, 17; as
    pro-corporate, 12, 86
Clinton, Hillary: "basket of deplorables,"
    121; and sexism, 10
Cobb, Jonathan, 94
Code Pink movement, 7

Coffin, William Sloan, 112
colleges. *See* universities and colleges
Collins, Chuck, 250n1
colonialism, European, 35–36, 79, 82–83,
    130
the Commons: definition of, 178;
    enclosure of, 81; protection of, 178
"common sense" of capitalist societies,
    26, 45, 80, 142–43
communism. *See* socialist and communist
    movements and systems
communities: activities offered in, 158;
    celebratory gatherings of empathy
    tribes, 158; changes in, as foundation
    for post-capitalist order, 14; decision
    making by, 16; and democratization
    of the economy, 179, 180; family
    support groups in, 158, 172; and global
    Generosity Plan/Marshall Plan,
    211–12; Green New Deal support for, 6;
    "of meaning," 172; security commit-
    tees and community forces, 191;
    workplace support groups in, 162–63
compassion: as central to revolutionary
    love, 56, 238; and crime, 222;
    government as manifestation of,
    148–49; as guiding principle in a
    caring society, 221–22; and the new
    bottom line, 51–52; for ourselves and
    others, 107; and the penal system,
    224; personal responsibility for, 58;
    slavery and lack of, 36; for those with
    distorted consciousness, 42, 184. *See
    also* respect for the shared humanity
    of all people
competitive marketplace. *See under*
    capitalism
Cone, James, 112
Congress, U.S., and regulation of money
    in politics, 205

consciousness: and ethos of respect, impact of, 58; as manifesting freedom and choice, 47; and qualitative research, 48; as unable to be reduced to deterministic laws, 46–47, 48–49. *See also* fear and domination worldview; love and generosity worldview

—TRANSFORMATION OF: as central idea for creation of the caring society, 149, 151, 158, 161; consciousness-raising meetings, 164; critical mass of, and appeal to people outside the Left, 159; ongoing effort required for, 161; ongoing openness to, 238; paths to, 238; prophetic empathy tribes and outreach for, 158; of selfishness and endless consumption, 200; social change movements as fostering, 58; the workplace and, 164

conservatism. *See* neoliberalism

Constitution, U.S.: amendments needed to save the environment, 13; Electoral College, 10, 205; elitism and fear of the majority in the authors of, 10; ESRA as overriding, 209; Trump and violation of separation of powers, 22. *See also* Environmental and Social Responsibility Amendment (ESRA); government; legal system; voting rights

consumerism. *See under* capitalism

corporations: defeat of climate change laws, 7–8; democratization of, 168; as discrediting fundamental change, 142–43; ESRA structuring of boards and charters, 203–4, 206–8, 209; fiduciary responsibilities to investors, 207–8; moving or closing businesses to maintain political

control, 201, 208; nationalization of, 208; personhood of, 202, 203; politicians' support for, 201; Supreme Court ruling that money in politics is free speech, 86, 202, 204–5; "triple bottom line," 207, 254n1. *See also* capitalism; Environmental and Social Responsibility Amendment (ESRA)

correctives needed for the Left to be more successful: overview, 100–101, 157; overcoming religiophobia (leftist disdain for religion and spirituality), 108, 109, 111–15; prophetic empathy tribes to teach how to engage in, 154–61; respect for the shared humanity of all people, 101–8, 116, 123, 133–34, 136–37. *See also* identity politics; institutional changes for building a Love and Justice movement; program proposals for the caring society

courts: ESRA as overriding, 209; transformation of, 181, 222–23. *See also* legal system; Supreme Court, U.S.

creative nonviolence, 137

Crenshaw, Kimberlé, 127, 252n2

crime: the caring society and reduction of, 222, 224; decriminalization of personal behavior not harming others, 224; hate crimes, rise of, 101–2. *See also* drugs; homeland security— and terrorism; legal system; violence

criminal justice system. *See* legal system

cultural hegemony, 66–68, 81, 251n1

cultural systems, 35–39, 80, 105

Dalai Lama, 239

Dawkins, Richard, *The Selfish Gene*, 68, 252n2

death instinct, 68

Declaration on the Rights of Indigenous Peoples, UN, 7

democracy: corporate power as subverting, 201–2; education for participation in, 185; futurist imagining of, 231–32; neoliberalism as barrier to, 54–55; U.S. Senate as barrier to, 243. *See also* democratization

Democratic Party: apologizing for nonsupport of working people's needs, 159; business as usual of, 12–14; campaigning on the wrong messages, 10; criticized as "weak" for caring about progressive ideas, 59–61; economic security and human rights as focus of, 141; elite loyalties of, 8; failure to address environmental problems, 12; failure to address fairness and economic inequality, 10–12, 87; failure to address psychological and spiritual meaning needs, 18, 20–21, 141–42, 143–44, 150, 227; failure to address racism, 11, 37; failure to campaign on a caring society, 151; funding strategies of, 8–10; Green New Deal and, 199; Love and Justice Party presence within, 227; and materialist reductionist discourse, 18, 87, 143; neoliberalism and, 54–55, 86, 159, 165, 199–200; New Democrats, 86; partial reforms of, 143, 243; primaries of, as opportunity to present progressive ideas, 227; respect for the shared humanity of all people, need for, 102, 135, 159; split of: pro-corporate vs. a more progressive force, 12–14, 20–21. *See also* correctives needed for the Left to be more successful

—ELECTIONS: 2010 midterms, 151; 2016 presidential, 10, 18, 28, 87–88, 109, 122–23; 2018 midterms ("Blue wave"), 12–13, 25, 122

—ELECTION OF 2020: and blaming and shaming, effects of, 145; and the ESRA, 209–10; and the global Generosity Plan, 211; and hope for meaningful change, 20–21; and lack of meaningful change, 243; and Love and Justice movement, 150; and progressive (Sanders-Warren) wing, 149–50; and the resistance movement, 76; and respect for the shared humanity of all people, 102, 135

Democratic Socialists of America, 15, 16

democratization: of corporations and institutions, 168; post-socialism and, 177. *See also* economic democratization

depression. *See* psychological depression

disabilities, persons with, prejudice against, 175

disaster capitalism, 42

Disciples of Christ, 113

discrimination and bigotry: as continuing, 124–25; family support and rejection of, 175; in hiring and pay, end of, 167; laws against, 124; legacy of, in liberal and progressive movements, 109. *See also* ageism; anti-Semitism; bigotry; classism; homophobia; Islamophobia; Others; racism; respect for the shared humanity of all people; sexism; xenophobia

district attorneys and assistants, 223

diversity, religious diversity ignored, 111

divorce, 90, 172

domination. *See* fear and domination worldview

Dreamers, 216

drugs: addiction treatment, 224; decriminalization of recreational, 224; overdose deaths, 127, 132

Earth. *See* environmental crisis; nature, experiences of

Eastern Europeans, as immigrants, 183

economic democratization: marketplace restrictions proposed, 180–81; measurement of productivity via human capacity development and care investment, 177–78; post-socialism and, 16–17; program proposals for transition to a caring economy, 173, 177–82; psychological and spiritual meaning needs as essential to, 17; socialist and communist systems and lack of, 15–16, 177, 180; worker cooperation, 179–80. *See also* Environmental and Social Responsibility Amendment (ESRA); Green New Deal; production of goods and services; work and the workplace

economic growth, 14, 200

economic inequality: overview of statistics, 175; as "common sense" of capitalism, 142–43; cross-race and cross-class alliances to challenge, 190; discretionary income and consumer goods market, 173–74; and economic planning for a caring society, 180; and elite loyalties of Democratic Party, 8; excessive executive pay and bonuses, 85, 170; failure of Democratic Party to address, 11–12; family support and decrease of, 175; futurist imagining of wealth redistribution, 233–34; global loan forgiveness, 213; and life expectancy, 33; lifetime earning

mobility, decline of, 84; as masked by "change yourself and the world will be changed" mentality, 54; maximum wage rules, 170, 188, 216–17; minimum wage erosion and, 85; and origins of capitalism, 220; overtime standards and, 85; and public policies and social norms of mid-twentieth century vs. current era, 85; wealth inequality, 33; website on, 250n1; worldwide, 33. *See also* old bottom line; self-blame

education: anti-oppression curriculum in, 11, 37; attainment in, and nature experiences, 193; of boys, 184; Christian colleges funded by the Right, 9; as discrediting the idea of fundamental change, 142–43; ESRA curriculum requirements, 204, 208; and fear vs. love worldviews, 72; futurist imagining of, 235–36; of girls, 184, 213; for health care practitioners, 187–88; level of attainment of, and decline in upward mobility, 84; liberal colleges and lack of challenge to capitalist worldview, 9–10; for prison inmates and ex-inmates, 224; privatization of, 165; program proposals re-envisioning, 182–87; public complaints about paying for Others, 187; and racism, dismantling, 182, 183, 189–90, 191; restorative justice and, 191; and social wealth, measurement of, 177–78; taxes and funding for, 177–78, 182, 187, 191; teacher salaries, 182; Trump administration's dismantling of public, 22. *See also* childrearing; universities and colleges

Edwards, Michael, *Small Change: Why Business Won't Save the World*, 254n1

Eisenstein, Charles, *Sacred Economics*, 178
Eisler, Riane, 253nn5–6; Center for
    Partnership Studies, 177–78; *The
    Chalice and the Blade*, 174
elections: media prime time requirement
    for debates, 205; public funding of,
    205; removal of money from, 201,
    203, 204–5. *See also* Democratic
    Party– elections; voting rights
Electoral College, 10; abolishment of, 205
elitism: of authors of the U.S. Constitu-
    tion, 10; Democrats perceived as
    elites, 8; of the Left, 24, 100–101. *See
    also* classism; correctives needed for
    the Left to be more successful;
    identity politics; ruling elites
empathy, development of: education and,
    182, 183; Love and Justice movement
    and, 28. *See also* compassion;
    prophetic empathy
empirical approach, as foundation of
    scientific inquiry, 45. *See also* radical
    empiricism
energy. *See* fossil fuels; renewable
    energy
environmental and social responsibility:
    and economic planning for a caring
    society, 178, 180; futurist imagining
    of, 234–37
Environmental and Social Responsibility
    Amendment (ESRA): governmental
    contract requirements, 167–68; labor
    union support in, 166–67; and need
    to reach out to religious people, 114;
    and production of goods, 178–79;
    program proposals for, 199–210;
    public funding of elections, 205. *See
    also* environmental crisis
environmental crisis: extinction illness,
    21–22, 26, 74, 154, 202; futurist

imagining of mourning for losses due
    to, 237; goals for change, 4; govern-
    ment contracts supporting preven-
    tions of, 167–68; "growth economy"
    as contributor to, 200; habitat loss,
    199; and mass global migration, 215;
    Pope Francis's statement on, 215;
    scientists' statements on seriousness
    of, 3–4, 200, 249n2; Trump adminis-
    tration dismantling laws to prevent,
    22; unemployment and, 170, 209;
    wildlife deaths since 1970, 199. *See
    also* environmental and social
    responsibility; Environmental and
    Social Responsibility Amendment
    (ESRA); nature, experiences of; new
    bottom line
—CLIMATE CHANGE: denial of, 4; natural
    disasters resulting from, 177;
    Rightwing dismissal of science of,
    46; scientist statements on serious-
    ness of, 3–4, 200, 249n2; temperature
    rise, effects of, 199
Environmental Protection Agency (EPA),
    and Green New Deal, 6
Episcopal Church, 112
equality, "equal under the law," 82
Equal Rights Amendment (ERA), 198
ESRA. *See* Environmental and Social
    Responsibility Amendment
ethics: as dismissed by scientism, 46;
    feminist ethic of care, 62–63; and
    hope for the future, 229; methodo-
    logical principle of, 46; mocked as
    "idealistic" and "unrealistic," 98
Europe: colonialism of, 35–36, 79, 82–83,
    130; Others in, 117–18; re-emergence
    of fascistic movements in, 15. *See also*
    neoliberalism; socialist and
    communist movements and systems

—AND THE RISE OF NAZISM: and the
danger of silent "good people," 76,
136–37; the Holocaust, 22, 23,
129–30, 136–37, 183; pre-Holocaust,
and psychotherapy, 22, 23; and
rationality of fear and dominance
worldview, 74–75
evolution, racism justified through, 68
extinction illness, 21–22, 26, 74, 154, 202

Fair Deal, 147
fair wages, feudal religious requirement
for, 220
families: definition of, as inclusive,
171–72; importance of, to LGBTQ
people, 150; investment in, as
measure of social wealth, 177–78;
love within, revolutionary love as
encompassing, 40, 43; and the
partnership society, 174–75,
253nn5–6; program proposals for
support of, 162–63, 171–77, 189; the
Right's claim to support of, 171;
separation of, as Trump administration policy, 44, 73–74, 195–96. See also
childrearing; education; friendships;
marriage; personal love relationships; personal solutions; single
people
—DYSFUNCTION OF: competitive
marketplace dynamics and, 28, 83,
95–96, 105, 117, 136, 171; prophetic
empathy tribes teaching the systemic
nature of, 157; and self-blame,
development of, 92–94, 104. See also
economic inequality; psychological
and spiritual meaning needs
fascism: confrontation of, 136–37; cruelty
of, utilized to discredit social change,
79; re-emergence of, 15, 135, 253n4.

See also Europe— and the rise of
Nazism; Right, the
fear and domination worldview:
overview, 65–66; childrearing and,
69–70, 71–72, 174–75; countering the
social conditioning of, 104–5; as
cultural hegemony supporting the
ruling elites, 66–68, 251n1; framing
of events and, 76–78; global
Generosity Plan/Marshall Plan as
alternative to, 210, 211; and homeland security, 66, 210; vs. love and
generosity worldview, as continuum,
70–75; "necessity and inevitability
of", as scientism, 67–68, 252nn2–3; at
personal level, 65–66; as rational
choice in some situations, 74–75;
religion and, 66–67; and self-blame
dynamic, 94–95; social energy as
pushing towards fear or towards love,
72, 75–78, 79–80, 153–54, 238, 252n5;
as winning out instead of love and
justice, 242–43. See also instrumen-
tal/utilitarian worldview; love and
generosity worldview
feminism: as arising from a tiny group,
25; as belying scientism, 48;
"bourgeois feminism," 61–62;
care-oriented/ethic of care, 61–64;
and consciousness-raising groups,
164; decrease of self-blame and, 97,
98–99; and discourse of psychological and spiritual meaning needs,
143–44; legacy of bigotry in, 109;
meritocracy myth and token hires
due to, 81; as most significant
revolution, 144; the Right's defining
as "special interest," 118; the Right's
refusal to see the humanity of
women, 101; and self-blame as a

feminism *(continued)*
　　systemic problem, 157; shortcomings
　　of, 25; taken seriously, as next stage
　　of healing, 64. *See also* gender;
　　sexism; women
feudalism, 82, 220
financial institutions, 87, 207, 252n1
financial transactions, tax on, 216
First Amendment fundamentalism, 192
Forbes, James, 112
foreign policy. *See* global Generosity Plan/
　　Marshall Plan; homeland security
fossil fuels: phaseouts of, 5, 6, 7, 208;
　　Standing Rock protest against Dakota
　　pipeline, 40, 102, 252n1; subsidies
　　for, ending, 5
Fourth of July, reconstructed as global
　　Interdependence Day, 194–97
Frankfort School of Critical Theory, 23
Frank, Thomas, *Listen, Liberal*, 8
fraternity. *See* social solidarity
freedom: as belying scientism, 47–49; as
　　constrained by capitalism, 81,
　　220–21; as constrained by societal
　　norms, 47; negative, and Anglo-
　　American legal system, 220–21;
　　positive, and a caring and coopera-
　　tive legal system, 221
free trade. *See* trade agreements
Freud, Sigmund, 23, 68, 71
Friedman, Thomas, 199–200
friendships: difficulties in sustaining
　　under global capitalism, 28, 83, 95,
　　105, 117; and selfishness, 89–90
Fromm, Erich, 23; *The Anatomy of Human
　　Destructiveness*, 68, 252n3
funding: of education, 182, 187, 191; of
　　education, as measure of social
　　wealth, 177–78; for global Generosity
　　Plan/Marshall Plan, 211, 212, 213,

216–17; of inventions to support the
　　new bottom line, 163; the Left and
　　inept strategies for, 8–10; for Love
　　and Justice movement, 161, 242;
　　public funding of elections, 205; the
　　Right and strategies for, 8–9; of
　　Tikkun and the Network of Spiritual
　　Progressives, 241. *See also* repara-
　　tions; taxes
futurist imaginings: overview, 228,
　　230–31; dystopian visions as not
　　inevitable, 228–30
—A REPORT FROM THE NEXT CENTURY:
　　environmental responsibility,
　　234–37; government, 231–32;
　　international solidarity, goodbye to
　　all borders, and unity of all being,
　　237; Jubilee— redistribution of
　　wealth, 233–34

Gabel, Peter, 51, 252n5
Galea, Sandro, 33
Gandhi, Mahatma, 41, 112
gender: as both a lived experience and a
　　social construct, 64; and caring
　　viewed as "weak" and devalued,
　　59–64, 174; education and challeng-
　　ing of assumptions of, 184; nonbi-
　　nary/non-gender-conforming
　　people, 62, 64; payment for house-
　　work and hierarchical relations of,
　　174; transgender people, 64, 124, 126,
　　183. *See also* sexism
Gilligan, Carol, 62, 63, 251n8
Ginsberg, Allen, 137
Giroux, Henry, 253n4
Glasmeier, Amy K., 166
global Generosity Plan/Marshall Plan:
　　futurist imagining of, 237; and
　　homeland security, 215–17; imple-

mentation of, 212, 217–18, 241; and
need to reach out to religious people,
114; program proposals for, 210–19;
rural communities as beneficiaries
of, 160; as term, 211; website for more
information on, 254n2

global Interdependence Day, Fourth of
July reconstructed into, 194–97

globalization of selfishness (ethos of
capitalism), 50–51, 53–54, 59, 89–90,
94, 98, 200

global South and East, Western society's
role in undermining, 84, 183,
190, 237

"God-ing", revolutionary love as, 43

Gorz, Andre, *Strategy for Labor*, 145

government: bureaucracy as deliberate
impediment to caring society, 148;
contracts from, environmental and
social responsibility in, 167–68;
futurist imagining of, 231–32, 236;
legal system emergence to protect
overreach of, 220–21; Republican
Party goal to dismantle, 147;
separation of church and science and,
192–93; the U.S. Senate as undemocratic, 243; as vehicle for the people
to create the caring society, 148–49.
See also Caring Society—Caring for
Each Other and Caring for the Earth;
Constitution, U.S.; elections;
Environmental and Social Responsibility Amendment (ESRA); Green
New Deal; homeland security; legal
system; New Deal; politicians; ruling
elites; voting rights

Graeber, David, *Bullshit Jobs: A Theory*, 125

Gramsci, Antonio, 66

Great Deprivation (psychological and
spiritual pain), 34–39, 54, 61, 125,

144. *See also* psychological and
spiritual meaning needs

Great Recession (2007–2011), 87, 123, 128,
151

Great Society, 147

greed. *See* selfishness

Green New Deal, 5–7, 199–200

Green Party, 227

guaranteed basic income, 166–67, 170,
204, 209, 217, 222; futurist imagining
of, 230

gun control, 185

Harari, Yuval Noah, *Homo Deus: A Brief
History of Tomorrow*, 229

hate crimes, rise of, 101–2. *See also*
homeland security— and terrorism

hate groups, people who leave, 116

health care system for the caring society,
187–89, 253n10

Hebrew Bible: choose life, 26; and
domination vs. generosity worldview, 71; Jubilee— redistribution of
wealth, 233; love the Other/the
stranger/neighbor as yourself, 40, 69,
233; and revolutionary love, 160

hegemony, cultural, 66–68, 81, 251n1

Hendrickson, David C., *Republic in Peril*,
194

Heschel, Abraham Joshua, 112, 141–42;
The Prophets, 55

high-tech industry, 85, 88, 163, 170

Hindu countries, 118

Hobbes, Thomas, 67

Hochschild, Arlie Russell, *Strangers in
Their Own Land*, 10–11, 18

Holocaust, 22, 23, 129–30, 136–37, 183

homeland security: and anger at Western
societies, 214, 215; definition of, 66;
and fear and domination worldview,

homeland security *(continued)*
66; and love and generosity worldview, 69; and Western society's role
in undermining the global South and
East, 84, 183, 190, 237. *See also* global
Generosity Plan/Marshall Plan
—AND TERRORISM: causes of international
terrorism, 214, 219; domestic
terrorists as mainly white males, 215;
and framing of events, 76–77; the
global Generosity Plan and, 214–15,
219; Obama drone strikes, 74, 75;
public education to undo messages of
hate, 185–86; September 11, 2001, 59,
76–77
homeless people, 29, 167, 217
homophobia: decrease of self-blame and
ability to acknowledge, 97; education
and dismantling of, 183; Love and
Justice movement as undermining, 28,
175; percentage of voters who are
deeply homophobic, 100; progressive
religious activism against, 109; in
religious communities and secular
movements, 109; of right-wing voters,
as assumed by the Left, 10; violence
and, 183. *See also* LGBTQ people
hospice, 189
housework and homemaking, valuing of,
174, 177
housing and housing programs, 167, 176,
217; futurist imagining of, 234
human capacity development, 177–78
humanity of all people, respect for, 101–8,
116, 123, 133–34, 136–37
human rights: Anglo-American legal
system and rights of the individual,
220–21; Democratic Party as focused
on, 141–42; divorce of, from
psychological and spiritual meaning

needs, 142; same-sex marriage, and
love- vs. rights-based discourse, 150
humility, 29, 58, 115, 154, 217–18, 238
hunger, 217; worldwide, 33
hunter-gatherer tribes, 66

ICE (U.S. Immigration and Customs
Enforcement agency), 44
identity politics, 117–38; overview,
118–19, 138; advent of and continued
need for, 124–25, 128–30; intersectionality and, 127, 252n2; political
correctness, 134, 221; and transformative consciousness, development of, 126–27; and welcoming of
white people and cis men, 131–34
—BLAMING AND SHAMING: of anyone even
slightly benefiting from systems of
oppression, 39; as destroying
solidarity of social change movements, 144–45; education and
overcoming of, 183–84; examples of,
119–23; and hierarchies of suffering
(less/more oppressed), 127, 131; vs.
need to respect our shared humanity,
123; prophetic empathy tribes
teaching how to avoid, 155–56; social
media behavior of, 119; and turn to
the Right, 122–23, 145; of working
class whites and men, 127–28,
155–56. *See also* respect for the shared
humanity of all people
—AND CLASS OPPRESSION: overview, 125;
class differences within identity
groups, 131; classism as harming
everyone, 128, 130–32, 137–38;
Democratic Party as ignoring
suffering of working people, 126;
dismissed as white- or male
privilege, 126–27, 134–35, 196;

economic success as no protection from oppression, 129–30; the system as to blame for, 127–28; and turn to the Right, 126, 134–35; and whiteness, invention of, 130; women and people of color as getting a worse deal than white men, 128. *See also* classism

—THE RIGHT AND: blaming people's pain on "special interests" (Others), 117–18, 126, 127; relief from self-blaming promised by, 117, 135; sense of community promised by, 117

immigration and immigrants: assaults on immigrants, 14; causes of, 213, 215; the global Generosity Plan and, 213, 215–16; neoliberal policies and, 86; Obama expulsion of, 113; prejudice against, 183, 195; the Right's refusal to see the humanity of, 101; as "special interest" in right-wing discourse, 118; Trump and, 44, 60, 195–96; undocumented immigrants, 113, 115, 215–16; and whiteness, invention of, 130. *See also* refugees

income inequality. *See* economic inequality

Indigenous Peoples: domination worldview not flourishing under, 66; genocide of, 36, 194; Green New Deal support for, 7; UN Declaration on the Rights of, 7. *See also* Native Americans

individualism, 53

inequality. *See* classism; economic inequality; Great Deprivation

Institute for Labor and Mental Health: "Honor the Worker" day, 64; occupational stress groups, 23, 49–50, 88, 95, 119, 158

institutional changes for building a Love and Justice movement: democratiza-tion of institutions, 168; promotion of, 198. *See also* Environmental and Social Responsibility Amendment (ESRA); global Generosity Plan/Marshall Plan; legal system

instrumental/utilitarian worldview: dystopian futurism and, 228; Love and Justice movement and overcom-ing of, 106–7, 159, 218, 230; new bottom line and transcendence of, 2, 51–52, 151–52; post-socialism and overcoming of, 106; prophetic empathy tribes as teaching skills to overcome, 159; and relationships, 90

intelligence agencies, 145

intentional communities, 172

Intergovernmental Panel on Climate Change, UN, 3–4, 249n2

internationalism, 196–97

international relations. *See* global Generosity Plan/Marshall Plan; homeland security

intersectionality, 127, 252n2

Irish people, as immigrants, 183

Islamophobia: Love and Justice move-ment as undermining, 28, 175; percentage of voters who are deeply Islamophobic, 100; in religious communities and secular move-ments, 109; of right-wing voters, as assumed by the Left, 10

Israel, kibbutzim, 168–69, 172

Italians, as immigrants, 183, 195

Japanese immigrants, 183, 195

Jewish spiritual wisdom: choose life, 26; disputes "for the sake of heaven," 232; every person created in the image of God, 116; love and caring as echoed in social change movements,

Jewish spiritual wisdom *(continued)*
113; love the Other/the stranger/
neighbor as yourself, 40, 69, 233;
prophetic anger, 29; Sabbath day of
rest, 178; Seder, 239; *teshuva*
(returning to one's own highest
vision of the good), 239; *tikkun olam*,
24, 43, 59, 104, 148, 238
Jews: as identity, 128–29; as not white,
130; and psychotherapy, 22, 23. *See
also* anti-Semitism; Jewish spiritual
wisdom
Jim Crow, 183
jobs. *See* work and the workplace

kibbutzim, 168–69, 172
King, Martin Luther Jr.: the arc of the
universe bends towards justice, 64;
"Darkness cannot drive out
darkness," 144; "I Have a Dream"
speech, 134, 141; and lack of
Democratic Party understanding of
the Great Deprivation, 141–42; and
nonviolence, 41; as religious figure,
112; "Testament of Hope," 36
Klein, Naomi, 42
Kohlberg, Lawrence, 62
Koran, 71
Krugman, Paul, 243
Ku Klux Klan, 116

labor movements: economic security and
human rights as focus of, 141; failure
to address psychological and spiritual
meaning needs, 142, 143–44; legacy
of bigotry in, 109; materialist
reductionist view and, 17–18, 143;
militant New Deal support by, 87–88;
Reagan/Bush presidencies and
abandonment of, 88. *See also* labor
unions; work and the workplace

labor unions: and ESRA protections,
166–67; and honoring worker events,
165; neoliberalism and destruction of,
55; strength of, and mid-twentieth
century economic expansion, 85;
volunteer activities selected not to
undercut, 166; and worker support
groups, 163. *See also* workers
Latinos: affirmative action and, 37; as
Others in right-wing churches, 115;
prejudices against immigrants, 183,
195; as "special interest" in right-
wing discourse, 118. *See also* asylum
seekers; immigration and immigrants
lawyers, in a caring legal system, 222–23
the Left: definition of, 249–50n4; elitism
of, 24, 100–101; and materialist
reductionist discourse, 143, 144. *See
also* correctives needed for the Left to
be more successful; Democratic
Party; labor movements; liberal and
progressive social change movements; program proposals for the
caring society; socialist and
communist movements and systems
legal system: adversarial system, 222–23;
decriminalization of personal
behavior not harming others, 224;
and dismantling racism, 189, 191;
ESRA and, 209; history of Anglo-
American, as "negative freedom,"
220–21; penal system transformation, 191, 223–24; program proposals
for a cooperative and caring system,
219–25; restorative justice, 191,
222–23. *See also* Constitution, U.S.;
crime; government; police; Supreme
Court, U.S.; voting rights
Lerner, Rabbi Michael, invitation to
contact and contact information,
241, 247

LGBTQ people: and church inconsist-
ency/hypocrisy, 113; ethos of respect
for, 58; family support for, 171;
fascist attacks on, 136–37; as
Others/"special interest" in
right-wing discourse, 115, 117–18; the
Right's refusal to see the humanity
of, 101; right to marry, 124, 150, 171.
See also homophobia
liberal and progressive social change
movements: abandonment of,
beginning in Reagan/Bush years, 88;
elitism of, 24, 100–101; and fear of
being perceived as "weak," 60–61,
63; historical legacy of bigotry and
prejudice in, 109; and private
solutions, turn to, 145; psychological
and spiritual meaning needs as
unaddressed by, 142, 143–45;
Resistance to Trumpists, 25, 76; rise
of, in second half of the twentieth
century, 143–44; transitional
demands ("nonreformist reforms")
of, 145; undercover agents in, 57, 107,
145, 250–51n4; and working within
the system, 146–47; wounded
individuals in, 94. *See also* antiwar
movements; civil rights movement;
identity politics; Left, the
Liberation Theology, 112
liberty, equality, and fraternity, 81
life expectancy, 33
life support system of Earth. *See*
environmental crisis
Lifton, Robert Jay, 23
living wage, 165–66, 209, 219, 253n4,170
local communities. *See* communities
"looking out for number one" (selfishness
as ethos of capitalism), 50–51, 53–54,
59, 89–90, 94, 98, 200
#Love&JusticeParty, 246

love and generosity worldview: overview,
65, 68–70; childrearing and, 69–70,
71–72, 174–75; vs. fear and domination worldview, as continuum,
70–75; and self-blame dynamic,
94–95; social energy as pushing
towards love or towards fear, 72,
75–78, 79–80, 153–54, 238, 252n5;
and subjective care ("good enough
mothering") vs. objective care,
69–70. *See also* fear and domination
worldview; revolutionary love
Love and Justice movement: overview,
28–29, 64, 138; annual celebration of
liberation, 239; balance of life and
work and, 239–40; compassion for
ourselves and others in, 107; and
confrontation of violence, 136–37;
critical mass of, and creation of the
caring society, 150; donors for, 161,
242; as embodiment of yearning for a
life of love, respect, and higher
meaning, 108, 148–49, 197, 222;
experience joy, 197, 225, 227, 239; fear
and domination as winning out
instead of, 242–43; hiring workers
for, 160–61; joining, 241; phony
versions of the message, avoidance
of, 241–42; prophetic empathy tribes
as foundation for, 161; and respect for
the shared humanity of all people,
106–7, 116, 123, 133–34; the ruling
elites and attempts to ignore,
ridicule, and repress, 107; standing
up against oppressive or environmentally destructive behaviors,
101–2, 123, 136–37, 157, 159; study
groups and formation of chapters,
241, 242; vanguard of, and wish to
bring about the caring society,
153–54; weekly trainings to

Love and Justice movement *(continued)*
overcome the capitalist ethos, 107; as
welcoming secular humanists,
atheists, and people from every
non-oppressive branch of every
world religion, 116. *See also* Caring
Society—Caring for Each Other and
Caring for the Earth; institutional
changes for building a Love and
Justice movement; program
proposals for the caring society
Love and Justice Party: overview, 28, 225,
246–47; asking questions of
candidates, 227; creating a presence
within the Democratic Party and the
Greens, 227; discussion of issues as
expanding the realm of the possible,
226–27; experience joy, 197, 225, 227,
239; #Love&JusticeParty, 246; media
and social media writings, 226;
prophetic empathy tribe trainings,
225, 226; and the reality police,
rejection of, 226–27; and revolutionary love worldview, 225; running for
office, 226–27; study groups and
formation of chapters, 225–26; *Tikkun*
magazine as communication vehicle
for, 164, 225; website for joining, 225
love, romantic. *See* personal love
relationships
love- vs. rights-based discourse, 150
Loy, David, 239; "Beyond McMindfulness," 55
Lukacs, Martin, 54–55
Lutheran Church, 112

McKibben, Bill, 199
Malcolm X, 38
Mandela, Nelson, 133
Mander, Jerry, *The Capitalism Papers*,
254n1

Marcuse, Herbert, 23
Markey, Ed, 5
marriage: divorce/dissolution of, 90, 172;
same-sex, 150; and self-interest/
selfishness, 90. *See also* families;
personal love relationships; single
people
Marshall Plan. *See* global Generosity Plan/
Marshall Plan
Marxism, 17–18
Marx, Karl, 71, 105
mass incarceration, 113
mass media: and childhood, corporate
control of, 182; and consumerism,
80; as discrediting the possibility of
fundamental change, 79, 142–43;
ESRA proposal for prime-time
election debates on, 205; and fear vs.
love worldviews, 68, 72, 73; and girls,
education of, 184; and honoring
workers events, 165; Love and Justice
Party material published in, 226; and
meritocracy myth, 81, 83–84; and the
old bottom line, 50; and perception
of caring as "weak," 60–61; public
education about terrorism, 185–86;
and racism, dismantling, 189, 191;
and sexuality, 177, 184; shaming and
blaming by the Left in, 119; working
class people rarely represented in,
125. *See also* social media
mass shootings, 14, 38, 185
materialist reductionist view: and denial
of psychological and spiritual
meaning needs, 18, 19, 46, 142;
discourse of the Left and, 143, 144;
"It's the economy, stupid," 17–18, 97.
See also radical empiricism; scientism
material needs, focus on: Democratic
Party, 141–42; labor movements,
141–42; socialist and communist

systems, 16–17. *See also* psychological and spiritual meaning needs; subjective caring

maximum wage rules, 170, 188, 216–17

meaning needs, 16–17. *See also* psychological and spiritual meaning needs

media. *See* mass media; social media

Medicare for All, 187, 253n10

men: and caring viewed as "weak," 59–64; education of boys on sexism and gender, 184; and patriarchal masculinity, 184; sexual abuse and, 52, 124, 183, 194; and suicide, 4, 127, 132, 170. *See also* feminism; gender; identity politics; whites

Mennonites, 112

mentoring, education in, 185

meritocracy as myth, 80–81, 83–85, 93, 156–57, 221

Metzger, Deena, "Extinction Illness: Grave Affliction and Possibility," 26

Mexicans, as immigrants, 195. *See also* asylum seekers; immigration and immigrants

Middle East, drone attacks in, 74

middle income people: and cross-class, cross-race alliances, 190; decline in upward mobility among, 84; and the "realistic", limitations of, 23; shamed and blamed by the Left, 10, 24; taxes for global Generosity Plan not affecting, 217. *See also* classism; identity politics; respect for the shared humanity of all people

military: budget for, 210, 216, 217; civilian peace teams in place of, 213; the global Generosity Plan and role of, 216, 217; jobs program for job losses due to cuts in, 217; nonviolence retraining of, 213; service in, 82, 104. *See also* war and war preparations

mindfulness, 55, 58

minimum wage, erosion of, 85

monarchies, 67–68, 220

money: futurist imagining of, 233–34, 236; removal from elections, 201, 203, 204–5

Muslims: anti-Semitism and, 129; assaults on, 14; as immigrants, 195; as "special interest"/Others in right-wing discourse, 101, 115, 118. *See also* Islamophobia

mythology, 34, 66

narcissistic defenses, taken as sign of strength, 95

National Council of Churches of Christ, 112

National Institute of Mental Health, 23, 88

nationalism: and blaming Jews, 129; and colonialist wars, 82–83, 194; as obliterating brutal histories of national formation, 194; reconstructing Fourth of July as global Interdependence Day, 194–97; right-wing promotion of, 195; and shaming and blaming, 127; Trump/Pence regime utilizing, 195–96; turn to, as misunderstood by the Left, 143; white nationalism, 12, 24, 29, 38, 127. *See also* Right, the

Native Americans: acting in solidarity with, 189–90, 252n1; dismantling racism against, 190; education about genocide against, 183, 190; genocide of, 183, 190, 194; as Others in right-wing churches, 115; reparations for, 190; as "special interest" in right-wing discourse, 118; Standing Rock protests, 40, 102, 252n1. *See also* Indigenous peoples nature, experiences of: and educational attainment, 193; futurist imagining of relationship with, 235; as path to distancing from consumerism, 178; as resisting the Great Deprivation, 35; science education and, 185. *See also* environmental crisis

Nazism. *See* Europe— and the rise of Nazism

neoliberalism, 54–55, 86, 159, 165, 199–200

Network of Spiritual Progressives: and development of proposals for the caring society, 154; donations to, 241; and Green New Deal, 5; as ignored by the Left, 111; online training program of, 241, 253n2; professions as vocation, leaflets for, 253n3; prophetic empathy, 103, 155; and prophetic empathy tribe trainings, 225–26; and revolutionary love, 107; universalist solidarity work of, 38

New American Movement, 15, 146

new bottom line: as basis of proposals for a caring society, 151–52; as challenge to the old bottom line, 152; defined as judging institutions, policies, and actions by their capacity to produce the caring society, 2, 51–53, 151–52; and economic planning for a caring society, 177–78; and the global Generosity Plan, 216, 218–19; and scientific research, 192–93; talking to people about, 152–54, 226–27. *See also* Caring Society—Caring for Each Other and Caring for the Earth; psychological and spiritual meaning needs; work and the workplace

New Deal: gradual weakening of, 33, 147; and militancy of the labor move-ment, 87–88; objective caring and bureaucracy as weakness of, 17, 148. *See also* Green New Deal

New Left, 143, 144, 146

New Testament, both fear and love worldviews expressed in, 71

Newton, Huey, 38

Next System Project, 180, 253n9

Nixon administration: and Seattle Seven trial, 38, 250–51n4; and Southern Strategy, 37

Noddings, Nel, 63

nonbinary/non-gender-conforming people, 62, 64

nonviolence: military retraining in, 213; revolutionary love as committed to, 41, 136–37, 197, 217; in school curriculum, 182, 204; and social change activism, 196

Obama, Barrack Hussein: drone attacks in the Middle East, 74, 75; failure to address economic inequality, 11–12, 87; failure to address racism, 37; failure to campaign for the caring society, 151; failure to stand up for Native Americans at Standing Rock, 102; Great Recession bailouts, 87, 123; and illusion of equality, 37; immigrants expelled by, 113; as pro-corporate, 12, 86; racism and election of, 10, 120; and social energy moving toward fear, 75–76

objective caring. *See* material needs; subjective caring

Ocasio-Cortez, Alexandria, 5, 199

occupational stress groups (research): methodology of research, 88; and question of middle income people turning to the right, 23–24; and self-blame for failures, 89, 95–99; and selfishness as worldview, 89; and shaming and blaming by the Left, 119–22, 127–28; and yearning for a world of love and justice, 96–97

Occupy Wall Street movement, 19–20, 120

offshoring, 86

oil. *See* fossil fuels

old bottom line, 49–50, 51, 146–47, 152. *See also* capitalism— "realistic" ideas and policies of; new bottom line

open borders, 237

opioid overdose deaths, 127, 132

oppression. *See* systems of oppression

Others: decreases in self-blame leading to less blaming of Others, 97–98; fear and domination worldview and, 67; Hebrew Bible teaching to love the Other, 40, 69, 233; public complaints about paying for education of, 187; the Right and blame of, 115–16, 117–18

ownership as concept, futurist imagining of, 233, 234–35. *See also* private property

Palast, Greg, *The Best Democracy Money Can Buy*, 86

parenting. *See* childrearing

Paris Agreement (2018), 13, 16

Paris rebellion (1968), 143

partnership societies, 174–75, 253nn5–6

patriarchal societies: childrearing assigned to women in, 62; education and challenges to, 184; families and, 174–75; and fear vs. love worldviews, 73; pessimism as intrinsic to, 15; violence as intrinsic to, 34, 35. *See also* classism; feminism; sexism

people of color: acting in solidarity with, 189–90; discrimination against, 124; ethos of respect for, 58; meritocracy myth and, 81; the Right's refusal to see the humanity of, 101; Trump administration undermining rights of, 22. *See also* African Americans; economic inequality; racism

"The Personal is Political," 105, 144

personal love relationships: difficulties of sustaining under global capitalism, 105; and fear vs. love worldviews, 72; revolutionary love as encompassing, 40, 43; single people, support for, 176; yearning for love, 96–97. *See also* families; friendships; marriage; personal solutions; single people

personal responsibility: overview, 56; for compassion, 58; ethos for, vs. legislation, 58; gratitude and forgiveness, 57; and insight on personal path to a life of deeper meaning/purpose, 58–59; for mistakes, 56–57, 58, 98, 239; for population control, 56; for violence in one's name, 57–58

personal solutions: both internal and external change needed, 55–56; changing one's self won't create the world we want, 53–56, 58, 145; as compensation for Great Deprivation, 51; as parallel universes, 51; self-fulfillment through consumption, 80

pessimism: as intrinsic to class and patriarchal societies, 15; and Trump/re-emergence of fascistic movements, 15

pharmaceutical companies, 188

Physicians for a National Health Plan, 253n10

Pittsburgh synagogue mass shooting (2018), 38, 137

Plaskow, Judith, 112

police: dismantling and replacing with neighborhood security committees, 191, 225; violence against antiwar demonstrators, 250–51n4; violence against people of color and the poor, 37, 124, 132, 224–25; whites as safer in the presence of, 127, 132. *See also* crime; legal system

Polish people, as immigrants, 195

political correctness, 134, 221

politicians: as discrediting the possibility of fundamental change, 142–43; and fear vs. love worldviews, 72; and honoring worker events, 165; and money in elections, 201; and support for corporations, 201. *See also* Democratic Party; Love and Justice Party; Republican Party

politics of meaning, 144. *See also* psychological and spiritual meaning needs

Pope Francis, 112; *Laudato Si*, 215

population growth, need for limits on, 3, 56, 213–14

post-socialism (socialism of the heart/ spiritual socialism): and democratization of the economy, 15–17; and differentiation from focus on material well-being and rights, 105–6; as term, 15, 17, 147–48. *See also* economic democratization; love and generosity worldview; program proposals for the caring society

poverty. *See* classism; economic inequality; global Generosity Plan/

Marshall Plan; homeless people; hunger; legal system; police

"Power to the People," 144

Presbyterian Church, 112

President's Day, replaced with celebration of liberation, 239

prices, 178, 220

prisons and prisoners, changes to system of, 191, 223–24

private life, futurist imagining of, 231

private property, 81. *See also* ownership as concept

production of goods and services: and global Generosity Plan, 217; that contribute to protection/repair of the environment and the well-being of all people, 173–74, 177, 178–79, 180–81

professionals: as vocation, 163, 253n3; yearning for love, respect, and a higher meaning assumed to be the realm of, 97. *See also* work and the workplace

program proposals for the caring society: as always in progress, 149; as aspirational for a loving society, 149; and critical mass of Love and Justice movement, 150; as democratically created, 154; feedback invited on, 154; futurist imagining of results of, 228–37; and love- vs. rights-based discourse, 150; and mistakes, addressing of, 161; the new bottom line as basis of, 151–52; partial victories of, 150–51; and political campaigning in terms of a caring society, 151; and progressive (Sanders/Warren) wing of the Democratic Party, 149–50; and the reality police, rejection of, 154;

talking about the proposals with others, 152–54; transformation of consciousness as central idea of, 149, 151, 158, 161

—SPECIFIC PROGRAMS: economic system transition, 173, 177–82; educational system, 182–87; family support, 162–63, 171–77, 189; Fourth of July reconstructed as global Interdependence Day, 194–97; health care system, 187–89, 253n10; prophetic empathy tribes, 154–61, 226; racism, challenging and dismantling, 189–92; separating church, state, and science, 192–93; work and the workplace, 162–70. See also Love and Justice movement

Progressive National Baptist Convention, 113

progressive religious communities. See religious and spiritual progressive communities

prophetic empathy: as affirming the humanity of all people, 103–5; compassion and, 103; countering the fear and domination worldview, 104–5; definition of, 103, 155; in education of children, 183; framing social values in terms of yearning for the caring society, 105–6; and genuine curiosity about what underlies a person's political commitments, 103–4; and individuals as embodiment of the sacred, 159; and rethinking the Left's perpetuation of self-blame, 104; and seeing the real suffering of people who may appear to be privileged, 104; tribes for teaching and training in, 154–61, 226

prophets: anger at religious hypocrisy, 29; and need for both internal and external transformation, 55; revolutionary love at heart of teachings of, 59

proposals. See program proposals for the caring society

Protestant Reformation, 220

psychological and spiritual meaning needs: and apparently irrational political behavior, 18–19; capitalism as unable to acknowledge or satisfy, 14; definition of, 16–17; and democratization of economy, as essential to, 17; and the global Generosity Plan, 218–19; Great Deprivation of, 34–39, 54, 61, 125, 144; the Left as tone deaf to, 14, 18, 19–21, 142, 143–44, 150; the Right as manipulating, 18, 21; socialism and communism as not addressing, 16–17, 143–44

—YEARNING FOR LOVE/RESPECT/ MEANING: as assumed to be the realm of upper middle class professionals, 97; denial of need, 93–94; framing of leftist social values in terms of, 105–6; helping others to get in touch with, 246; and liberal and progressive social change movements, 94; Love and Justice movement as embodiment of, 108, 148–49, 197, 222; prophetic empathy tribes to teach about, 156; speaking our truth of, as necessity, 108; as suppressed but still existent, 104; working class people and, 96–97, 156

psychological depression: extinction illness, 21–22, 26, 74, 154, 202; increase of, 4; unemployment and, 170 psychotherapists: expense of, and class differences in healing, 125; and the larger pathologies of society, 21–23; as prophetic empathy tribe members, 156; and self-blaming, overcoming, 98–99

public transportation, 6

Purser, Ron, "Beyond McMindfulness," 55

Quakers, 112

racism: acting in solidarity with those affected by, 38–39, 189–90, 252n1; and Barrack Obama, 10, 120; and cross-class alliances, 190; decrease of self-blame and ability to acknowledge, 97; failure of the Democratic Party to address, 11, 37; failure to focus on dismantling the assumptions of, 36–37; and fear vs. love worldviews, 73; intersectionality and, 127; and the legal system, 189, 191; Love and Justice movement as undermining, 28, 175; and media, 189, 191; percentage of voters who are deeply racist/unreachable, 100, 116, 123, 134–35, 136; and perceptions of injustice exaggerated by the Right, 11; program proposals for challenging and dismantling, 189–92; progressive religious activism against, 109; prophetic empathy tribes teaching the systemic nature of, 157; in religious communities and secular movements, 109; reparations and, 190; resurgent, and Republican Party, 37; of right-wing voters, as assumed by the Left, 10; slavery and the slave trade, 35–36, 183; Social

Darwinism/"survival of the fittest" and, 68; universalist vision in solidarity against, 38–39; and voting rights, 191; white supremacy, 10, 24, 43, 190, 196. *See also* classism; economic inequality; immigration and immigrants; refugees

radical empiricism, 45–46; and "impossibility" of human emancipation, 47, 48–49. *See also* scientism

Reagan, Ronald, and administration, 37, 54, 87, 88, 147

"realistic" ideas and policies. *See under* capitalism

reality police: definition of, 154; vs. hope for the future, 229, 241; rejection of, and imagining the caring society, 154, 162; rejection of, and running for office, 226–27

Reconstructing Judaism, 112

red states: guaranteed basic income and, 167; prophetic empathy tribe outreach to, 159–60. *See also* respect for the shared humanity of all people; rural Americans

Reformed Church in America, 113

refugees: alleviation of, and the global Generosity Plan, 213, 215–16; as Others in right-wing churches, 115; and religious hypocrisy, 29; the Right's refusal to see the humanity of, 101; as "special interest" in right-wing discourse, 118; Trump administration policy of abuse of, 44, 73–74, 195–96; Trump administration's manipulation of issue of, 22

religion: both fear and love worldviews expressed in, 71; and consumerism, 80; and domination worldview, 66–67; feudal constraints for fair wages and prices, 220; futurist imagining of, 237; hypocrisy and, 29, 113; old bottom line as kind of, 49, 152; as path to distancing from consumerism, 178; religiophobia (leftist disdain for religion and spirituality), 108, 109, 111–15; as resistance to Great Deprivation, 34–35; revolutionary love at heart of teachings of, 59; right-wing preaching about Others, 115–16; scientism as dismissing, 46; scientism as kind of, 46, 52, 109–10; as undermined by subservience to ruling elites, 34–35. *See also* Jewish spiritual wisdom; psychological and spiritual meaning needs; religious and spiritual progressive communities

religiophobia (leftist disdain for religion and spirituality), 108, 109, 111–15

Religious Action Center (of Reform Judaism), 112

religious and spiritual progressive communities: growth of activism of, 109; as ignored/marginalized by the Left, 109, 111–12; importance of contributions to progressive thought, 112–13; progressive religious groups, as ignored or marginalized due to leftist disdain for religion, 109, 111–12; and prophetic empathy tribe outreach to red states, 160; and right-wing plausible portrayals of progressives as anti-religious, 115

renewable energy: and fossil fuel phaseouts, 5, 6, 7, 208; Green New Deal policy for, 5–6; for vehicles and public transportation, 6

renters, tax breaks for, 175

reparations: for destruction of Native American populations, 190; for enslavement of African Americans, 190; Great Recession and proposal of, for citizen losses during, 151; for job losses due to corporate offshoring or downsizing, 208; for Western dominance of the planet, 218; for working class jobs, 169

Republican Party: criticizing Democrats as "weak," 59–60; government dismantling as goal of, 147, 148; as influenced by white nationalists and Christian fundamentalists, 29; and midterms (2018), 109; resurgent racism and, 37; rural Americans as voters for, 19; Southern Strategy, 37; Tea Party, 20, 37; voter suppression by members of, 86. *See also* Right, the

respect, for the shared humanity of all people, 101–8, 116, 123, 133–34, 136–37. *See also* psychological and spiritual meaning needs— yearning for love, respect, and a higher meaning

responsibility. *See* environmental and social responsibility; Environmental and Social Responsibility Amendment (ESRA); personal responsibility

restorative justice, 191, 222–23

retirement benefits, neoliberalism and loss of, 86

retirement communities, 189, 191

Reuther, Rosemary Radford, 112

revolutionary love: compassion as central to, 56, 238; definition of, 1–2, 39–44; and economic planning for the caring society, 181–82; as ethical psycho-spiritual strategy, 53–56; as fundamental transformation, 25, 26, 43,

revolutionary love *(continued)*
238; as "God-ing," 43; love the
oppressors, 41–42; love your neighbor/
Other/the stranger as yourself, 40, 69,
233; and nonviolence, 41, 136, 137; as
not a New Age variant, 2, 25, 150; and
tikkun, reawakening of, 43; toughness
in standing up for, 63; and unity/
interconnectedness of all being, 24,
39, 40, 43–44; urgency of need for,
2–4. *See also* Caring Society—Caring
for Each Other and Caring for the
Earth; correctives needed for the Left
to be more successful; Great
Deprivation (psychological and
spiritual pain); love and generosity
worldview; personal solutions;
program proposals for the caring
society

the Right: churches of, 115–16; definition
of, 249–50n4; and the family, claims
to support, 171; funding strategies of,
8–9; growth of, and despair of
fundamental change, 14; injustice of
affirmative action as exaggerated by,
11; as manipulating psychological
and spiritual meaning needs, 18, 21;
Others, blaming as "special
interests," 117–18, 126, 127; percentage of voters who are deeply racist/
sexist/etc., 100; those we cannot
hope to reach, 100, 116, 123, 134–35,
136; two-country solution, 243–46;
the values of capitalism as hated by,
110–11, 115–16, 118; white male
domestic terrorists, 215. *See also*
nationalism; Republican Party

Roma people, 118, 136–37

Roosevelt, Franklin Delano, 88

Rousseau, Jean-Jacques, 67–68

ruling elites: cultural hegemony of,
66–68, 81, 251n1; and expansion of
American Empire, 194; fear of labor
movements and welcoming of
McCarthyism, 79–80; and hiding of
the tradition of Jubilee— redistribution of wealth, 233; Love and Justice
movement ignored, ridiculed, and
repressed by, 107; as manipulating
men and whites into believing the
system works for them, 128; systemic
practices and consciousness used by,
to divide the workforce, 24; and
whiteness, invention of, 130. *See also*
capitalism; cultural systems; Great
Deprivation (psychological and
spiritual pain)

rural Americans: anger at liberals, 19;
definition of, 19; ethos of mutual
support and care among, 81, 114;
Generosity Plan/Marshall Plan to
benefit, 160; "moral communities" of
caring among, 19, 160; prophetic
empathy tribe outreach to, 159–60;
as Republican voters, 19; Senate as
overweighting representation for,
243. *See also* red states; respect for the
shared humanity of all people;
working class people

Sabbath day of rest, 178; futurist
imagining of, 235

Sabbatical Year, futurist imagining of,
235–37

Sandel, Michael, *What Money Can't Buy*,
254n1

Sanders, Bernie, 28, 88, 149–50

Schwarzenegger, Arnold, 59–60

science: anti-science teaching of religious
communities, 109; and awe and

wonder at Earth, 185; defense of, 192–93; as dismissed by the Right, 46; education in, 182, 185; empirical approach as foundation of, 45; the new bottom line and research in, 192–93; scientism distinguished from, 45; statements on climate change and environmental danger, 3–4, 200, 249n2; support for, while criticizing scientism, 46, 110

scientism: consciousness as belying, 46–49; definition of (everything real must be measurable or empirically verifiable), 45–46; and denial of psychological and spiritual meaning needs, 142; distinguished from science, 45, 192; ethics as dismissed by, 46; fear and domination worldview justified via, 68, 252n2–3; as methodological principle, 46; the old bottom line as backed by, 152; as religion in itself, 46, 52, 109–10; replacement of humans with robots as justified under, 229

Seale, Bobby, 38

Seattle Seven, 38, 250–51n4

secular humanists, 59, 67, 153

self-blame: overview, 89; childrearing and development of, 92–94, 104; and constrained choice, 95–96, 220; decrease of, and ability to acknowledge systemic oppressions, 97–98; denial of, 93–94, 95; and failure of self-fulfillment through consumerism, 80; feminism's recognition of systemic problem of, 157; healing of, via empathic communication and discussion groups, 95–99; and humiliation, avoidance of, 93–94; the Left as perpetuating, 104; and

meritocracy myth, 93, 156–57; occupational stress groups and, 89, 95–99; prophetic empathy tribes as teaching skills to overcome, 156–57, 158; the Right as alleviating, by blaming "special interests" (Others), 117–18, 126, 127; and wounded individuals, 94–95

selfishness as ethos of capitalism, 50–51, 53–54, 59, 89–90, 94, 98, 200

Senate, U.S., as undemocratic, 243

Sennett, Richard, 94

September 11, 2001 attacks, 59, 76–77

sex education, 171

sexism: and caring viewed as "weak," 59–64; as cultural system, 38–39; decrease of self-blame and ability to acknowledge, 97; education and dismantling of, 183, 184; Equal Rights Amendment and campaign against, 198; failure of the Democratic Party to address, 11; and Hillary Clinton, 10; intersectionality and, 127; Love and Justice movement as undermining, 28, 175; percentage of voters who are deeply sexist, 100; progressive religious activism against, 109; in religious communities and secular movements, 109; of right-wing voters, as assumed by the Left, 10; Trump administration support for, 22. *See also* economic inequality; gender; patriarchal societies; women

sexual abuse, 52, 124, 183, 194

sexuality: cheapening of, and capitalist marketplace, 177; family support and, 176, 177

shaming. *See* identity politics—blaming and shaming; self-blame shared humanity of all people, respect for, 101–8, 116, 123, 133–34, 136–37

Silicon Valley. *See* high-tech industry

single people: dating and self-interest of, 90, 176; housing options for, 176; and sexuality, 176, 177; single-parent families, 171; social support for, 176–77

slavery and the slave trade, 35–36, 183, 190, 194, 243

small groups of people creating change together: as challenging the "realists," 23–24; feminism and, 25

Social Darwinism, 68

social energy, 72, 75–78, 79–80, 153–54, 238; definition of, 75, 252n5; and framing of events, 76–78

socialist and communist movements and systems: failure to address psychological and spiritual meaning needs, 16–17, 143–44; fascist attacks on socialists, 136–37; lack of democratic control over the economy of, 15–16, 177, 180; legacy of bigotry in, 109; McCarthyism/anti-communism, 79–80; material well-being and rights as focus in, 16–17, 105–6; repression of, 79–80, 82–83; and totalitarian leadership, 15–16, 106, 144, 146. *See also* post-socialism (socialism of the heart/spiritual socialism)

social media: dating apps and websites, 90; and fear vs. love worldviews, 73; Love and Justice Party material posted on, 226; shaming and blaming by the Left on, 119; Trump and, 42. *See also* mass media

social responsibility. *See* Environmental and Social Responsibility Amendment (ESRA)

social sciences: fear and domination worldview supported by scientism of, 68; inability to construct laws of human behavior, 46–49; qualitative research, 47–48

social services, defunding of, 165

social solidarity: capitalism and destruction of, 82; with those affected by racism, 38–39, 189–90, 252n1; universalist vision of, 37–39, 129

solar energy. *See* renewable energy

South Africa, Truth and Reconciliation Commission, 133

Soviet Union, 79

spiritual needs. *See* psychological and spiritual meaning needs; religion

Spitz, René, 69

Standing Rock protests, 40, 102, 252n1

subjective caring: definition of, 147–48; as demonstrating that society is filling with caring people, 219; global Generosity Plan reflecting both types of caring, 213, 214; love and generosity worldview and, 69–70; objective caring without, 27, 148, 243. *See also* psychological and spiritual meaning needs; revolutionary love

suicide: assisted, 188–89; rates of, 4, 127, 132, 170

Supreme Court, U.S.: corporate power and the super-rich as supported by, 201, 202; denial of class action suits to employees, 86; and pornography, problem of, 52; as right-leaning, 13; ruling that corporate money in elections is a form of free speech (Citizens United), 86, 202, 204–5; same-sex marriage and love- vs.

rights-based discourse, 150; Voting
Rights Act, dismantling of, 86
"survival of the fittest," 68
systems of oppression: as loss in the quality
of life for most people, 39; racism as,
35–39; universalist consciousness in
solidarity against, 37–39, 129

taxes: carbon emissions, 7–8, 216–17; cuts
for the super-rich, 165; and decreas-
ing economic inequality, 175; for
education, 182, 187; and maximum
wage rules, 170, 216–17; and renters,
tax breaks for, 175; to support the
global Generosity Plan, 216–17. *See
also* funding; reparations
Taylor, Keeanga-Yamahtta, 12, 36, 37–38
terrorism. *See under* homeland security
teshuva, 239
Thatcher, Margaret, 54
theology: and domination worldview, 66.
See also religion
350.org, 20
Tikkun: donations to, 241; ongoing
changes to text of ESRA, 204
Tikkun magazine: and Green New Deal, 5;
and proposals for the caring society,
154; proposal to link federal support
of education to anti-oppression
curriculum, 11; subscription to, 241;
urging Obama to campaign on the
caring society, 151; as vehicle of
communication for Love and Justice
movement, 164, 225. *See also* Network
of Spiritual Progressives
tikkun olam (healing and repairing our
world), 24, 43, 59, 104, 148, 238
Torah, 26, 40, 233
trade agreements: global Generosity Plan
and, 212; neoliberalism and, 86

transgender people, 64, 124, 126, 183
tribal worlds: and joy of spiritual
experiences of, 66–67; and relative
equality in human origins, 34
tribes, prophetic empathy. *See under*
prophetic empathy
T'ruah, 112
Trump administration: climate change
report, 4; destructiveness of, 11–12,
22; and Paris Agreement, withdrawal
from, 13; and pessimism, 15;
Resistance to, 25, 76; separation and
abuse of families seeking asylum at
the Mexican border, 44, 73–74,
195–96; and social energy moving
toward fear, 75
Trump, Donald: America First ideology,
196; climate change denial by, 4;
election of (2016), 87; Evangelicals
supporting, 109; and government
shutdown (2018–2019), 60; hate
mongering by, 42; and immigration,
44, 60, 195–96; "Make America Great
Again," 85; as malignant narcissist/
sociopath, 22; as reality show
star, 73
Truth and Reconciliation Commission
(proposed for USA), 190
Truth and Reconciliation Commission
(South Africa), 133
twelve-step programs, 158, 193

undocumented immigrants. *See*
immigration and immigrants
unemployment. *See under* work and the
workplace
unions. *See* labor unions
Unitarian Universalists, 113
United Church of Christ, 112
United Methodist Churches, 112, 113

unity of all being, futurist imagining of, 237

universal basic income. *See* guaranteed basic income

universal healthcare, 187–89, 253n10

universalist consciousness, 37–39, 129

universities and colleges: accreditation policies and the caring society, 186; admissions policies and the caring society, 186; as discrediting the possibility of fundamental change, 79; elite power supported by, 68; and meritocracy myth, 81, 83–84; national service corps for graduates of, 186–87; prophetic empathy tribe teach-ins at, 158; tuition, free/reduced/cost-of-living stipends, 186–87, 188. *See also* education

upper middle class people: defined as upper 20 percent of income earners, 53; and retirement communities, 189; and selfishness, 53–54; upward mobility of, 83; yearning for a caring society assumed to be the realm of, 97. *See also* classism; ruling elites

utilitarian worldview. *See* instrumental/utilitarian worldview

values: of capitalism, as hated by the Right, 110–11, 115–16, 118; of the Left, framed in terms of the caring society, 105–6

veganism, futurist imagining of, 237

vehicles, 6, 208

Vietnam War, 60, 112, 137, 142. *See also* antiwar movements

violence: confrontation of, and protection of the vulnerable, 136–37; domestic violence, reduction of, 222; of European Nazism, 136–37; hate crimes, rise in, 101–2; homophobic violence, 183; increase of, and movement of social energy towards fear, 75; mass shootings, 14, 38, 185; personal responsibility for violence done in one's name, 57–58; police violence, 37, 124, 132, 224–25, 250–51n4; racist violence, 14, 37, 38, 124, 137, 183; used to coerce people into the Great Deprivation, 34, 35–36. *See also* homeland security— and terrorism

voluntary simplicity, futurist imagining of, 234–35

voting rights: in ESRA, 203, 205; futurist imagining of, 232; for incarcerated and former prisoners, 191, 224; protection of, 191; voter suppression by Republicans, 86

Voting Rights Act, 86

wages. *See under* work and the workplace

Wallace-Wells, David, "Time to Panic," 199

war and war preparations: Congressional sponsors for, 5; discrediting the possibility of social change in aftermath of, 79–80; embraced by religion, 67; and framing of events in fear vs. hope worldviews, 76–79; and social energy moving toward fear, 75–76; transition away from, 7; and U.S. expansion, 194; and the working class, promises to, 82. *See also* antiwar movements; homeland security; military

Warren, Elizabeth, 149–50

Washington State, carbon emissions tax (proposed), 7–8

Wasow, Arthur, 112

wealth inequality. *See* economic inequality

White Lives Matter movements, 11

white nationalists, 12, 24, 29, 38, 127

whiteness: and blaming of privilege, 127, 196; invention of, 130; problematization of, 130. *See also* classism; identity politics

whites: advantages of, 132; domestic terrorism as mainly committed by white men, 215; fear that the system of oppression will be turned on them, 132–33; as manipulated into adopting racism, 183; opioid overdose deaths of, 127, 132; as safer in the presence of police, 127, 132; suicide rate of, 127, 132; working class men and disdain for liberals, 10–11; working class men, liberal and progressive demeaning of, 127–28, 155–56. *See also* respect for the shared humanity of all people; Right, the

white supremacy, 10, 24, 43, 190, 196

Winnicott, Donald, 70

women: discrimination against, 124; education and empowerment of girls, 184, 213; ethos of respect for, 58; meritocracy myth and, 81; as Others in right-wing churches, 115; and rights under capitalism, 220–21. *See also* families; feminism; gender

Women's March, 20

women's movement. *See* feminism

work and the workplace: and ethos of caring for other people, 168–69; futurist imagining of, 230, 231, 235–37; program proposals re-envisioning with a new bottom line, 162–70; worker-owned workplaces, 16, 179–80, 209. *See also* classism; labor unions; production of goods and services; workers

—UNEMPLOYMENT: depression and suicide and, 170; due to corporate offshoring or downsizing, 208; due to military cuts, 217; and the environmental crisis, 170, 209; fear of, as reinforcing politician support for corporations, 201; futurist imagining of, 230; job losses due to robotics and other technical advances, 170; neoliberalism and, 86; program proposals to combat, 166, 167, 170, 217; training and jobs programs, 167, 217; volunteerism and, 166

—WAGES: discrimination in, end of, 167; feudalism and the religious requirement for "fair wage," 220; guaranteed basic income, 166–67, 170, 204, 209, 217, 222; for housework/homemaking, 174, 177; living wage, 165–66, 209, 219, 253n4,170; maximum wage rules, 170, 188, 216–17; minimum wage, erosion of, 85; and work week reductions, 173

workers: Anglo-American legal system and abandonment of, 220–21; Green New Deal support for, 6; group support for, 162–63, 164; honoring, proposals for, 164–65; systemic practices and consciousness used by ruling elites to divide, 24; yearning for sense of meaning and purpose, 96–97. *See also* labor movements; labor unions; occupational stress groups (research); work and the workplace; working class people

working class people: Great Deprivation (psychological and spiritual pain)

working class people *(continued)*
and, 125; and meritocracy myth, 83,
84–85; middle-class identification of,
84; promises of trickle-down wealth
to, 82–83, 147; psychological and
spiritual meaning needs and, 18; and
reparations for generations of
underpaid and under-recognized
working class jobs, 169; white men,
disdain for liberals of, 10–11; white
men, liberal and progressive
demeaning of, 127–28, 155–56. *See
also* classism; identity politics— class
oppression and; psychological and
spiritual meaning needs— yearning
for love, respect, and a higher
meaning; red states; respect for the
shared humanity of all people; rural
Americans; whites
World War II: and hope for change as
discredited, 79–80; and Marshall
Plan, 211; and weakening of
colonialism, 82
wounded individuals, 94–95
Wuthnow, Robert, *The Left Behind: Decline
and Rage in Rural America*, 19, 114

xenophobia: education and dismantling
of, 182–84; Love and Justice
movement as undermining, 28; of
right-wing voters, as assumed by the
Left, 10. *See also* discrimination and
bigotry

yearning for love/respect/higher
meaning. *See under* psychological and
spiritual meaning needs
younger people: as having no historical
experience of large-scale change, 25;
progressiveness of, 14

Zavis, Cat, 103, 155, 241